Abby
Hurson

Voo Doo Lounge

Todds' Unique
Dining

ZAGATSURVEY®

2007

LAS VEGAS RESTAURANTS & NIGHTLIFE

Local Editors: Heidi Knapp Rinella and Jason Bracelin

Staff Editor: Curt Gathje

Published and distributed by
ZAGAT SURVEY, LLC
4 Columbus Circle
New York, New York 10019
Tel: 212 977 6000
E-mail: lasvegas@zagat.com
Web site: www.zagat.com

Acknowledgments

We thank the following members of our staff: Emily Parsons (associate editor), Sean Beachell, Maryanne Bertollo, Reni Chin, Larry Cohn, Victoria Elmacioglu, Andrew Eng, Jeff Freier, Shelley Gallagher, Roy Jacob, Natalie Lebert, Mike Liao, Dave Makulec, Andre Pilette, Becky Ruthenburg, Thomas Sheehan, Kilolo Strobert, Donna Marino Wilkins, Sharon Yates and Kyle Zolner.

Contents

About This Survey

This *2007 Las Vegas Restaurant & Nightlife Survey* is an update reflecting significant developments as reported by our editors since our last *Survey* was published. For example, we have added 60 important new restaurants and nightlife spots, as well as indicated new addresses, chef changes and other major alterations. All told, this guide now covers 596 of the Las Vegas area's best restaurants, bars, clubs and lounges. To help you find the best meals and best buys, we have prepared a number of lists. See Most Popular and Key Newcomers (page 9), Top Ratings (pages 10–14) and Best Buys (page 15) as well as a total of 76 handy indexes. Nightlife lists begin on page 127.

This marks the 28th year that Zagat Survey has reported on the shared experiences of diners like you. What started in 1979 as a hobby involving 200 of our friends rating NYC restaurants has come a long way. Today we have over 250,000 active surveyors and now cover dining, entertaining, golf, hotels, movies, music, nightlife, resorts, shopping, spas, theater and tourist attractions around the world. All of these guides are based on consumer surveys. They are also available by subscription at zagat.com, and for use on BlackBerry, Palm, Windows Mobile devices and mobile phones.

By regularly surveying large numbers of avid customers, we hope to have achieved a uniquely current and reliable series of guides. More than a quarter-century of experience has verified this. In effect, these guides are the restaurant industry's report card, since each place's ratings and review are really a free market study of its own customers.

For this book, over 4,100 restaurant- and club-goers responded, bringing roughly 848,000 meals and evenings out worth of experience to this *Survey*. Our editors have done their best to synopsize these surveyors' opinions, with their direct comments shown in quotation marks. We sincerely thank each of these people; this book is really "theirs."

We are especially grateful to our editors, Heidi Knapp Rinella, the restaurant critic and a features writer for the *Las Vegas Review-Journal,* and Jason Bracelin, the entertainment writer at the newspaper.

Finally, we invite you to join any of our upcoming *Surveys*. To do so, just register at zagat.com, where you can rate and review any restaurant or nightspot at any time during the year. Each participant will receive a free copy of the resulting guide when it is published. Your comments and even criticisms of this guide are also solicited. There is always room for improvement with your help. You can contact us at lasvegas@zagat.com.

New York, NY
December 6, 2006

Nina and Tim Zagat

What's New

If Madonna were a city, she'd be Las Vegas. The Neon Metropolis has long been known for continually reinventing itself and its booming, star chef–driven restaurant scene is responsible for its most recent incarnation as a leading dining destination.

The Bar Keeps Rising: Just when Las Vegas foodies were convinced that the city's culinary reach couldn't extend any further, it did. This year, that lift was provided by Parisian super-toque Guy Savoy, whose eponymous restaurant (and first U.S. foray) was unveiled at Caesars Palace. Other notable new arrivals included a Michael Mina steakhouse, StripSteak, at Mandalay Bay; Fin, Japonais and Stack at the Mirage; Nove Italiano, in the Palms' Fantasy Tower; and Social House at Treasure Island. By year's end, Caesars will open a spin-off of NYC's legendary Rao's, a larger version of the 55-seat original that will hopefully be easier to get into.

Suburban Spillover: The growing number of top-quality restaurants on the tourism corridor has had a positive effect in the areas frequented by Las Vegas residents. Locals' casinos continue to include a variety of great dining opportunities in their resorts, such as Salt Lick Bar-BQ and T-Bones Chophouse at Red Rock Casino. The poker bar of old was reborn as an upscale restaurant (with barely noticeable video-poker machines) at Becker's Steakhouse. Auld Dubliner and Bistro Zinc were the latest arrivals in the ever-growing Lake Las Vegas. And the continuing popularity of sushi has prompted a boom in that genre at places like I Love Sushi, Sapporo and Sen of Japan.

The Bigger the Better: As for the nightlife scene, subtlety remained as foreign a concept as sobriety. Even by the city's outsized standards, the new clubs were more over the top than ever. The mammoth, multi-tiered Jet landed at the Mirage with three dance floors and four bars. At the Wynn, the equally lavish Tryst (built at a reputed cost of $40 million) arrived complete with its own nine-story waterfall. The Fantasy Tower of the Palms was home to two splashy newcomers: Moon, with a high-tech retractable roof, as well as the first Playboy Club in 25 years, where lounging, gambling and Playmate centerfold wallpaper coexist. Off the Strip, Cherry at Red Rock Casino boasted a gleaming, nickel-plated look right down to its conversation-starting urinals.

Cost Check: At $38.38, the average price of a meal in Sin City is somewhat easier to swallow than NYC's $39.43, though decidedly above San Francisco ($35.96) and Los Angeles ($31.93), not to mention the national average of $32.86.

Las Vegas, NV
December 6, 2006

Heidi Knapp Rinella
Jason Bracelin

Ratings & Symbols

Name, Address, Phone Number & Web Site

Zagat Ratings

Hours & Credit Cards

	F	D	S	C
Tim & Nina's ◑ 🚫 ⧸	▽ 23	9	13	$150

88 Wile E. Coyote Dr. (Roadrunner Blvd.), 702-555-1212; www.zagat.com

"You're more likely to see Tim and Nina at the slots" than run into them (let alone "sniff out a server") at their African-, Asian-, Armenian-, Aleutian-accented steakhouse off the Strip, where the "ambitions are as frighteningly elevated as the prices"; maybe the staff got "waylaid by baccarat" during the "long, forced march through the casino" to get to this "chintz-infested tomb" where "a table by the peephole" offers a "glimpse of the construction site" next door.

Review, with surveyors' comments in quotes

Top Spots: Places with the highest overall ratings, popularity and importance are listed in BLOCK CAPITAL LETTERS.

Hours: ◑ serves after 11 PM
      🚫 closed on Sunday
      Ⓜ closed on Monday

Credit Cards: ⧸ no credit cards accepted

Ratings are on a scale of **0** to **30**.

F	Food	D	Decor	S	Service	C	Cost
23		9		13		$150	

0–9 poor to fair	**20–25** very good to excellent
10–15 fair to good	**26–30** extraordinary to perfection
16–19 good to very good	▽ low response/less reliable

Cost (C): Reflects our surveyors' average estimate of the price of a dinner with one drink and tip and is a benchmark only. Lunch is usually 25% less.

For newcomers or survey write-ins listed without ratings, the price range is indicated as follows:

I	$25 and below	**E**	$41 to $65
M	$26 to $40	**VE**	$66 or more

Most Popular

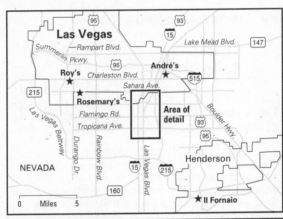

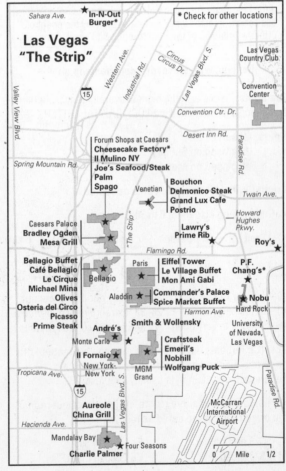

Las Vegas

- Rampart Blvd.
- Roy's ★
- André's ★
- Rosemary's ★
- Il Fornaio ★

NEVADA

Henderson

0 Miles 5

Sahara Ave.
In-N-Out Burger* ★

* Check for other locations

Las Vegas
"The Strip"

Las Vegas Country Club

Convention Center

Convention Ctr. Dr.

Desert Inn Rd.

Forum Shops at Caesars
Cheesecake Factory*
Il Mulino NY
Joe's Seafood/Steak
Palm
Spago

Venetian ★

Bouchon
Delmonico Steak
Grand Lux Cafe
Postrio

Caesars Palace ★
Bradley Ogden
Mesa Grill ★

Lawry's Prime Rib ★

Roy's ★

"The Strip"

Flamingo Rd.

Bellagio Buffet
Café Bellagio
Le Cirque ★
Michael Mina
Olives
Osteria del Circo
Picasso
Prime Steak

Bellagio

Paris ★
Aladdin ★

Eiffel Tower
Le Village Buffet
Mon Ami Gabi

P.F. Chang's* ★

Commander's Palace
Spice Market Buffet

Nobu ★
Hard Rock

André's ★

Smith & Wollensky ★

University of Nevada, Las Vegas

Monte Carlo

Il Fornaio ★
New York-New York

MGM Grand ★

Craftsteak
Emeril's
Nobhill
Wolfgang Puck

Tropicana Ave.

McCarran International Airport

Aureole
China Grill ★

Hacienda Ave.

Mandalay Bay ★
Charlie Palmer

Four Seasons

0 Mile 1/2

8

subscribe to zagat.com

Most Popular

Each surveyor has been asked to name his or her five favorite places. This list reflects their choices.

1. Picasso	21. Cheesecake Factory
2. Aureole	22. P.F. Chang's
3. Delmonico Steak	23. Eiffel Tower
4. Bellagio Buffet	24. Nobhill*
5. Prime Steak	25. Osteria del Circo
6. Commander's Palace	26. Postrio
7. Mon Ami Gabi	27. André's
8. Emeril's	28. Charlie Palmer
9. Le Cirque	29. Craftsteak*
10. Spago	30. Smith & Wollensky
11. Nobu	31. Joe's Sea/Steak
12. Bouchon	32. China Grill
13. Bradley Ogden	33. Roy's
14. Olives	34. Il Fornaio
15. Michael Mina	35. Il Mulino NY
16. Palm	36. Café Bellagio
17. Grand Lux Cafe	37. In-N-Out Burger*
18. Le Village Buffet	38. Lawry's Prime Rib
19. Rosemary's	39. Spice Mkt. Buffet
20. Mesa Grill	40. Wolfgang Puck

If popularity were calibrated to price, many other restaurants would join the above ranks. Therefore, we have added a list of 80 Best Buys on page 15. These are restaurants that give real quality at extremely reasonable prices.

Key Newcomers

Here are 10 of the year's most notable arrivals.
For a full list, see page 107.

Becker's Steak	Japonais
Chandelier	Origin India
Fin	Social House
Guy Savoy	Stack
I Love Sushi	StripSteak

---

* Indicates a tie with restaurant above

Top Ratings

Excluding places with low voting.

Food

28 Rosemary's	Shintaro
Lotus of Siam	Bartolotta
27 Nobu	Alizé
Picasso	**25** Daniel Boulud
Michael Mina	Austin's Steak
André's	Luxor Steak
Prime Steak	Steak House (Treasure Is.)
26 Steak House (Circus)	Commander's Palace
Delmonico Steak	Hyakumi
Sterling Brunch	Michael's
SW Steak	Fiore Steak
Fleur de Lys	Hugo's Cellar
Alex	Craftsteak
Medici Café	Jean Philippe
Le Cirque	N9ne Steak
Nobhill	Morton's Steak
Bradley Ogden	Sushi Roku
Okada	Mayflower Cuisinier
Pamplemousse	Lawry's Prime Rib
Todd's Unique Dining	Capital Grille

By Cuisine

American (New)
- **28** Rosemary's
- **26** Medici Café
- Bradley Ogden
- **25** Aureole
- **24** Verandah

American (Traditional)
- **26** Sterling Brunch
- **23** Fix
- **21** Cheesecake Factory
- Triple 7
- Egg & I

Asian
- **28** Lotus of Siam
- **25** Roy's
- **24** Japengo
- **23** 808
- China Grill

Chinese
- **25** Mayflower Cuisinier
- **24** Shanghai Lilly
- Pearl
- **22** Jasmine
- Empress Court

Eclectic
- **26** Todd's Unique Dining
- **24** Bellagio Buffet
- **23** Ortanique
- Simon Kitchen
- **22** Spice Mkt. Buffet

French
- **27** André's
- **26** Alex
- Pamplemousse
- **24** Bouchon
- **23** Le Village Buffet

French (New)
- **27** Picasso
- **26** Fleur de Lys
- Le Cirque
- Alizé
- **25** Daniel Boulud

Hamburgers
- **24** In-N-Out Burger
- **23** Burger Bar
- **21** Fatburger
- **20** All-American B&G
- **17** Big Dog's

Top Food

Italian
26 Bartolotta
25 Fiore Steak
    Il Mulino NY
    Osteria del Circo
24 Nora's

Japanese
27 Nobu
26 Okada
    Shintaro
25 Hyakumi
    Sushi Roku

Mexican
22 Isla
    Diego
21 Taqueria Canonita
    Border Grill
20 Chipotle

Pizza
22 Metro Pizza
21 Le Provençal
    Canaletto
20 Trattoria del Lupo
    Sammy's Pizza

Seafood
27 Michael Mina
26 Nobhill
    Bartolotta
25 Luxor Steak
    Craftsteak

Steakhouses
27 Prime Steak
26 Steak House (Circus)
    Delmonico Steak
    SW Steak
25 Austin's Steak

By Special Feature

Breakfast
26 Medici Café
    Jean Philippe
24 Verandah
    Bouchon
    Bellagio Buffet

Brunch
26 Steak House (Circus)
    Sterling Brunch
    Medici Café
25 Commander's Palace
24 Mesa Grill

Buffet (Hotel)
26 Sterling Brunch
24 Verandah
    Bellagio Buffet
23 Le Village Buffet
    Gaylord's

Business Dining
28 Rosemary's
27 Prime Steak
26 Delmonico Steak
    SW Steak
    Bradley Ogden

Child-Friendly
25 Roy's
24 Bouchon
23 Burger Bar
21 Grape St. Cafe
    Paymon's Med. Café

Cigars Welcome
27 André's
26 Delmonico Steak
    Medici Café
25 Fiore Steak
    Craftsteak

Dining Alone
28 Rosemary's
    Lotus of Siam
25 Daniel Boulud
    Jean Philippe
24 Verandah

Hotel Dining
27 Nobu
    Hard Rock
    Picasso
    Bellagio
    Michael Mina
    Bellagio
    André's
    Monte Carlo
    Prime Steak
    Bellagio

Late Dining
27 Nobu
24 Ruth's Chris
    In-N-Out Burger
23 Smith & Wollensky
    Osaka Bistro

Top Food

Offbeat
21 Yolie's Brazilian
19 Crown & Anchor
   Pink Taco
18 Melting Pot
16 Quark's

Outdoor Dining
26 SW Steak
   Bartolotta
25 Daniel Boulud
24 Verandah
   Boa Steak

People-Watching
27 Nobu
   Picasso
   Michael Mina
26 Steak House (Circus)
   Delmonico Steak

Quick Bite
25 Jean Philippe
24 In-N-Out Burger
23 Capriotti's
21 Fatburger
   Paymon's Med. Café

Trendy
25 N9ne Steak
   Aureole
23 Simon Kitchen
19 Kona Grill
   Pink Taco

Winning Wine List
27 Picasso
   Michael Mina
   André's
26 SW Steak
   Alex

By Location

Downtown
27 André's
25 Hugo's Cellar
22 Makino
   Redwood B&G
   Binion's Steak

East of Strip
28 Lotus of Siam
27 Nobu
26 Pamplemousse
25 Morton's Steak
   Lawry's Prime Rib

East Side
24 In-N-Out Burger
   Fellini's
23 Capriotti's
22 Metro Pizza
21 Fatburger

Henderson
26 Medici Café
   Todd's Unique Dining
24 In-N-Out Burger
   Japengo
23 Osaka Bistro

North Las Vegas
25 Austin's Steak
21 Fatburger
   Memphis BBQ
18 Outback Steak
17 Feast Around World

Northwest/Summerlin
24 In-N-Out Burger
   Spiedini
23 Capriotti's
21 Marché Bacchus
   Grape St. Cafe

Strip
27 Picasso
   Michael Mina
   André's
   Prime Steak
26 Steak House (Circus)

West of Strip
26 Alizé
25 Fiore Steak
   N9ne Steak
24 In-N-Out Burger
23 Capriotti's

West Side
28 Rosemary's
25 Mayflower Cuisinier
   Roy's
24 Nora's
   Fleming's Prime

Top Decor

28 Picasso	Shintaro
27 Alex	Verandah
Mix	André's
Aureole	Nobhill
Prime Steak	Japengo
Okada	**24** Michael Mina
26 Alizé	Shanghai Lilly
SW Steak	Boa Steak
Le Cirque	Quark's
Fleur de Lys	Bradley Ogden
Medici Café	Bouchon
Eiffel Tower	Fiamma Trattoria
Bartolotta	Empress Court
25 Panevino	Mon Ami Gabi
Daniel Boulud	Craftsteak
AquaKnox	Charlie Palmer
Osteria del Circo	Agave
Little Buddha	**23** VooDoo Cafe
Jasmine	Delmonico Steak
Top of the World	Fix

Outdoors

Border Grill	Mayflower Cuisinier
Bouchon	Mon Ami Gabi
Cafe Ba Ba Reeba!	Okada
Daniel Boulud	Olives
Firefly	Picasso
Kona Grill	Spiedini
Lucille's BBQ	Verandah

Romance

Alex	Le Cirque
Alizé	Michael's
André's	Mix
Becker's Steak	Nobhill
Eiffel Tower	Pamplemousse
Fleur de Lys	Sensi
Hannah's	Top of the World

Rooms

Alex	Le Cirque
Aureole	Nine Fine Irishmen
Fleur de Lys	Picasso
Hannah's	Sensi
Joël Robuchon	Stack
L'Atelier/Joël Robuchon	Zeffirino

Views

Alizé	Mix
Capital Grille	Mon Ami Gabi
Eiffel Tower	Range Steak
Jimmy Buffett's	Top of the World
Maggiano's	VooDoo Cafe

Top Service

27 Picasso

26 Alex
Prime Steak
Rosemary's
Verandah
Todd's Unique Dining
Michael Mina
André's
Medici Café
Hugo's Cellar
Michael's

25 Austin's Steak
Luxor Steak
Le Cirque
Nobhill
Delmonico Steak
Fleur de Lys
SW Steak
Bradley Ogden
Pamplemousse

Commander's Palace
Alizé
Charlie Palmer

24 Fiore Steak
Steak House (Circus)
Aureole
Bartolotta
Craftsteak
Lawry's Prime Rib
Okada*
Pearl
Capital Grille
Daniel Boulud

23 Osteria del Circo
Joe's Sea/Steak
Steakhouse46
Range Steak
Shintaro
Valentino
Morton's Steak

Best Buys

Top Bangs for the Buck

1. In-N-Out Burger
2. Capriotti's
3. Chipotle
4. Fatburger
5. Rubio's Mexican
6. Baja Fresh
7. Egg & I
8. Jean Philippe
9. Paradise Buffet
10. Chocolate Swan
11. Crown & Anchor
12. Garden Court
13. Metro Pizza
14. Feast, The
15. Tintoretto Bakery
16. Feast Around World
17. Big Dog's
18. La Salsa
19. Mr. Lucky's 24/7
20. Buffet (Golden Nugget)
21. Triple 7
22. French Mkt. Buffet
23. Carson St. Cafe
24. Paymon's Med. Café
25. 'wichcraft
26. Roadrunner
27. Chicago Brewing
28. Lotus of Siam
29. Guadalajara B&G
30. Burger Bar
31. Chili's G&B
32. Memphis BBQ
33. Coco's
34. Famous Dave's
35. Don Miguel's
36. Garduño's
37. Paradise Garden
38. Courtyard Buffet
39. Quark's
40. Elephant Bar

Other Good Values

Agave
Archi's Thai
Bootlegger Bistro
Cafe Ba Ba Reeba!
Chandelier
Cheesecake Factory
Doña Maria
Eliseevsky
El Sombrero Café
Enrico's
Firefly
Fix
Florida Cafe
Full Ho
Grand Lux Cafe
Hard Rock Cafe
Hilltop House
Hush Puppy
Kathy's Southern
Kona Grill
Little Buddha
Lou's Diner
Pasta Mia
Pasta Shop
P.F. Chang's
Ping Pang Pong
Pullman Grille
Red, White & Blue
Redwood B&G
Rincon Criollo
Sammy's Pizza
Sam Woo BBQ
Second St. Grill
Spice Mkt. Buffet
Steak House (Treasure Is.)
Tenaya Creek
Tinoco's Bistro
Toby Keith's B&G
Todd's Unique Dining
Ventano

vote at zagat.com   **15**

Restaurant Directory

Agave ◐

20 | 24 | 18 | $27

Pavilion Ctr., 10820 W. Charleston Blvd. (Hwy. 215), 702-214-3500;
www.agavelasvegas.com

Both the "blindingly pink" decor and the sips from the "extensive tequila menu" are "stunning" at this "trendy" cantina bringing "new flair to Mexican" fare in Summerlin; the "striking" exterior sporting one of the "best outdoor patios in town", the "casual but hip" interior and the "upscale", "tasty" *comidas* are "quickly becoming popular with the locals", while a few "great margaritas" blur complaints about "spotty service."

Ah Sin

21 | 21 | 19 | $40

Paris Las Vegas, 3655 Las Vegas Blvd. S. (bet. Flamingo Rd. & Harmon Ave.), 702-946-7000; www.parislasvegas.com

"Ah, full!" is what you'll be after grazing on "everything from dim sum to chow mein to fancy whole fish" to "fresh, abundant sushi" at the Paris' "total Asian experience"; still, critics say the kitchen could "try a bit" harder to turn out "more creative" plates for the "silly waiters" to ferry; the "patio seating is barely one step up from picnic tables" in comparison to the "beautifully decorated" room, but dine alfresco anyway for "great views of the Bellagio fountains."

AJ's Steakhouse ⊠Ⓜ

22 | 21 | 22 | $54

Hard Rock Hotel, 4455 Paradise Rd. (bet. Flamingo Rd. & Harmon Ave.), 702-693-5500; www.hardrockhotel.com

A "Dean Martin kind of restaurant" in a Van Halen kind of hotel, the Hard Rock's "retro" chophouse serves up "the swankiest, sexiest nods to Rat Pack culture"; in the "cozy, cool '50s"-style room, "gorgeous" "eye candy" caddies "incredible martinis" and "rocking steaks" for a dining experience that's "truly hip in its own quiet way"; "be sure to tip the piano player", and maybe he'll have an answer when you ask him "where's Frank?"

Alan Albert's ◐

21 | 17 | 20 | $60

3763 Las Vegas Blvd. S. (bet. Harmon & Tropicana Aves.), 702-795-4006

"You feel like you've been transported back in time" at this "old-fashioned, romantic" steakhouse on the Strip where the "filet mignon is as big as a softball" and much more "delicious"; the "views of the lobster tank can be creepy" while the service simply creeps: "it took a long time for them to clear away plates" tut tourists who add that taking a "picture with an extremely large crustacean" is more "fun" than eating it.

al Dente Ⓜ

19 | 18 | 20 | $42

Bally's Las Vegas Hotel, 3645 Las Vegas Blvd. S. (Flamingo Rd.), 702-967-7999; www.ballyslasvegas.com

"As is indicated by the name, pasta is the specialty" of this Northern Italian in Bally's where the only complaint about the "very good" linguine with baby clams is that there isn't enough of it; "small portions" aside, the "routine" plates are "ok for a fast meal", and the "courteous staff" obliges you in your rush, while the "blah" decor has you yearning to leave quickly; those with no time at all for the place ask "why go here when there are far better choices?"

ALEX ⓜ   26 | 27 | 26 | $114
Wynn Las Vegas, 3131 Las Vegas Blvd. S. (Desert Inn Rd.),
702-770-9966; www.wynnlasvegas.com
One of Sin City's "very best" chefs, Alex Stratta, has earned the first-name clout to head up this "Wynn top draw" where diners "descend a grand staircase" "Dolly Levi"–style to a "lavish" room to savor "extraordinarily conceived" French-Med meals served on "gorgeous china"; the staff "goes out of its way to ensure a wonderful evening", and "perfect touches" like "the seat-side purse ottoman" for a clientele "who actually remembers to dress" guarantee a reprieve from "the shorts-and–flip-flops" "Vegas culture"; N.B. no children under five allowed.

ALIZÉ   26 | 26 | 25 | VE
Palms Casino Hotel, 4321 W. Flamingo Rd. (Arville St.),
702-942-7777; www.alizelv.com
"Against all the out-of-town invaders", local institution André Rochat "holds his own" at his "magical" New French "splurge" atop the Palms Hotel where, "if you can tear your eyes away from the chef's stunning plates", you're treated to "an awesome, infinite view of the lights and sights"; in fact, "it's hard to decide which is more fabulous: the food, the vista", the "impeccable service" or "a wine list that would make Bacchus cry" – each is "off the charts"; N.B. they prefer if you don't bring your children under 10.

All-American Bar & Grille ☻   20 | 17 | 18 | $31
Rio All-Suite Hotel, 3700 W. Flamingo Rd. (bet. I-15 &
Valley View Blvd.), 702-777-7767; www.playrio.com
"We're talkin' half-pounder cooked to order, juicy, with a great bun" at this "easy" "all-American spot" at the Rio for "big" burgers or "solid steak", "chops and chix" that make "decent late-night meaty snacks"; the vibe is "laid-back", the "cost isn't bad" and a "positive" remodeling has some-what improved decor that's centered around "upbeat sports plasma screens."

America ☻   14 | 15 | 14 | $24
New York-New York Hotel, 3790 Las Vegas Blvd. S.
(Tropicana Ave.), 702-740-6451; www.arkvegas.com
The eponymous "land of abundance" is amply repre-sented by the "plethora of choices" "from each state in the country" at this 24/7 New York-New York themester; though "slow service leaves time to view" the "gigantic U.S. map" dominating the "red, white and blue" room, it

can seem that the "waiters are actually going to some of those far-reaching places to get the food" – and, if they are, it's "not worth the trip" for "pedestrian" "coffee-shop fare" that "doesn't make one proud to be an American."

Amlee Gourmet
▽ 20 | 14 | 20 | $25

3827 E. Sunset Rd. (Sandhill Rd.), 702-898-3358
Sinophiles fly to "the other side of the airport" on the East Side to chow down on "basic" but "very well-prepared Chinese food" brought by a "very sweet" staff at this "nice neighborhood" spot; the "shredded chicken salad is a locals' fave", the "glazed bananas are great" and the strawberry chicken? – that's just "too good for words."

Andiamo
22 | 19 | 20 | $45

Las Vegas Hilton Hotel, 3000 Paradise Rd. (bet. Desert Inn Rd. & Karen Ave.), 702-732-5664; www.lvhilton.com
If you're "going to the Manilow show", a "great find" for a pre-'Mandy' meal is this "hidden gem in the maze of the Las Vegas Hilton" with a "wonderful, open-kitchen ambiance" and "roomy seating" ripe for ripping through "reliably good" pasta and other Northern Italian–Med specialties; the "attentive, assertive staff" will get you out in time for Barry, but barring the chance to hear 'Copacabana' one more time, critics "wouldn't go out of their way" for the "uninspired" eats.

ANDRÉ'S
27 | 25 | 26 | $69

Monte Carlo Resort, 3770 Las Vegas Blvd. S. (bet. Harmon & Tropicana Aves.), 702-798-7151
401 S. Sixth St. (bet. Bonneville St. & Bridger Ave.), 702-385-5016 ⌺
www.andrelv.com
"Go to the original for homey and the hotel for classy", but enjoy the same "fantastic" French fare at André Rochat's eponymous eateries in a "rustic, charming" "cottage" Downtown and tucked behind "soundproof doors" in a "Louis XIV–style" room in the Monte Carlo; "everything is rich, rich, rich", but diners "basking in the full glory of butter, cream and foie gras" "done to perfection" and presented by a "gracious" staff find it all *"magnifique!"*

Anna Bella
▽ 24 | 17 | 25 | $27

Pebble Mkt., 1000 N. Green Valley Pkwy. (I-215), Henderson, 702-434-2537
"Thank God they're back!" blubber "relieved" *bambini* who rely on this "traditional Italian" when they "miss their mommy" and her "terrific meatballs" and other "good, simple" standards; this Henderson location is "modern, spacious and noisy", but the "warm and welcoming service" makes you "feel like you're part of the family", even if some complain that "the food was better before they moved."

Antonio's   23 | 22 | 23 | $49

Rio All-Suite Hotel, 3700 W. Flamingo Rd. (bet. I-15 & Valley View Blvd.), 702-777-7777; www.playrio.com

The "kitchen is very accommodating to requests", and so is the wine cellar (at prices up to $200,000 a bottle) at the Rio All-Suite's "marvelous New York–style" Italian; complete with "strolling musicians" and "cordial service", this "comfortable setting" for "heavenly" signature onion soup and "excellent veal dishes" "looks like a scene from *The Godfather*, but with a happier ending."

Applebee's   13 | 12 | 16 | $19

Best of the West, 2070 N. Rainbow Blvd. (Lake Mead Blvd.), 702-648-1065
Boulevard Mall, 3340 S. Maryland Pkwy. (Desert Inn Rd.), 702-737-4990
820 E. Warm Springs Rd. (I-215), 702-837-8733
5010 S. Fort Apache Rd. (Tropicana Ave.), 702-221-1061
Smith's Shopping Ctr., 500 N. Nellis Blvd. (Stewart Ave.), 702-452-7155
3501 S. Rainbow Blvd. (Spring Mountain Rd.), 702-220-3070
8730 W. Charleston Blvd. (Durango Dr.), 702-946-6104
Westland Fair, 4605 W. Charleston Blvd. (Decatur Blvd.), 702-870-5973
1501 N. Green Valley Pkwy. (Pebble Rd.), Henderson, 702-914-2691
699 N. Stephanie St. (Sunset Rd.), Henderson, 702-433-6339
www.applebees.com
Additional locations throughout the Las Vegas area

"If you're looking for a quick lunch" after days of haute fressing, "you could do worse than a salad" from the "great Weight Watchers menu" at this "low-end" Traditional American chain that's "thriving like fungus" in Vegas; "if the service were any worse, it would be a buffet", but at least it "beats standing in line at a hotel coffee shop."

AquaKnox   24 | 25 | 23 | $58

Venetian Hotel, 3355 Las Vegas Blvd. S. (bet. Flamingo & Spring Mountain Rds.), 702-414-3772; www.aquaknox.net

"Catch a star" falling upon the "brilliant" fish and raw-bar items at the Venetian's "über-cool", celebrity-infested crustacean house where the glass-enclosed circular room features "cascading water" and "lighting changes from blue to green that make you feel as if you were deep in the ocean"; it "doesn't cost like Fort Knox", but your "waiter might wander for 40 years between appetizer and entree."

Archi's Thai Kitchen Ⓜ   ∇ 24 | 15 | 17 | $21

6360 W. Flamingo Rd. (Jones Blvd.), 702-880-5550

"Excellent curry and pad Thai" are on order at this tiny West Side Thai where "gullible Americans" should be forewarned that "spicy means spicy" – "with a vengence"; it's a "small" strip-mall "shack", but "they do a lot with it" to create a "peaceful" atmosphere.

Auld Dubliner Irish Pub NEW   – | – | – | M

MonteLago Vlg., 40 Via Bel Canto (Via Brianza), 702-567-8002;
www.aulddubliner.com

Like a wandering expat, this bit of the auld sod adds some diversity – if only faux – to the Med-themed MonteLago Village at Lake Las Vegas; the 'cottage-style' furnishings imported from Dublin evoke the cozy feel of an Emerald Isle public house, and it follows through with traditional Irish dishes washed down with free-flowing Guinness.

AUREOLE   25 | 27 | 24 | $76

Mandalay Bay Resort, 3950 Las Vegas Blvd. S. (Mandalay Bay Rd.), 702-632-7401; www.charliepalmer.com

"Book your bachelor party" in the "vaulted" front of Charlie Palmer's Mandalay Bay outpost for a "super-sexy" "dining fantasy" complete with "acrobatic" "angels" "on bungees" "who fetch the good stuff" from the "extravagant wine tower", or let the "attentive" staff usher you to the back for a "romantic dinner"; either way, "bring your bank book", as the bill for the "sublime" New American offerings "can rise as high as those lovely ladies" soaring for your vino.

Austin's Steakhouse   25 | 22 | 25 | $48

Texas Station Hotel, 2101 Texas Star Ln. (bet. Lake Mead Blvd. & Rancho Dr.), North Las Vegas, 702-631-1033;
www.stationcasinos.com

If "you're tired of buffets and food courts" – heck, if you need "a break from the Strip" altogether – high-tail it to North Vegas where "wonderful steaks", a "nice atmosphere" and "outstanding service" await at this Texas Station chophouse; when you're done with your meal, "you can hit the $2 craps tables" in the hotel's "locals' casino."

Baja Fresh Mexican Grill   19 | 12 | 15 | $11

3347 E. Russell Rd. (Pecos Rd.), 702-212-6800
Mission Ctr., 1380 E. Flamingo Rd. (Maryland Pkwy.), 702-699-8920
4343 N. Rancho Dr. (Craig Rd.), 702-396-2553
Sahara Pavilion, 4760 W. Sahara Ave. (Decatur Blvd.),
702-878-7772
4190 S. Rainbow Blvd. (Flamingo Rd.), 702-876-4193
Summerhill Plaza, 7501 W. Lake Mead Blvd. (Buffalo Dr.),
702-838-4100
Target Shopping Ctr., 1292 S. Nellis Blvd. (Charleston Blvd.),
702-641-6770
The Lakes, 8780 W. Charleston Blvd. (bet. Durango Dr. & Rampart Blvd.), 702-948-4043
The Tropicana Beltway, 4916 S. Fort Apache Rd. (W. Tropicana Ave.), 702-871-4260
7930 W. Tropical Pkwy. (Centennial Center Blvd.), 702-307-2345
www.bajafresh.com
Additional locations throughout the Las Vegas area

"Fresh fast food" might sound like an "oxymoron", but given the "healthy" staples "made right in front of you" and a "rapidly replenished fixings bar", the cuisine at this Mexican chainster fits the description; ok, it's "not a place for a romantic dinner", but it's "simple", "inexpensive" and turns out your "delicious, filling" order quicker than you can throw "two thumbs up for its Burrito *Dos Manos*."

Bally's Steakhouse　　　　22　19　21　$52

Bally's Las Vegas Hotel, 3645 Las Vegas Blvd. S. (Flamingo Rd.), 702-739-4111; www.ballyslasvegas.com
"If it's raining and you don't want to leave the premises", you're in luck at Bally's where "solid" beef and lobster come "with all the comforts you would expect" from "a man's steakhouse out of the '60s" (1973, to be exact), including "old-world service" and a "clubby" ambiance; perhaps the "decor and menu are dated, but the food is good", not only for dinner but during the "quintessential old-school" champagne-and-caviar Sunday brunch.

Bamboleo　　　　　∇　21　20　19　$27

Rio All-Suite Hotel, 3700 W. Flamingo Rd. (bet. I-15 & Valley View Blvd.), 702-247-7983; www.playrio.com
"Sit at the bar and watch the carnival floats" during the free Show in the Sky at this "decent Mexican" upstairs in the Rio's Masquerade Village; monster signature margaritas in souvenir glasses go well "with the Mardi Gras entertainment outside", and as for the "standard" south-of-the-border bites, the "chips and salsa are very tasty", and those who "recommend the fish tacos" are "right on" the *dinero*.

Bartolotta Ristorante di Mare　　26　26　24　$70

Wynn Las Vegas, 3131 Las Vegas Blvd. S. (Desert Inn Rd.), 702-770-9966; www.wynnlasvegas.com
Namesake chef Paul Bartolotta's Italian seafood palazzo in the Wynn offers "exceptional" dining thanks to Mediterranean fish previously "unheard of west of Appalachia" that's flown in daily and oven-roasted or charcoal-grilled; the neo-rustic interior is "lovely", but "eat outside, as it's beautiful" on the property's exclusive lake; P.S. wherever you sit, "if you watch what you order", your meal "can be reasonably priced for the high-end."

Battista's Hole in the Wall　　16　16　18　$27

4041 Audrie St. (bet. Flamingo Rd. & Las Vegas Blvd.), 702-732-1424; www.battistaslasvegas.com
"Finally", "something with soul" in Sin City sigh surveyors stuffing themselves on "red-sauce" "package deals" including soup or salad, "great garlic bread and as much wine as you can drink" at this "old Vegas" "dive" that offers "no uppity claims", just "passable" Italian with faux "Queens ambiance" on the side; sure, it's "tacky" and "out of date", but everyone "treats you like a human", including the "campy" "accordion guy" who "has a song and something to say about each state" in the nation.

Bay Side Buffet   21 | 19 | 18 | $25
Mandalay Bay Resort, 3950 Las Vegas Blvd. S.
(Mandalay Bay Rd.), 702-632-7402; www.mandalaybay.com
"Lots of choices" – including "roasted meats", a "good
pasta station" and a "nice selection of desserts" – might
sound heavy, but it's balanced by the "light and airy" view
of the "amazing" Mandalay Bay pools and gardens at this
Eclectic buffet that's "above and beyond" the pack of wolf-
downs on the Strip; still, even fans admit "it is what it is":
"just another cafeteria" in which to "use your comps to get
a free meal."

Becker's Steakhouse ● NEW   – | – | – | E
2400 N. Buffalo Dr. (Smoke Ranch Rd.), 702-216-2700
This meat-mavens' mecca on the West Side comes courtesy
of a family long in the gaming biz, but the video-poker
machines built into the bar don't detract from the well-
executed steakhouse favorites, elegant interior, polished
service and live entertainment that all conjure up Old Las
Vegas; N.B. no one under 18 admitted.

BELLAGIO BUFFET   24 | 19 | 19 | $31
Bellagio Hotel, 3600 Las Vegas Blvd. S. (Flamingo Rd.),
702-693-8255; www.bellagio.com
"Loosen your belt good" because "all anyone could want"
to eat is "deftly prepared" and "well presented" at the
Bellagio's "high-end" Eclectic paean to "pigging out"; the
"feast" (from "unlimited cracked crab" and Kobe beef to
"Asian specialties like congee" and "exotic choices such
as venison") is so "fresh and flavorful", it "elevates the
genre", so despite "hungry" "hordes" and a "banquet-
hall" atmosphere, gourmands ask "can I live here?"

Bella Luna   – | – | – | E
7905 W. Sahara Ave. (Buffalo Dr.), 702-227-7900;
www.bellaluna.us
The name means 'beautiful moon' in Italian, and the
Sardinian chef-owner of this West Sider brings a touch of
elegance to the suburbs with seafood creations and thin-
crusted pizzas that make you feel like you've escaped to a
serene Mediterranean island; smooth service at a relaxing
pace adds the grace notes.

Benihana   18 | 19 | 20 | $39
Las Vegas Hilton Hotel, 3000 Paradise Rd. (bet. Desert Inn Rd. &
Karen Ave.), 702-732-5334; www.benihana.com
Amid an east-of-the-Strip landscape "replete with
koi ponds, waterfalls and replica huts" lies the "most
lavish" link in this "standard-model chop 'n' dice"
Japanese chain; the "chefs put on quite a show" for "con-
ventioneers" slurping "umbrella drinks", but the fare is
"trite", so the "shrimp-and-knives juggling" act quickly
becomes "old-hat."

Bertolini's
|19| |19| |18| |$33|

Forum Shops at Caesars Palace, 3500 Las Vegas Blvd. S. (Flamingo Rd.), 702-735-4663
Village Sq., 9500 W. Sahara Ave. (Fort Apache Rd.), 702-869-1540
www.mortons.com

"Watch the indoor sky change colors from day to night" from your terrace seat "in the middle of the mall at Caesars" at the Strip branch of this "fast, friendly" chain serving a "generous", if "run-of-the-mill", Italian meal; it's "noisy if you're close to the fountain", but it's a "great place to people-watch" – "for a quieter dinner, try inside", or cab it over to the West Side location.

Big Al's Oyster Bar ●
|19| |12| |17| |$27|

Orleans Hotel, 4500 W. Tropicana Ave. (Arville St.), 702-365-7111; www.orleanscasino.com

"Sit at the counter and watch 'em make your meal" in the open kitchen at this raw bar/casual seafooder in a "heavily trafficked area of the Orleans" west of the Strip where fans claim the "affordable" eats are "not damn bad at all"; critics, however, aren't nearly as "friendly" toward the place as the staff is toward them: asked "how can you mess up an oyster?", they suggest visiting this "perfect combination" of "disappointing" fare and "unending racket" to find out.

Big Dog's ●
|17| |14| |17| |$16|

1511 N. Nellis Blvd. (bet. Owens & Washington Aves.), 702-459-1099
4543 N. Rancho Dr. (Craig Rd.), 702-645-1404
6390 W. Sahara Ave. (Torrey Pines Dr.), 702-876-3647
www.bigdogsbrews.com

"Great for Green Bay Packer cheeseheads", this "pub-grub" trio wags the tail with "Wisconsin specialties", including the "best hot dogs in town"; the "cute roadhouses" serve "nothing fancy", just "tasty", "modestly priced" comfort food (plus "their own beer brewed on-site" at Rancho Drive) dished out in a four-legged-friend-themed "sports-bar" atmosphere – bring "earplugs" lest the howling "during playoffs" nips at your nerves.

Big Kitchen Buffet
|16| |11| |16| |$20|

Bally's Las Vegas Hotel, 3645 Las Vegas Blvd. S. (Flamingo Rd.), 702-967-4930; www.ballyslasvegas.com

It's "not the newest kid on the block", but "if you want a hearty meal (and who doesn't when they're losing money?)", this matron of "midlevel buffets" in Bally's churns out the "usual" belt-buster suspects, from "regular American" to Chinese; the "sterile room" feels like a "cafeteria", and "nothing will knock your socks off", but it might make you pop your pants — eat enough of the "home-town potluck" cuisine, and you'll "have to buy a sweat suit to be comfortable for the rest of the day."

Billy Bob's   ▽ 22 17 19 $34
Sam's Town Hotel, 5111 Boulder Hwy. (S. Nellis Blvd.),
702-454-8031; www.samstownlv.com
For an "economical" beef feast, check out this "cowboy"-
themed surf 'n' turfer in Sam's Town on the East Side,
where they don't take the words "come hungry" lightly –
the portions are "big enough to fill the Hoover Dam"; still,
given the "typical" tastes, critics ask "even if you could
eat this much, why would you want to?"

Binion's Ranch Steakhouse   22 17 19 $40
Binion's Hotel, 128 Fremont St., 24th fl. (bet. Casino Center Blvd. &
1st St.), 702-382-1600; www.binions.com
Though "the World Series of Poker has moved away" from
the legendary Downtown casino that Benny built, the
"ghosts of gamers past still linger" over the steak-and-
lobster dinners served at this "good, old-fashioned" chophouse in Binion's; those who "remember it as being better"
before the "Harrah's acquisition" say if you think "you can
still smell Sinatra" here, it might just be the "musty" decor.

Bistro Zinc NEW   – – – E
MonteLago Vlg., 15 Via Bel Canto (Via Brianza), 702-567-9462;
www.bistrozincrestaurant.com
A more casual counterpart to Como's steakhouse – its
sister restaurant also in Lake Las Vegas' MonteLago
Village – this lakeside newcomer already has a reputation
as a place for laid-back dining (particularly on the patio
with an alfresco jazz concert nearby); its French-flavored
American menu is the handiwork of Joseph Keller, brother
of über-chef Thomas.

Black Mountain Grill ●   18 17 19 $27
11021 S. Eastern Ave. (Sun Ridge Pkwy.), Henderson,
702-990-0990; www.blackmountaingrill.com
"For a solid meal without the tourists", hang out with
Henderson "locals" at this "rustic", "lodge-style" Eclectic
covering everything from steakhouse specialties to wood-
fired pizzas to Pacific Rim flavors; "the fireplace is a nice
touch", and "the food is good, but it takes forever for it to
come out of the kitchen" – lucky that the place is open 24
hours a day.

Blackstone's Steak House   23 21 22 $53
Monte Carlo Resort, 3770 Las Vegas Blvd. S. (bet. Harmon &
Tropicana Aves.), 702-730-7405; www.montecarlo.com
"When you want to be part of the old boys' network", sink
into a "high-backed armchair" or "deep booth" at this
"dark" beefery in the Monte Carlo on the Strip, have an
"excellent" waiter bring you the "stellar wine list", an
"incredible T-bone" or "fantastic prime rib" and enjoy a
"quiet", "classic" meal; the only diners "disappointed"
here are the ones "who order fish."

Boa Steakhouse   24   24   22 $60

*Forum Shops at Caesars Palace, 3500 Las Vegas Blvd. S.
(Flamingo Rd.), 702-733-7373; www.innovativedining.com*
A "California favorite comes to Vegas" at this Forum Shops
steakhouse that "exceeds all expectations" with a "fabulous" menu: start with a "perfect-10 martini", finish with
"dessert to die for" and dig in between to "heavenly" cuts,
"delicious" fish and "appetizers with flair"; you can settle
in amid "interesting", "ancient hardwood" decor or out on
the "great patio" – though it's "trendy", it "doesn't have
that here's-your-hat-what's-your-hurry feeling."

Bob Taylor's Ranch House   ▽ 17   15   18 $38

*6250 Rio Vista St. (Ann Rd.), 702-645-1399;
www.bobtaylorsranchhouse.com*
Neighboring Northwest suburban lawns have supplanted
tumbleweeds, and yet this 52-years-young "bastion" is
"still standing", serving chophouse chow and "old-time"
vibes; a meal by the fire amid the well-aged git-along-little-
doggy decor can be "relaxing", if you don't mind "average"
eats and service "lacking in personality" – culinary sheriffs
shoot it up, drawling "it should be called Raunch House."

Bonefish Grill **NEW**   –   –   –   M

*10839 S. Eastern Ave. (Horizon Ridge Pkwy.), Henderson,
702-228-3474; www.bonefishgrill.com*
Seafood in the desert is no oxymoron at this Florida-based
chain that's landed in a South Henderson strip center; look
for a daily changing variety of fresh fish (including its
signature Bang-Bang Shrimp, a pile of crustaceans served
in a spicy, creamy sauce) served in an airy atmosphere
with – you guessed it – fish-themed art.

Bootlegger Bistro ◗   18   18   18 $29

*7700 Las Vegas Blvd. S. (Robindale Rd.), 702-736-4939;
www.bootleggerlasvegas.com*
"Relive the early years" of Sin City at this south-of-the-
Strip "hangout" "where the real deals were made back in
the day", a 24/7 "red-sauce" Italian "hoot" complete with
"leather booths, mood lighting" and "entertainers dining
after the shows let out"; regulars stick around until the sun
comes up to "try their breakfast pizza", even though
foodies would rather "pass on the menu and stick with the
entertainment and libations."

Border Grill   21   18   18 $33

*Mandalay Bay Resort, 3950 Las Vegas Blvd. S.
(Mandalay Bay Rd.), 702-632-7403; www.bordergrill.com*
"Don't look for the Taco Bell dog" at this "elevated
Mexican" by TV's *Two Hot Tamales* where "reasonably
priced", "creative" *comidas* are created with "plenty of
spice" and "a dash of tradition"; the "margaritas could
knock you on your ass" – if you weren't already sitting

down in the "tacky" interior or outside "overlooking the Mandalay Bay pool gardens" slur "crowds" who cause such a ruckus that "a bullfight ring is more subdued"; those who say it "ain't that sizzling anymore" think it's "time to run from the Border."

BOUCHON 24 | 24 | 23 | $57

Venetian Hotel, 3355 Las Vegas Blvd. S. (bet. Flamingo & Spring Mountain Rds.), 702-414-6200; www.bouchonbistro.com

"Genius" Thomas Keller "graces Vegas" with this French bistro, an outpost of the Yountville "classic" in the Venetian's "new tower" "far away from the razzmatazz"; "casual gourmands" flock here for "power breakfasts" featuring "light-as-a-feather sourdough waffles" or dinner's "luscious rotisserie chicken", nesting in the "Parisian" interior or on the "lovely" patio; service might be "so-so" so far, but the kitchen earns its "buzz" by "proving you don't have to be expensive to be excellent."

BRADLEY OGDEN 26 | 24 | 25 | $80

Caesars Palace, 3570 Las Vegas Blvd. S. (Flamingo Rd.), 702-731-7731; www.caesarspalace.com

"What a treat" it is to dine at this "wonderful" Caesars casino destination where the "celebrity" namesake "is actually in", "working his wonders" with an "always changing menu" of "deliciously innovative" New American dishes; the "portions are small" but the "flavors are big", and the "impeccable" staff is "without pretension" – they might even give you a "tour of the kitchen" for a "charming" topper to an "elegant" evening that's "worth your hard-earned dollars."

Broiler ▽ 21 | 15 | 20 | $26

Boulder Station Hotel, 4111 Boulder Hwy. (Lamb Blvd.), 702-432-7777 ☾
Palace Station Hotel, 2411 W. Sahara Ave. (Rancho Dr.), 702-367-2408
www.stationcasinos.com

"Adding an entree can be gilding the lily" when the "excellent soup-and-salad bar" is this "extensive", but make room anyway for the "good" meat and "great" seafood at this "solid, casual" surf 'n' turf duo in the Station casinos on the East Side and west of the Strip; they're "fantastic values" for a "reliable" meal, with plenty left over to "wrap up and take away."

Buffet, The 18 | 16 | 17 | $17

Golden Nugget Hotel, 129 Fremont St. (Main St.), 702-385-7111; www.goldennugget.com

"A very good combination" of "clean, casual" environs and "fulfilling" fare awaits at this Golden Nugget buffet; the "traditional Downtown setting" and "safe-for-American-tastes" cuisine might be "nothing special", but Friday's seafood is "plentiful", Sunday brunch's "champagne flows freely" and, as opposed to other "cheap" spreads, "some of the food here even has flavor" – particularly the "to-die-for bread pudding."

Buffet, The   16 | 12 | 15 | $19
Las Vegas Hilton Hotel, 3000 Paradise Rd. (bet. Desert Inn Rd. & Karen Ave.), 702-732-5111; www.lvhilton.com
Even if "cabbies and locals" recommend this all-you-can-eat chowdown amid the "flashing lights and singing slots" of the Las Vegas Hilton's sportsbook east of the Strip, tourists find it "nothing to write home about"; there's "lots of variety" to the "decent" Eclectic offerings, but like others of its ilk, it's "known for speed, not quality dining."

Burger Bar   23 | 17 | 18 | $23
Mandalay Place, 3950 Las Vegas Blvd. S. (Mandalay Bay Rd.), 702-632-9364; www.mandalaybay.com
From the "Zen-like simplicity" of a plain patty to the "baroque opulence" of "Kobe beef with foie gras and black truffles", the "possibilities are unlimited" for "building your own" version of that "old American favorite" at this "great concept" in Mandalay Place; not only can you choose from "an array of tasty toppings", but the burgers themselves come in a "huge variety" – at a "wide range of prices"; beyond monitors broadcasting sports events, the "casual" place isn't nearly as well dressed as the namesakes.

Buzio's   22 | 20 | 21 | $42
Rio All-Suite Hotel, 3700 W. Flamingo Rd. (bet. I-15 & Valley View Blvd.), 702-252-7697; www.playrio.com
The "cioppino is wonderful" and a "bargain, for all you get" at this "terrific" fish house in the Rio that also offers "oversized cocktails" and the "biggest lobster ever"; still, those who knew it when feel it's "getting a bit dated", citing the kitchen's "lack of imagination", not to mention "slow service" and a "so-so setting."

Cafe, The   19 | 19 | 18 | $26
The Hotel at Mandalay Bay, 3950 Las Vegas Blvd. S. (Mandalay Bay Rd.), 702-632-9250; www.mandalaybay.com
This "cut-above" cafe in The Hotel at Mandalay Bay is a "stylish" setting for "casual" but "relaxing" dining; though the menu choices are "standard" for this type of Traditional American, they're "well prepared" and it's a "hoot" watching the "parade of interesting people going to Mix" while remaining at a safe distance from the "hustle and bustle."

Cafe Ba Ba Reeba!   23 | 21 | 21 | $34
Fashion Show Mall, 3200 Las Vegas Blvd. S. (Fashion Show Ln.), 702-258-1211; www.cafebabareeba.com
They "should open in Madrid and teach Spaniards how good their food can be" argue amigos of this Fashion Show Mall outpost of a Chicago institution serving "little morsels

of heaven"; there are "no bad picks" among their "amazing" paellas and "huge variety" of "excellent tapas", while the "indoor/outdoor" seating helps make it the "place for celebrating", "sampling" and "sipping sangria."

Café Bellagio ❂   20 | 20 | 19 | $28
Bellagio Hotel, 3600 Las Vegas Blvd. S. (Flamingo Rd.), 702-693-8255; www.bellagio.com
"Even at 3 AM" when "you want to get back to the tables quickly", the casual New American food is "fresh and plentiful" and the staff "accommodating" at this around-the-clock, "upscale coffee shop" that's the "most reasonable place to eat" in the namesake hotel; a "lovely view" of the conservatory's "ever-fabulous", ever-changing floral garden makes this "quiet oasis" all the more "pleasant."

Cafe Heidelberg   ▽ 21 | 15 | 20 | $25
610 E. Sahara Ave. (bet. Maryland Pkwy. & Paradise Rd.), 702-731-5310
"Not for the faint of appetite", this "fast, fun German" east of the Strip rolls out "huge portions" of "excellent" wurst, schnitzel and sauerbraten; a weekend band playing oompahs and "cheery maidens" who seem "fresh out of their show-girl costumes" bring on "Oktober in April" where "far too much of a good thing" includes takeaway tastes from the "nice" deli/grocery.

Cafe Lago   18 | 19 | 17 | $25
Caesars Palace, 3570 Las Vegas Blvd. S. (Flamingo Rd.), 702-731-7110; www.caesarspalace.com
"Slightly more sophisticated" than most "typical hotel cafes", this "mellow" spot in Caesars with "short waits" is a "good choice" for Traditional American and International selections served à la carte or at weekend dinner and brunch buffets; sit outside on the patio or inside by the "big windows" for a view of the "hot bodies surrounding the huge pool."

Cafe Tajine   ▽ 19 | 18 | 18 | $35
Hyatt Regency Lake Las Vegas, 101 Montelago Blvd. (Lake Las Vegas Pkwy.), 702-567-1234; www.hyatt.com
Though the fare is now more New American steakhouse than Mediterranean-influenced, this "casual" yet "attractive" indoor/outdoor venue at the Hyatt Regency on Lake Las Vegas still sports "lovely" Moroccan decor, with a "nice view" from the terrace; "considering the location", the tabs are "reasonable", but they still might not be worth it for "so-so food" and "slow" service.

Café Wasabi   ▽ 25 | 20 | 21 | $32
7365 W. Sahara Ave. (Tenaya Way), 702-804-9652
The "funky atmosphere" fits a menu filled with "unusual" "combinations that work like a charm" at this "hip place" where young "locals" feed on "creative" Pacific Rim

cuisine, "inventive sushi" and "delicious saketinis" served by a "smiling" staff; if you're wondering "why it's not busier", it's probably because the spot is "hidden" in a West Side shopping mall.

California Pizza Kitchen   19 | 14 | 17 | $21 |

Fashion Show Mall, 3200 Las Vegas Blvd. S. (Fashion Show Ln.), 702-893-1370
Mirage Hotel, 3400 Las Vegas Blvd. S. (Spring Mountain Rd.), 702-791-7357 ●
www.cpk.com

"Same ol', same ol'", but it's all "decent" at this "reliable chain" for "California twists" on pizza, pasta and salad on the Strip or in the Fashion Show Mall; the "reasonably priced", "kid-friendly" menu offers "enough options to please any crew", so "bring the gang", "especially to the Mirage location" where a "great view of the sportsbook" and "good people-watching" keep the urchins occupied during the "very long wait" for a table.

Canaletto   21 | 22 | 20 | $41 |

Venetian Hotel, 3355 Las Vegas Blvd. S. (bet. Flamingo & Spring Mountain Rds.), 702-733-0070; www.venetian.com

The "delicious" Northern Italian dishes "almost make the canal seem real" on the terrace of this "charming" trattoria in the Venetian's "'open-air' replica of St. Mark's Square"; delight your date with "a late lunch and a good bottle of wine" – accompanied by "faux sunsets", "singing gondoliers and lapping water", it's "as romantic as outdoors created indoors can get."

Canal Street   ▽ 20 | 17 | 19 | $35 |

Orleans Hotel, 4500 W. Tropicana Ave. (Arville St.), 702-365-7111; www.orleanscasino.com

A "good steak" "won't break the bank" at this surf 'n' turfer west of the Strip offering a "treasure trove of tasty value"; though it's "supposed to be the crown jewel of Orleans eateries", critics look elsewhere for culinary gems, citing "inconsistent" eats, "a has-been sort of style" and "irritating service."

Canter's Deli ●   18 | 12 | 13 | $18 |

Treasure Island Hotel, 3300 Las Vegas Blvd. S. (Spring Mountain Rd.), 702-894-7111; www.cantersdeli.com

"Skinny girls beware": though it's the "sister" of a Los Angeles institution, this "casual" joint doesn't peddle celebrity-diet fare; instead, "if you need a pastrami fix or a bowl of matzo-ball soup and can live with lining up to place your order", its deli dishes "meet expectations" for a "huge", "quick bite"; TI's take is "almost authentic", though it's "missing the attitude" and "gritty charm" of the SoCal original.

Canyon Ranch Cafe   20 | 17 | 19 | $28
*Venetian Hotel, 3355 Las Vegas Blvd. S. (bet. Flamingo &
Spring Mountain Rds.), 702-414-3633; www.venetian.com*
"Detox" from "gluttony" with a "light, delicious" meal at
this "healthy" New American next to Venetian's namesake
spa; it may seem "weird sitting next to bathrobed clients",
but an egg-white omelet in a "cool, chic" setting "without
the slot-machine noise" is a "nice way to start a day" in
which you've promised yourself you'll "follow through with
your workout", even if foes grumble "I had to go get some
breakfast after breakfast" here.

Capital Grille   25 | 23 | 24 | $58
*Fashion Show Mall, 3200 Las Vegas Blvd. S., 3rd fl.
(Spring Mountain Rd.), 702-932-6631; www.thecapitalgrille.com*
"They take their meat seriously" – and with "a list as long
as your arm", they treat their wines the same – at this
"white-tablecloth" chophouse chainster in the Fashion
Show Mall; "thick, flavorful" steaks prepared using "classic
techniques" combine with "super" service and a "typi-
cally clubby", "dark-wood" room to make for a "power-
lunch" destination, with a "phenomenal" city view to boot.

Capriotti's Sandwich Shop   23 | 8 | 16 | $10
*7440 Cheyenne Ave. (Buffalo Dr.), 702-656-7779
3981 E. Sunset Rd. (Sandhill Rd.), 702-898-4904
Paradise Mktpl., 3830 E. Flamingo Rd. (Sandhill Rd.), 702-454-2430
450 S. Buffalo Dr. (bet. Alta Dr. & Ducharme Ave.), 702-838-8659
4825 S. Fort Apache Rd. (Tropicana Ave.), 702-873-4682
Silverado, 9620 Las Vegas Blvd. S. (W. Gary Ave.), 702-407-5602
4747 S. Maryland Pkwy. (bet. Flamingo Rd. & Tropicana Ave.),
702-736-6166
4983 W. Flamingo Rd. (bet. Decatur Blvd. & Edmond St.),
702-222-3331
322 W. Sahara Ave. (bet. Industrial Rd. & Las Vegas Blvd.),
702-474-0229 ⊠
8450 W. Sahara Ave. (Durango Dr.), 702-562-0440
www.capriottis.com
Additional locations throughout the Las Vegas area*
The "Capastrami is awesome", the "cheese steaks are
heavenly" and the "famous Bobbie" (a turkey-and-
trimmings sub that's "like Thanksgiving without the work")
is "sooo delicious" at these "excellent sandwich shops"
dotting the desert; "what they lack in decor, they make up
for in the quality of the food", so get yours to go before you
leave Vegas – then unwrap an "enormous" feast on your
flight home and "receive a lot of envious stares."

Caribe Café ◐   18 | 16 | 18 | $24
*Mirage Hotel, 3400 Las Vegas Blvd. S. (Spring Mountain Rd.),
702-791-7356; www.mirage.com*
When you come down with gambling fever, try the "great
chicken noodle soup" for comfort at this "solid" all-nighter

in the Mirage; "more than a glorified hotel coffee shop"
but less than "special", it efficiently serves "reliable"
Traditional American eats that belie its name – in other
words, "there's nothing Caribe about it."

Carluccio's Tivoli Gardens Ⓜ   ▽ 20 | 19 | 19 | $23

Liberace Plaza, 1775 E. Tropicana Ave. (Spencer St.), 702-795-3236
If you "love a cheesy night out", "plastic grapes" and all,
you can get your "Liberace" on at this "old-school" Vegas
Italian/"giant piano bar" once owned and said to be
"haunted" by the besequined one himself; the "'70s-style"
setting and pricing are "so retro", you get a "good value"
on a "kitschy", "hearty", "red-tablecloth" meal, followed
by a tour of Mr. Showmanship's "attached museum."

Carnegie Deli ◑   20 | 13 | 15 | $22

*Mirage Hotel, 3400 Las Vegas Blvd. S. (Spring Mountain Rd.),
702-791-7310; www.mirage.com*
As "obscenely large" as its "towering" Gotham prototype,
a skyscraping sandwich from the Mirage's deli offshoot
"could literally feed three", if they had a "forklift" to handle
it; the corned beef and pastrami are "musts", but the soup
is also "rich and steaming" and the half-sours are "tart
and plentiful"; even New Yorkers who say "the original, it
ain't" concede that "it does the trick."

Carnival World Buffet   19 | 15 | 16 | $24

*Rio All-Suite Hotel, 3700 W. Flamingo Rd. (bet. I-15 &
Valley View Blvd.), 702-252-7757; www.playrio.com*
One G-rated reason to "undo your pants" in Vegas is this
"massive" International buffet west of the Strip where a trip
around the room takes you "around the world" cuisinewise;
be careful of the ballast you load at each of the "ethnically
grouped" ports of call, as the space can be "too difficult to
navigate to get back to your table" with all that "quantity
that supercedes quality."

Carson Street Cafe ◑   20 | 16 | 17 | $20

*Golden Nugget Hotel, 129 Fremont St. (Main St.), 702-385-7111;
www.goldennugget.com*
"As pleasant a coffee shop as you can find" "when nothing
else is open" Downtown is this 24-hour Eclectic in the
Golden Nugget where the "amazing variety" suits the
"wide range of visitors and locals"; "if you don't like buffets",
or you're too "hungover" to stomach the lines at the feeding
troughs, this sit-down is "good in a pinch" for breakfast or
lunch, despite sometimes "slow" service.

Cathay House   ▽ 20 | 15 | 18 | $26

*5300 Spring Mountain Rd. (bet. Decatur Blvd. & Lindell Rd.),
702-876-3838; www.cathayhouse.com*
"Nighttime dim sum! – that fact alone is enough to merit a
recommendation" for this "great find" on the West Side
where dumplings and other Chinese delights are "done

well" and accompanied by a view of the Strip; "it does get busy", so avoid it "in the middle of the lunch hour."

Center Stage   ▽ 19 19 18 $35
Plaza Hotel, 1 Main St. (Fremont St.), 702-386-2110;
www.plazahotelcasino.com
"Soak up old Vegas atmosphere" at this Italian-American set inside a glass dome in Downtown's Plaza Hotel; though the fare is "decent at a fair price" with a "bargain wine list" to boot, the "restaurant gets its cachet from its location", which gives you "a direct view of the Fremont light show."

Chandelier NEW   _ _ _ I
2980 St. Rose Pkwy. (Eastern Ave.), Henderson, 702-456-8643;
www.chandelierlasvegas.com
The hookah's the thing at most of the Med eateries that dot the Las Vegas Valley, and this Henderson newcomer jazzes up the genre with water-filled banquettes and piped-in jazz; the innovative menu ranges from venerable Middle Eastern dishes to specialties from Italy, India and Greece.

Chang's   20 17 19 $31
Bally's Las Vegas Hotel, 3645 Las Vegas Blvd. S. (Flamingo Rd.),
702-967-7999; www.ballyslasvegas.com
Palace Station Hotel, 2411 W. Sahara Ave. (Rancho Dr.),
702-221-6900; www.palacestation.com ●
4670 S. Decatur Blvd. (Tropicana Ave.), 702-362-3663
For the "real deal in Hong Kong–style" dining, "plenty of Asians" will direct you toward these "classy" Chinese restaurants where shark-fin soup and other "neat stuff" "only slightly modified for the Anglo palate" coexist with more "Americanized" dishes; the Palace Station site means you can get the same "fantastic food" west of the Strip now too.

Charlie Palmer Steak   25 24 25 $68
Four Seasons Hotel, 3960 Las Vegas Blvd. S. (Four Seasons Dr.),
702-632-5120; www.charliepalmer.com
Both the fare and the ambiance are "delicious" at the namesake chef's "sanctuary of beef" in the Four Seasons; the dining room's "well-spaced tables" and "peaceful, adult" atmosphere are "a nice change from places that scream 'notice me'", while the "comfy, clubby" lounge is "out of this world" for a "pre-show drink and cigar"; still, given the "high prices", some "expect more from Charlie."

Cheesecake Factory   21 18 19 $26
Forum Shops at Caesars Palace, 3500 Las Vegas Blvd. S.
(Flamingo Rd.), 702-792-6888 ●
750 S. Rampart Blvd. (Alta Dr.), 702-951-3800
The District, 160 S. Green Valley Pkwy. (Paseo Verde Pkwy.),
Henderson, 702-207-6372 NEW
www.thecheesecakefactory.com
"Cheesecake, cheesecake, oh my God, the cheesecake!" – "batten the hatches 'cause it fattens the britches", but boy,

is that "signature" dessert "super" at the Henderson, Strip and Summerlin links of this "steady nationwide chain" of Americans where the "menu reads like an encyclopedia", the "portions are huge" and the lines are "wayyy longgg"; at least at Caesars, you can "browse the Forum Shops" until you're ok'd for a landing in the "airport-ramp-noisy" room.

Chevys Fresh Mex 16 14 15 $21
Galleria Mall, 1300 W. Sunset Rd. (Stephanie St.), Henderson, 702-434-8323; www.chevys.com
For a "cheap" pit stop while cruising Henderson's Galleria, this California Mexican chainster rolls out a "filling" meal made of "fresh ingredients and tortillas" and sided by "light, crispy chips"; if the "cookie-cutter" "Americanized" *comidas* "lack in creativity", the fruity margaritas are "really good" for a Vegas-style refueling.

Chianti Café ∇ 21 20 19 $33
Trails Village Ctr., 1916 Village Center Circle (Trailwood Dr.), 702-228-3330 ● NEW
2895 N. Green Valley Pkwy. (Sunset Rd.), Henderson, 702-450-3232
"Attentive, personable" servers ferry "surprisingly good" Italian specialties to locals relaxing amid the rustic environs of this Henderson spot; the "nice wine list" includes a dozen by the glass to sip to the tunes tickled from the ivories of a "delightful piano that plays itself when the weekend talent isn't there"; N.B. the Summerlin branch opened post-*Survey*.

Chicago Brewing Company ● 17 16 19 $20
Four Queens Hotel, 202 Fremont St. (Casino Center Blvd.), 702-385-4011
2201 S. Fort Apache Rd. (bet. Charleston & Sahara Aves.), 702-254-3333
www.chicagobrewingcolv.com
The "garlic cheese knots rule" and the ales and lagers are "even better" at this "solid" West Side American microbrewery where the "typical pub grub" is a "great" accompaniment when "watching sports events", followed by a stogie in the cigar lounge; not all of those "giant vats" are filled with hops, though – they also make their own root beer.

Chicago Joe's ⊠ 21 14 19 $25
820 S. Fourth St. (bet. Gass & Hoover Aves.), 702-382-5637; www.chicagojoesrestaurant.com
Chicago Joes and Janes jump for the "real" Windy City chow at this "longtime locals' favorite" in a "tiny cottage nestled among the legal offices" Downtown; it might be a "hole-in-the-wall", but its "consistently good red-sauce Italian food" will "make your mouth happy", and the "genial *Goodfellas* vibe" clinches it as a "choice for a lawyers' power lunch" in the "old-fashioned" tradition.

Chili's Grill & Bar
| 17 | 15 | 18 | $20 |

7530 Las Vegas Blvd. S. (Warm Springs Rd.), 702-270-2818
2011 N. Rainbow Blvd. (Lake Mead Blvd.), 702-638-1482
2520 S. Decatur Blvd. (Sahara Ave.), 702-871-0500
10080 S. Eastern Ave. (bet. Ribbon Rd. & Rte. 146),
702-407-6924
9051 W. Charleston Blvd. (Rampart Blvd.), 702-228-0479
2751 N. Green Valley Pkwy. (Sunset Rd.), Henderson, 702-433-3333
www.chilis.com

"When you're too tired to cook or live it up" or even go for something that's not "predictable", this "good family chain" may be "nothing special", but it "does just what it says it will": serve "a decent fajita, a medium-rare burger" or some other Traditional American or Tex-Mex "standard" along with "great chips", salsa and margaritas at "moderate prices"; sometimes it's soothing to "know what you'll get."

China Grill
| 23 | 23 | 20 | $49 |

Mandalay Bay Resort, 3950 Las Vegas Blvd. S.
(Mandalay Bay Rd.), 702-632-7404; www.chinagrillmgt.com

"A lot of imagination" was sunk into the menu and decor at this "funky, loud" Asian fusion "madhouse" that "fits the bill" for fans of "hip places"; the Mandalay Bay outpost of the NYC original "beautifully presents" "family-style" "creativity" in entrees like signature Shanghai lobster followed by "Disney-esque desserts"; after a few "delicious" concoctions poured by the "talent" that stirs up the "outstanding bar scene", you'll want to stop into "the coolest bathrooms in town."

Chin Chin
| 18 | 15 | 17 | $27 |

New York-New York Hotel, 3790 Las Vegas Blvd. S.
(Tropicana Ave.), 702-740-6300; www.chinchin.com

A "Chinese breakfast is a good choice after all-night partying" at New York-New York, so stop into this Sino spot to soothe yourself with 7:30 AM dim sum; "bargain" pricing for "huge portions" is also a relief "after a long day of gambling" all your money away, but as for the flavor, critics aren't rushing to cash in their chips for "ersatz Asian-themed food."

Chinois
| 22 | 19 | 20 | $43 |

Forum Shops at Caesars Palace, 3500 Las Vegas Blvd. S.
(Flamingo Rd.), 702-737-9700; www.wolfgangpuck.com

"Life is not complete unless you've had the Chinois chicken salad" at the Forum Shops' "roomier" sibling to LA's original Peking Puck palace; though this satellite "doesn't have Wolfgang's personal touch, some of the magic can be sensed" in the Asian fare's "impressive flavor combinations"; a recent remodel made the "casual atmosphere" just the thing for "unwinding after shopping" with a "bowl of mai tais" along with "family-style" plates and "excellent sushi."

Chipotle   20 | 13 | 15 | $11 |

Food Court, 3475 Las Vegas Blvd. S. (Flamingo Rd.), 702-836-0804
7370 Las Vegas Blvd. S. (Warm Springs Rd.), 702-270-1973
4530 S. Maryland Pkwy. (Harmon Ave.), 702-436-9177
10251 S. Eastern Ave. (Sahara Ave.), Henderson, 702-361-6438
1311 W. Sunset Rd. (Stephanie St.), Henderson, 702-436-7740
www.chipotle.com

"Whether you're a high roller or just lost your shirt", you
get the same "cheap", "quick bites between bets" at this
Mexican chain where "high-quality ingredients" are rolled
into "spaceship-size burritos" right before your eyes; it's
"not exceptional", but if you're "drunk and hungry", it
"seems much more natural than McDonald's fare, even
though it's owned by them."

Chocolate Swan   22 | 16 | 17 | $15 |

Mandalay Place, 3930 Las Vegas Blvd. S., Ste. 121B
(Mandalay Bay Rd.), 702-632-9366; www.chocolateswan.com
The "hardest working kitchen" in a town of hard-working
kitchens just might lie in this "decadent" confection-and-
cake cafe at Mandalay Bay, a "pricey" but "great place to
satisfy your sweet tooth" on "delicious frozen custard",
"heavenly" pies and "kick-ass" cocoa-based creations;
it's an opportunity to "chocolate out" ("is that possible?"),
"sip coffee" or wine and "watch the world go by."

Coco's   14 | 12 | 15 | $16 |

169 E. Tropicana Ave. (Duke Ellington Way), 702-736-3936 ◑
9310 W. Tropicana Ave. (Fort Apache Rd.), 702-362-1897
9210 S. Eastern Ave. (Serene Ave.), Henderson, 702-614-2772
www.cocosbakery.com
"Dependable if unexciting", this "friendly" trio of "fair
stops" for coffee-shop fare is both "comforting" and "reasonably priced"; for breakfast, it's a "good option to soak
up any lingering alcohol and curb a potential hangover", if
the staff didn't "take forever" to bring your chow.

Coffee Pub   ▽ 17 | 12 | 18 | $18 |

2800 W. Sahara Ave. (Paseo Del Prado), 702-367-1913
"Politicos abound" in the "locals-only atmosphere" at this
place "to see and be seen eating breakfast" west of the
Strip, where "many business deals have been done" and
everyone who's anyone in Vegas gets their grub on; the
"food's not so good", the service needs help, but "just like
that bunny" on TV, it "keeps goin' and goin'."

COMMANDER'S PALACE   25 | 23 | 25 | $57 |

Desert Passage at Aladdin, 3663 Las Vegas Blvd. S.
(Harmon Ave.), 702-892-8272; www.commanderspalace.com
It's "not quite as good as New Orleans", but you can still
score "lick-the-plate-good" Creole cuisine in the desert at
the Aladdin's "excellent re-creation" of the Louisiana
"classic"; the dishes are "sinfully delicious", but there's

lots more to "put on your happy face" for: lunchtime's "hefty" martinis are a 25-cent "bargain", the band serves "mellow jazz with your turtle soup" during the "excellent" weekend brunch and the "service is so genteel", "it's straight out of the Big Easy."

Como's ▽ | 19 | 23 | 19 | $44 |

MonteLago Vlg., 10 Via Brianza (Lake Mead Dr.), 702-567-9950; www.comosllv.com

For an "excellent escape from the madness" on the Strip, enjoy a "lovely brunch in the breezy atmosphere" of this indoor/outdoor surf 'n' turfer where Thomas Keller's brother, Joseph, mans the stoves – then "stroll through the quaint village", and "you'll feel like you're in the Mediterranean"; still, the experience can be "inconsistent" at a place that has "so much potential", but it "needs better management" to be worth the trek to Lake Las Vegas.

Costa del Sol Ⓜ ▽ | 20 | 20 | 19 | $32 |

Sunset Station Hotel, 1301 W. Sunset Rd. (Stephanie St.), Henderson, 702-547-7814; www.stationcasinos.com

"A fish house is much needed" in Henderson's Sunset Station, and this one does a "better-than-average" job of it; net yourself an "imaginative special" along with some "great salad" or a dozen on the half-shell from the oyster bar for a "pleasant experience" at a "good value", even if the "slow" service and "just ok" eats disappoint foodies casting for the "top-notch."

Cottage Café ◗ | – | – | – | I |

4647 Paradise Rd. (bet. Harmon & Tropicana Aves.), 702-650-3395

Ethiopian cuisine remains a mystery to many locals but this user-friendly place east of the Strip makes it easy to learn the secrets of scooping up meat-based dishes with pancake-like injera bread (there's also spaghetti on the menu for the faint of heart); music videos from the homeland on a big-screen TV add to the transporting vibe.

Courtyard Buffet | 14 | 11 | 14 | $17 |

Stratosphere Hotel, 2000 Las Vegas Blvd. S. (north of Sahara Ave.), 702-380-7777; www.stratospherehotel.com

"They sometimes have good combination tickets for this buffet and a ride to the top of the tower", so "if you're at the Stratosphere" and you want to consume "mass quantities" before blasting off for a view of the Strip, the "average" Eclectic bites are "not bad" – if there aren't too many "tourists" in line ahead of you; gourmands go elsewhere, grumbling that this "feeding bin" "needs a lot of work."

Craftsteak | 25 | 24 | 24 | $70 |

MGM Grand Hotel, 3799 Las Vegas Blvd. S. (Tropicana Ave.), 702-891-7318; www.mgmgrand.com

"As expected", Tom Colicchio's MGM Grand chop-and-seafood house delivers "superior quality", "flawless execution" and dining empowerment: "choose what your cow ate before" it hit the plate, then "build your own meal with a bountiful selection" of sides to go with your "sublime" beef (or lamb, pork, fowl or fish); the wine list is "tremendous", the "groovy staff" is "helpful" and the "un-Vegas-like setting" ("not old boy, but metrosexual") is as "delightfully unadorned" as the meat; if you can afford the "high prices", you'll "enjoy it immensely."

Cravings   20 | 18 | 17 | $24 |
Mirage Hotel, 3400 Las Vegas Blvd. S. (Spring Mountain Rd.),
702-791-7355; www.mirage.com
On the heels of Adam Tihany's "hip" "makeover", the "Mirage buffet has left the 20th century and entered the 21st"; when you browse the dozen "separate stations" manned by chefs offering "personalized" dishes "from every corner of the world", "if you can't find something" to satisfy the "craving to fill your empty stomach without making a hole in your wallet", you're "food-phobic" say fans; those who find it "sterile" say the über-designer may have "taken the Zen, clean-lines thing a little too far."

Crown & Anchor British Pub ◑   19 | 19 | 18 | $16 |
1350 E. Tropicana Ave. (bet. Eastern Ave. & Maryland Pkwy.),
702-739-8676; www.crownandanchorlv.com
A "great place" to "meet friends after work", no matter what hours you keep, this 24/7 "real British pub" on the East Side is a "locals' favorite" for "traditional English fish 'n' chips" and "all kinds of ales" from across the pond; drop anchor in the "nice outdoor dining area", "watch rugby" on the tube or "have a go at the dartboards."

DANIEL BOULUD BRASSERIE   25 | 25 | 24 | $74 |
Wynn Las Vegas, 3131 Las Vegas Blvd. S. (Desert Inn Rd.),
702-770-9966; www.wynnlasvegas.com
"No matter where Daniel opens restaurants, you can be assured" of an "exceptional" experience, as evidenced by this "magical" New French namesake with a patio overlooking the Wynn's water wall; the "impressive dishes" (including the "famous" "burger stuffed with short ribs") have the "innovative yet traditional touches you would expect from a Boulud eatery", and the "chic" setting "is consistent with the db mode"; "the service is not perfected", but "give them time"; N.B. no children under five allowed.

Dan Marino's   – | – | – | E |
Fine Food & Spirits NEW
Hooters Hotel, 115 E. Tropicana Ave. (Las Vegas Blvd.),
866-584-6687; www.danmarinosrestaurant.com
The Dolphins' Hall-of-Fame quarterback may have retired from football, but like his former coach, Don Shula, he's touched down into the restaurant biz at this new surf 'n' turfer in the Hooters Hotel; be prepared to wade through

a sea of orange hot pants to reach the dining room, which offers a multitude of steaks and seafood (including some Florida favorites).

Del Frisco's   25 | 22 | 22 | $63
Double Eagle Steak House
3925 Paradise Rd. (Corporate Dr.); 702-796-0063; www.delfriscos.com
It's "a quick cab ride" east of the Strip to this "awesome" cow-palace chain link where you "tear a hunk of great hot bread and get ready" for "melt-in-your-mouth" "prime beef" and "amazing cold-water lobster tails"; the "masculine" setting includes a "nice cigar bar" and "waitresses dressed in sexy uniforms" who "send you thank you notes"; for the most in machismo, "ask to see the James Bond table", which holds magnum bottles etched with the film promos.

DELMONICO STEAKHOUSE   26 | 23 | 25 | $67
Venetian Hotel, 3355 Las Vegas Blvd. S. (bet. Flamingo & Spring Mountain Rds.); 702-414-3737; www.emerils.com
"Everything Emeril touches turns to gold", including this "hunk-of-meat heaven" in the Venetian; the beef is "impeccably aged" and "seasoned to perfection", the wine list is to "drool over" and the sides are so "orgasmic", "even the potato chips are divine"; what's more, the synchronized servers "know how to put on a great show", but the "dark, simple" room could be less "noisy" and "more interesting to match the quality of the fare" – book the pricey chef's table instead "for a feast to be remembered."

Diego   22 | 23 | 21 | $38
MGM Grand Hotel, 3799 Las Vegas Blvd. S. (Tropicana Ave.), 702-891-3200; www.mgmgrand.com
What's the specialty of this "snazzy" cantina in the MGM Grand?; "authentic Mexican with a flair" and even more so, to quote The Champs' 1958 classic, "tequila!" – 90 varieties, poured plain or stirred into the slurringly "bestest mahhhgaaahritas"; the "wonderful" fare is "more than tacos", so "look for the goat on the menu."

Doña Maria   ∇ 22 | 14 | 18 | $22
910 Las Vegas Blvd. S. (Charleston Blvd.), 702-382-6538
3205 N. Tenaya Way (Cheyenne Ave.), 702-656-1600
www.donamariatamales.com
Locals will tell you "the places for tamales" are in Central Vegas and the Northwest, where the "excellent" corn husk–wrapped specialties are "fresh-made" "in different varieties" including green chile or chicken; "the food is wonderful", the service "friendly" and both "surmount the warehouse ambiance" of the joints – they'll also bring in "mariachi music" if you're thinking of throwing a party.

Don Miguel's
19 | 15 | 18 | $21

*Orleans Hotel, 4500 W. Tropicana Ave. (Arville St.), 702-365-7111;
www.orleanscasino.com*
"At the end of a long day" of craps and slots when you
thirst for an "exceptional margarita", this casita in the
Orleans west of the Strip has 'em with "good, warm chips
served with nice salsa, guacamole and refried beans"; the
entrees are "ample" and "inexpensive", though "spotty
service" and "little innovation" in the kitchen lead south-
of-the-border intelligensia to label it "mindless Mexican."

Dragon Noodle Co.
20 | 18 | 20 | $27

*Monte Carlo Resort, 3770 Las Vegas Blvd. S. (bet. Harmon &
Tropicana Aves.), 702-730-7965; www.dragonnoodleco.com*
Noodles and other Cantonese dishes are "nicely prepped
and served" at this "casual" Asian in the Monte Carlo that
also offers some of "the best sushi on the Strip" in the evenings; it might be "a little pricey for what you get", but if
you don't want to "make the drive to Chinatown", the
lengthy tea list and fully feng-shui'd space make this convenient option all the more "pleasant."

Drai's ◐
22 | 22 | 22 | $58

*Barbary Coast Hotel, 3595 Las Vegas Blvd. S. (Flamingo Rd.),
702-737-0555; www.barbarycoastcasino.com*
The hold of the "tacky" Barbary Coast is an "unlikely venue"
for a "romantic" "rendezvous", but this New French "gem"
is "fabulous" for an "intimate" meal; the route through the
casino to get there might be more "ghastly" than walking
the plank, but the payoff is a "sexy, forbidden feeling" that
enhances the "marvelous food" and "candlelit" "house-
of-ill-repute decor"; after hours, you can "party" like the
"Rat Pack" when the place morphs into a "naughty" club.

Egg & I
21 | 12 | 19 | $14

*West Lake Plaza, 4533 W. Sahara Ave. (bet. Arville St. &
Decatur Blvd.), 702-364-9686; www.eggandi.com*
Yes, it's "in a strip mall", but "cast all fears aside" assure
"local celebrities" and plebians, because "breakfast in
Las Vegas doesn't get any better" than "perfect" "eggs
any way you like 'em" (including in "unusual" omelets, frit-
tatas and scrambles) at this Traditional American "family
place"; look for "interesting sandwich combinations"
during lunch and clues during Wednesday–Saturday
"murder-mystery dinner theater."

Eiffel Tower
22 | 26 | 22 | $70

*Paris Las Vegas, 3655 Las Vegas Blvd. S. (bet. Flamingo Rd. &
Harmon Ave.), 702-948-6937; www.eiffeltowerrestaurant.com*
Want to "fall in love again"? – ride the glass elevator to
this "romantic" "special-occasion" destination atop the
namesake at the Paris and "get a window seat facing the
Strip" because "watching the Bellagio water show is

dreamy" from above, particularly combined with a "classic"
French meal; you may even make "a trip to The Little White
Wedding Chapel" afterward, if your mood isn't dampened
by "prices as high as the view", "disappointing" dishes
and "lookie-loos who interfere with timely service."

| | 23 | 21 | 22 | $56 |

808

*Caesars Palace, 3570 Las Vegas Blvd. S. (Flamingo Rd.),
702-731-7731; www.caesarspalace.com*
The Pacific fusion fare is "exceptional in flavor and pre-
sentation" at this "piece of Hawaii"-meets-Europe in
Caesars; however, while the "imaginative" deconstructed
ahi roll and the New Wave bento box "wake up the
senses" and the "tranquil" room soothes the soul, the
"snotty" staff can get on the nerves.

| | 17 | 20 | 17 | $23 |

Elephant Bar

*The District, 2270 Village Walk Dr. (Green Valley Pkwy.),
Henderson, 702-361-7468; www.elephantbar.com*
"Your loud friends" in Henderson might trumpet this
"popular" Eclectic chainster in a "nice location" in The
District mall; it's "big, noisy and crowded", but it's a
"great place to meet at the bar" for a "quick bite" and a
cocktail in a "friendly atmosphere"; don't expect more
than a "just-average" meal, though: the "service is high-
school level", and as for the "inconsistent kitchen", "it's a
jungle in there."

| | ▽ 22 | 17 | 18 | $27 |

Eliseevsky ◑Ⓜ

4825 W. Flamingo Rd. (Decatur Blvd.), 702-247-8766
Every place in Vegas has a shtick, but this one's bona fide:
expats (including off-hours Cirque du Soleil performers)
will tell you this West Side spot is "almost like stepping into
a little eatery in the Ukraine" where the "good, basic
Russian food" pairs with "icy vodka shots" brought by
"surly" old-country waiters; it's so "authentic", "they
should give women babushkas when entering."

| | – | – | – | M |

**El Jefe's Mexican
Restaurant & Cantina** NEW

*594 N. Stephanie St. (Sunset Rd.), Henderson, 702-433-7579
9925 S. Eastern Ave. (St. Rose Pkwy.), Henderson, 702-453-5333
www.eljefesrestaurant.com*
These two Henderson siblings near the mall offer casual,
cantina-style atmospheres, but they go well beyond
the salsa-chips-and-enchiladas norm with creative takes
on south-of-the-border cuisine; the broad selection of
margaritas alone may make you swear you're wastin'
away in Guadalajara.

| | ▽ 21 | 9 | 21 | $19 |

El Sombrero Café Ⓢ

807 S. Main St. (Gass Ave.), 702-382-9234
"The best Mexican dive" in town might be this "Sonoran-
style" "institution" where the "sinful" carnitas are in keeping

with the general civic vibe; "the owner cooks, his wife serves" and the joint's "been around longer than most of the casinos", all of which makes it real enough to be worth the trip to its "frightening" Downtown neighborhood.

EMERIL'S NEW ORLEANS FISH HOUSE

23 | 19 | 22 | $55

MGM Grand Hotel, 3799 Las Vegas Blvd. S. (Tropicana Ave.), 702-891-7374; www.emerils.com

"Kick your dinner plans up a notch" at this MGM Grand spot for "oh-my-God"-good, "spicy, down-home Louisiana" seafood, a "bam! bam!" "sign of the times that you can get fantastic food of all sorts in Vegas"; dishes "bursting" with "flavors, colors and textures" match a "trendy" "remodel" (which may outdate the Decor score), while the staff manages to lend "a smaller feel to the huge" space; still, those who find the "TV chef's" empire "spread thin" and "overhyped" say "the trouble with Emeril's is there's no Emeril here."

Empress Court ⓜ

22 | 24 | 22 | $54

Caesars Palace, 3570 Las Vegas Blvd. S. (Flamingo Rd.), 702-731-7731; www.caesarspalace.com

This "Hong Kong regional" restaurant in Caesars offers "beautifully served" Cantonese and "great dim sum" amid "nice comfort" graced with "a touch of elegance"; still, "kung pao with no pow", "impassive waiters" and an "old-style" vibe have modernists urging "get with it!"

Enrico's Italian Bistro ⓜ

– | – | – | M

4864 W. Lone Mountain Rd. (Decatur Blvd.), 702-645-9495

In an "out-of-the-way strip mall" in the Northwest corner of town lies this "nicely decorated, family-owned" Italian offering "huge portions" of traditional eats; it may be "a little pricey" for the location, but you can dig into a "gold mine" of "deliciousness" for your dough.

Envy Steakhouse

▽ 22 | 25 | 21 | $54

Renaissance Las Vegas Hotel, 3400 Paradise Rd. (Desert Inn Rd.), 702-733-6533; www.envysteakhouse.com

Convenient for a conference break, this east-of-the-Strip steak place near the Convention Center "does very well" with a casual breakfast or lunch and an upscale dinner; the menu's "many delectable items" include a "must-try" tuna-and–crab meat dynamite, and the only glitch is service from "waiters too young for the cuisine."

Ethel's Chocolate Lounge NEW

– | – | – | M

Fashion Show Mall, 3200 Las Vegas Blvd. S. (Fashion Show Ln.), 702-796-6662; www.ethelschocolate.com

This new dessert lounge in the Fashion Show Mall is dedicated to all things chocolate, in the form of bonbons, fondues and beverages, though non-chocolate drinks are also available; the candy box setting (think overstuffed

couches in peppermint and cocoa tones) includes a sign
on the wall proclaiming 'chocolate is its own reward.'

Famous Dave's   20 | 17 | 19 | $23
1951 N. Rainbow Blvd. (Lake Mead Blvd.), 702-646-5631;
www.famousdaves.com
"Come early or expect a wait" at this Northwest outpost of
the Minnesota-based 'cue chain, where "smiling" servers
deliver "filling" plates of "melt-in-your-mouth" smoked
goods in a backwoods lodge setup; a choice of six different
sauces and "a lot of food for the buck" clinch its claim to
fame, causing "long lines on weekends."

Fatburger   21 | 9 | 13 | $10
Albertson's Shopping Ctr., 2845 S. Nellis Blvd. (Vegas Valley Dr.),
702-457-1727
3763 Las Vegas Blvd. S. (bet. Harmon & Tropicana Aves.),
702-736-4733 ◗
4525 N. Rancho Dr. (Craig Rd.), 702-658-4604 ◗
Santa Fe Station Hotel, 4949 N. Rancho Dr.
(bet. Lone Mountain Rd. & Rainbow Blvd.), 702-839-9610 ◗
4851 W. Charleston Blvd. (Decatur Blvd.), 702-870-4933 ◗
6775 W. Flamingo Rd. (Rainbow Blvd.), 702-889-9009 ◗
4663 E. Sunset Rd. (bet. Green Valley Pkwy. &
Mountain Vista Rd.), Henderson, 702-898-7200
Green Valley Ranch, 2300 Paseo Verde Pkwy.
(Green Valley Pkwy.), Henderson, 702-617-2209 ◗
Sunset Station Hotel, 1301 W. Sunset Rd. (Stephanie St.),
Henderson, 702-450-7820 ◗
Texas Station Hotel, 2101 Texas Star Ln. (bet. Lake Mead Blvd. &
Rancho Dr.), North Las Vegas, 702-638-4175 ◗
www.fatburger.net
Additional locations throughout the Las Vegas area
"Best burger west of the Mississippi" sigh devotees of this
"classic" fast-food chain, where "phat" patties, "perfectly
greasy" onion rings and "amazing" shakes are "hangover
cure" and "cardiac nightmare" all rolled into one; ok, "service can be slow" (the grub's "cooked to order", after all), so
"bring your quarters" to play the "great jukebox" while you
wait, or crank up your own car radio at the 24/7 drive-thru.

Feast, The   13 | 13 | 16 | $13
Boulder Station Hotel, 4111 Boulder Hwy. (Lamb Blvd.),
702-432-7777
Palace Station Hotel, 2411 W. Sahara Ave. (Rancho Dr.),
702-367-2411
Red Rock Casino, 11011 W. Charleston Blvd. (Hwy. 215),
702-797-7777
Sunset Station Hotel, 1301 W. Sunset Rd. (Stephanie St.),
Henderson, 702-547-7777
www.stationcasinos.com
"Very popular with local retirees", these Eclectic buffets are
"not for gourmets", but "value-seekers" can run amok amid

the steam trays, grabbing at "average" eats; they're "homey places", meaning unless you "luck out" and miss the "crowds", you'll have to contend with "crying children."

Feast Around the World Buffet   17 | 13 | 16 | $15 |
Green Valley Ranch, 2300 Paseo Verde Pkwy.
(Green Valley Pkwy.), Henderson, 702-617-7777
Texas Station Hotel, 2101 Texas Star Ln. (bet. Lake Mead Blvd. &
Rancho Dr.), North Las Vegas, 702-631-1000
www.stationcasinos.com
"There is a lot of variety at these budget-friendly buffets" with live-action cooking areas in Henderson's Green Valley Ranch and North Vegas' Texas Station, but there's also plenty of interest among "locals", so "go at off-times, as it gets busy", and "the wait" for the "constantly rotated" items "can make you even hungrier than you already are."

Fellini's   24 | 20 | 21 | $39 |
Sam's Town Hotel, 5111 Boulder Hwy. (S. Nellis Blvd.),
702-454-8041
Stratosphere Hotel, 2000 Las Vegas Blvd. S.
(north of Sahara Ave.), 702-380-7777
5555 W. Charleston Blvd. (bet. Decatur & Jones Blvds.),
702-870-9999 🅢
www.fellinislv.com
Promising a taste of la dolce vita are these "old-world" Italians where "friendly" servers ferry "large portions" of "traditional" but "very good" fare, at prices that "delight" penny-pinchers; depending on the night, wedding parties ("I had my reception here and loved it!") and "great singing artists" who "drop by to perform" may be part of the scenery.

Ferraro's   23 | 20 | 22 | $51 |
5900 W. Flamingo Rd. (bet. Decatur & Jones Blvds.),
702-364-5300; www.ferraroslasvegas.com
"If Dean, Sammy or Frank were still with us, they would kick back on a night off" with plates of "fall-off-the-bone osso buco, pasta dishes that make your head spin" and "amazing" wines at this West Sider serving "excellent traditional Italian fare prepared in a way that you just have to appreciate"; run by a "family as fantastic as their food", it's a "laid-back" "locals' favorite" with "no casino crowd to bother you during a great meal."

Festival Buffet   ∇ 15 | 12 | 14 | $13 |
Fiesta Rancho Hotel, 2400 N. Rancho Dr. (Lake Mead Blvd.),
702-631-7000
Fiesta Henderson Hotel, 777 W. Lake Mead Pkwy. (S. 4th St.),
Henderson, 702-558-7000
www.fiestacasino.com
"Saturday brunch is the buy of the century" rave hyperbolic types clamoring for the "cheap" eats at these Eclectic gorgefests in the Northwest and Henderson; if you happen

to be at either of the Fiestas, they'll do just "fine", particularly given "some excellent baked goods that lend them something to stand above the crowd" of joints at the "low end."

Fiamma Trattoria   24 | 24 | 23 | $55

MGM Grand Hotel, 3799 Las Vegas Blvd. S. (Tropicana Ave.), 702-891-7600; www.brguestrestaurants.com

"The MGM Grand is definitely putting itself on the food map of late", and Steve Hanson's "sexy" SoHo import is helping with "upscale" Italian dishes like "lobster gnocchi to dream about"; the "dark, ultramodern decor is perfect for a first date", whom you could even meet amid "an awesome bar scene filled with hip people" sipping "to-die-for specialty cocktails"; unfortunately, you might "part with more money than you should" for "small portions."

Fin NEW   – | – | – | E

Mirage Hotel, 3400 Las Vegas Blvd. S. (Spring Mountain Rd.), 702-792-7800; www.mirage.com

The name refers to the restaurant's fresh tank, the denizens of which may include several varieties of crab, but there's plenty more at this intimate Mirage Chinese seafooder; the self-described decor lies somewhere 'between edgy and elegant' with hand-painted rice-paper backdrops of Japan on the walls coexisting with decorative glass, china and crystal on the tables.

Fiore Steakhouse   25 | 23 | 24 | $55

Rio All-Suite Hotel, 3700 W. Flamingo Rd. (bet. I-15 & Valley View Blvd.), 702-777-7702; www.playrio.com

"Hidden off the Strip" in the Rio is this "rock-solid" Northern Italian chophouse whose "old-style menu", featuring "first-rate" mesquite-grilled meat, is enhanced by "one of the biggest wine lists around"; they "don't rush you" through, so it's a real "escape from the casino hustle."

Firefly ◑   23 | 17 | 21 | $29

3900 Paradise Rd. (bet. Flamingo Rd. & Twain Ave.), 702-369-3971; www.fireflylv.com

"Tasty little plates" of "easy-to-share" tapas "keep on comin'" to your table thanks to "helpful" servers at this East Side Spaniard that's "nowhere near as stuffy or expensive" as its Strip counterparts, and does without those "ringing slot machines" too; decorwise it may be a bit "blasé" inside, so "sit on the patio" instead, where pitchers of "dangerous" sangria go down easier.

Firelight Buffet   ▽ 14 | 13 | 15 | $14

Sam's Town Hotel, 5111 Boulder Hwy. (S. Nellis Blvd.), 702-454-8044; www.samstownlv.com

Like moths to the light, "locals throng" this "typical", "cheap buffet" in Sam's Town on the East Side; luckily, "the serving area has a good flow and doesn't bunch people up" on "don't-miss steak night" and other special evenings;

still, "you pay for what you get", so if you're seeking something "outstanding", "don't make a special trip here."

Fix ●　　　　　23　23　21　$57
Bellagio Hotel, 3600 Las Vegas Blvd. S. (Flamingo Rd.),
702-693-8400; www.bellagio.com
"Could the crowd or decor be any groovier" at this "eye-catching", dinner-only American "hot spot" that opens onto the Bellagio casino?; "sink into a deep booth" beneath an "artistic, wooden" ceiling that's "as curvy as the hostess" and order up a fix of "brilliant" "gourmet" comfort grub to "see and be seen" with – though the "flash" of the "loud" "bar scene blurs the palate", a "damn-hot staff serving great-looking", "young" "bachelorette partiers" makes the "people-watching" a "total experience."

Flavors Buffet　　　　16　12　16　$19
Harrah's Las Vegas, 3475 Las Vegas Blvd. S. (Flamingo Rd.),
702-369-5000; www.harrahs.com
Folks who stay at Harrah's "enjoy the buffet breakfast" at this Eclectic smorgasbord, and it's "great for a quick meal" at lunchtime, but because there's "lots of room for improvement" in its "utilitarian", "'50s-style" fare and "average decor", they "keep on walking" for dinner; critics crack "if you have a snout or happen to resemble any animal that does, you will feel perfectly at home" feeding at this "quality-over-quantity" trough.

Fleming's Prime　　　　24　22　22　$56
Steakhouse & Wine Bar
8721 W. Charleston Blvd. (bet. Durango Dr. & Rampart Blvd.),
702-838-4774; www.flemingssteakhouse.com
"Huge", "shockingly delicious" filets paired with "giant" sides ("it was practically a head of broccoli") and an "excellent" selection of wines by the glass help make this "clubby" satellite of the "high-end" national beef chain "the social hub of the West Side" (read: it's "very loud"); there may be "better ones on the Strip", but if you're caught further out, this one will make the cut.

FLEUR DE LYS　　　　26　26　25　$90
Mandalay Bay Resort, 3950 Las Vegas Blvd. S.
(Mandalay Bay Rd.), 702-632-9400;
www.fleurdelyssf.com
Chef-owner Hubert Keller "nourishes all the senses" at the "Vegas branch of his SF legend", this "dreamy" "jewel box" in Mandalay Bay where the "out-of-this-world" New French fare is "artistically impressive", the "spectacular service" helps ensure a "peaceful" experience and the "sexy" decor features "3,000+ roses on the wall"; choose a three-, four- or five-course "exquisite" prix fixe and pair it with a flight from the "amazing wine list" to "impress anyone from a date to a client."

Florida Cafe   ▽ 18 13 12 $18
Howard Johnson Hotel, 1401 Las Vegas Blvd. S.
(bet. Charleston & Oakley Blvds.), 702-385-3013;
www.floridacafecuban.com
Despite residency in a Howard Johnson's on a "seedy" stretch of Las Vegas Boulevard, this "Cuban oasis" manages to be "*the* place for ex-Miamians" to feast on "exemplary *croquetas*" and satisfy "cafe con leche cravings"; drivers take note: parking can be "hard to find" and the entrance/exit is dubbed "dangerous."

Francesco's   21 20 23 $50
Treasure Island Hotel, 3300 Las Vegas Blvd. S.
(Spring Mountain Rd.), 702-894-7348;
www.treasureisland.com
If you're "going to see *Mystére*", TI's "dependable if unspectacular" Italian works for a "reasonable" pre-show meal featuring Tuscan favorites ("go here for the veal") ferried by an "attentive" staff; decked out like a "bordello"-ish Mediterranean villa, it proudly displays artwork by Vegas legends Tony Curtis, Tony Bennett and Phyllis Diller.

French Market Buffet   18 14 17 $18
Orleans Hotel, 4500 W. Tropicana Ave. (Arville St.),
702-365-7111; www.orleanscasino.com
You can score "some really tasty" "treats" at this "excellent-value" Eclectic extravaganza situated west of the Strip, but "the trick is to catch it" at the "right" time – for example, Sunday for brunch, Monday night for seafood or Wednesday evening for steak; plus, there's always "a decent variety of American, BBQ, Chinese, Italian" and other types of dishes available for your "not-so-discerning palate."

Full Ho Chinese Cuisine Ⓜ   ─ ─ ─ | |
240 N. Jones Blvd. (I-95), 702-878-2378
Sure, the "weird name" and "dilapidated strip-mall" location couldn't be less enticing, but gung-ho fans say it's "worth the drive" to this Northwest Chinese for "consistently delicious" eats ("the best pan-fried won tons in town") and "friendly" hospitality commandeered by an owner who "remembers her customers."

Fusia   ▽ 20 22 20 $39
Luxor Hotel, 3900 Las Vegas Blvd. S. (Tropicana Ave.),
702-262-4774; www.luxor.com
The most recent addition to the Luxor's gourmet dining roster is this "very nice" Asian fusionist in a gold-hued, vaulted space; surveyors are split on whether the "food as art" concept works, with fans swearing the fare "cannot be beat" and detractors dissing a "mind-numbing blend of East, West and everything in between" brought by a staff whose "lack of know-how" only helps to con-fusia.

Gaetano's
23 | 22 | 23 | $38

Siena Promenade, 10271 S. Eastern Ave. (Siena Heights Dr.),
Henderson, 702-361-1661; www.gaetanoslasvegas.com
"Real class act" 'Tano' Palmeri "makes you feel at home" in
his "wonderfully friendly" yet "elegant" "family-operated"
namesake in Henderson where "the customer is first" on
the list for "personal care"; "it's not the cheapest Italian in
town", but it's "worth the price" for "excellent", "authentic
Northern" standards and "innovative specials" – even
snobs call it "not bad for a neighborhood place."

Gallagher's Steakhouse
23 | 18 | 21 | $56

New York-New York Hotel, 3790 Las Vegas Blvd. S.
(Tropicana Ave.), 702-740-6450; www.nynyhotelcasino.com
On your way into this "dark", "authentic" New York-New
York chophouse (a takeoff on the Gotham "original"), "you
can see" the "incredible" cuts "hanging in the windows"
"in giant coolers", and they're "exactly what you would
hope for", i.e. "mouthwateringly aged" and "big" say supporters who "can't believe they ate the whole thing"; "disappointed" carnivores counter that "there are better
options at Vegas' top-tier steak level" than the "tough"
chews in this "noisy" "blah environment."

Gandhi India Cuisine
▽ 20 | 15 | 18 | $22

4080 Paradise Rd. (Flamingo Rd.), 702-734-0094
If you tire of the town's many all-American pig-outs, a
"great place for an Indian buffet" is this "quiet", "spacious" spot east of the Strip where "hot, hot, hot" refers to
both the spice in some of the dishes and the temperature
of the "good variety of great naan and other breads" fresh
from the oven; at $9.95 for the lunch "deal", the prices are
as "friendly" as the atmosphere.

Garden Court Buffet
20 | 19 | 18 | $17

Main Street Station Hotel, 200 N. Main St. (Ogden Ave.),
702-387-1896; www.mainstreetcasino.com
"There are so many different tasting stations that you can't
sample all the varieties of foods in just one day" at this
"shockingly good" Downtown multidisher's depot say repeat
eaters who pop in on "specialty nights" like seafood Friday
or "go early to avoid the big crowds" "in line for the good
stuff at the grill"; "one of the most pleasant buffet dining
environments" in town also includes a gardenlike setting.

Garduño's
20 | 18 | 18 | $23

Fiesta Rancho Hotel, 2400 N. Rancho Dr. (Lake Mead Blvd.),
702-631-7000
Palms Casino Hotel, 4321 W. Flamingo Rd. (Arville St.),
702-942-7777
www.gardunosrestaurants.com
West of the Strip and in the Northwest, these Mexican/
Southwestern cantinas originally out of Albuquerque are

"great for drinks and gabbing" with gringos while gobbling "spicy", traditional grub; "sopapillas plus a salsa bar" "with some kickin' margaritas to boot" "equals a very happy tummy" tout amigos who "like it *mucho*" for a "reasonably priced" dinner, while the word on the "great Sunday buffet" is "*que bueno!*"

Gaylord's   23 | 21 | 19 | $41

Rio All-Suite Hotel, 3700 W. Flamingo Rd. (bet. I-15 & Valley View Blvd.), 702-777-2277; www.playrio.com
"A place to take cranky vegetarians" and whisper to them sweet nothings like "do you vindaloo?" is this Indian west of the Strip where the "excellent range of dishes and tastes" includes "sublime lentil soup" and other non-meat offerings; the "old-school atmosphere" sates the desire to "get out of Vegas without really leaving", and the staff will give you "advice if you need it" – when it's not having one of its "slow, forgetful" moments.

Giorgio Caffè & Ristorante   18 | 16 | 18 | $40

Mandalay Place, 3930 Las Vegas Blvd. S. (Mandalay Bay Rd.), 702-920-2700; www.caffegiorgio.com
"It's nice to sit and watch the shoppers go by" Piero Selvaggio's "comfortable", "cute place for lunch" in Mandalay Place where a "reasonably priced" Italian meal might include antipasto, "well-prepared" pasta and wine from the 20-strong by-the-glass list; it's a "winner", if you don't mind that it's "a serious step below" Valentino, the restaurateur's upscale spot.

Golden Steer Steak House   22 | 18 | 21 | $53

308 W. Sahara Ave. (bet. Fairfield Ave. & Tam Dr.), 702-384-4470; www.goldensteerlv.com
This former "Rat Pack hangout" is "as close to an eternal institution" as this town has, so "check your gun at the door" (proverbially speaking), "cozy up in a leather booth and enjoy a good piece of meat", a "massive baked potato" and a healthy dose of "Old West–bordello" "kitsch" west of the Strip; it's "great for bachelor parties", but some former regulars "no longer shine the banquettes with their bottoms" because the "service is marginal" compared to the "dozens of great steakhouses" competing with it now.

GRAND LUX CAFE ◐   21 | 19 | 19 | $26

Venetian Hotel, 3355 Las Vegas Blvd. S. (bet. Flamingo & Spring Mountain Rds.), 702-414-3888; www.venetian.com
Though the "huge portions" of Eclectic fare found on "the best 80-page menu on the Strip" might seem "eerily similar" to those of its relative, the Cheesecake Factory, this "wealthy cousin" delivers a "more refined dining experience" with culinary "complexity layered on the mundane", and the decor? – "such beautiful marble! such vaulted ceilings!"; conveniently located in the Venetian and open

24 hours a day with service that's "down to a science", it "doesn't take you away from the action for too long."

Grape Street Cafe   21 | 21 | 20 | $30

Summerhill Plaza, 7501 W. Lake Mead Blvd. (Buffalo Dr.), 702-228-9463; www.grapestreetcafe.com

The "fantabulous flights" are "made in heaven" at this "local" wine lover's "paradise" in the Northwest; the "super" Mediterranean entrees, "fun-to-share"-and-"rave-about" chocolate fondue and 75 "interesting" grapes by the glass are "good for a yuppie dinner out", particularly if you avoid the "crowded" inside (where "they play the music too loud at dinner") and take a table on the "adorable" patio.

Guadalajara Bar & Grille   18 | 15 | 16 | $19

Boulder Station Hotel, 4111 Boulder Hwy. (Lamb Blvd.), 702-432-7777
Palace Station Hotel, 2411 W. Sahara Ave. (Rancho Dr.), 702-367-2411
Sunset Station Hotel, 1301 W. Sunset Rd. (Stephanie St.), Henderson, 702-547-7777
www.stationcasinos.com

A "great family dining spot" for clans composed of "people of differing heat tolerances" is this "inexpensive" Mexican with locations in the "noisy" Station Casinos where "the top-notch salsa bar" runs the gamut from blistering to mellow; "if you don't want authentic", the "Americanized" menu is "not bad", and the "big" margaritas suffice for a buzz, if you can get served – the staff seems to "make a point of looking the other way all night."

Guy Savoy Ⓜ NEW   – | – | – | VE

Caesars Palace, 3570 Las Vegas Blvd. S. (Flamingo Rd.), 877-346-4642; www.caesarspalace.com

The renowned Parisian chef introduces his haute New French cuisine to the U.S. with this branch of his eponymous establishment housed in Caesars Palace; the sleek yet intimate space includes three private dining rooms, a chef's table, champagne and wine bar, and a glass-enclosed patio overlooking the Roman Plaza and the Strip; the bill of Savoy fare features a 10-course tasting 'menu prestige' at $290 and a four-course option for $190, while the wine list boasts some 1,500 labels, primarily from France.

Hamada   21 | 16 | 18 | $36

365 E. Flamingo Rd. (Paradise Rd.), 702-733-3005 ◑
Flamingo Las Vegas, 3555 Las Vegas Blvd. S. (Flamingo Rd.), 702-733-3455
Rio All-Suite Hotel, 3700 W. Flamingo Rd. (bet. I-15 & Valley View Blvd.), 702-777-2770
www.hamadaofjapan.com

"Three restaurants in one", the branches of this Vegas "classic" offer "good" "Benihana-style, sushi-bar and sit-down-Japanese" dining, all at "affordable prices"; no, there's "no karaoke", but the east-of-the-Strip original entertains with "fantastic people-watching after 10 PM"; since many say it's "nothing special" with "decor in need of upkeep", those who knew it when say "expansion has not helped" it.

Hank's   _ _ _ E

Green Valley Ranch, 2300 Paseo Verde Pkwy.
(Green Valley Pkwy.), Henderson, 702-617-7515;
www.greenvalleyranchresort.com

Marble floors, a freighter's worth of crystal chandeliers and drapery-swathed booths add neo-vintage glamour to this gray-and-silver steakhouse lined with a glass-fronted wine cellar, the latest upscale addition to Henderson's Green Valley Ranch; the accent's on beef, of course, but seafood, a slew of salads and sides round out the meal, preceded by (what else?) a martini to the strains of the piano in the lounge.

Hannah's Euro Asian Cuisine   _ _ _ M

1050 S. Rampart Blvd. (Charleston Blvd.), 702-932-9399;
www.hannahslv.com

Suburban Vegas dining is flavored with both style and substance at the An family's multifeatured Pan-Asian in the Northwest; as in the Beverly Hills branch of the clan's Crustacean, customers literally walk on water, prancing across a glass-topped aquarium floor as they make their way to the sushi-and–Far East tapas bar or the patio to sample satay and signature garlic noodles alfresco at off-Strip prices.

Hard Rock Cafe   14 22 16 $25

4475 Paradise Rd. (Harmon Ave.), 702-733-7625;
www.hardrock.com

For diners who love rock 'n' roll, this "typical" East Side branch of the music-themed chain is still singin' that same old song, with "lots of memorabilia", "loud" tunes, "overpriced T-shirts" and "juicy burgers"; the rest of the American menu is "hackneyed" and the service "indifferent", but when you're itching to mix with "hungover twentysomethings", "older biker types" and "festive tourists", "ya just gotta go there."

Harley-Davidson Cafe   15 19 16 $22

3725 Las Vegas Blvd. S. (Harmon Ave.), 702-740-4555;
www.harley-davidsoncafe.com

Don't dare tell the hog riders here that they're drinking out of "adult sippy cups"; not only are the mugs unusual, but with "a U.S. flag made of chain taking up an entire wall", motorcycles "whirling overhead" and the chance to snap "your very own pic as a Harley babe", the entire vibe at this easy-ridin' American "gimmick" is "interesting"; "get out your temporary tatoos and leather" for "cheap", "heaping burgers, a mishmash of bar food" and "lots of 'tude on the Strip."

Hash House A Go Go NEW — | — | — | M
6800 W. Sahara Ave. (Rainbow Blvd.), 702-804-4646; www.hashhouseagogo.com
'Twisted farm food' is promised by this West Side American – spun off from the San Diego original – and the result is farmer-boy-size portions of homestyle favorites served on platter-size plates; the only jarring note is decor that's dominated by decidedly un-countryish riveted steel.

Hilltop House Supper Club Ⓜ — | — | — | M
3500 N. Rancho Dr. (Jay Ave.), 702-645-9904
"The best steakhouse"-type place "left on this side of town", say Northwesterners, is this "outstanding" Traditional American, a "real old Vegas eatery in a converted house"; the "homemade items on the little salad bar" and the "pan-fried lobster tails" would have surveyors "eating here more often", if it weren't "so smoky."

Hilton Steakhouse ▽ 22 | 21 | 23 | $53
Las Vegas Hilton Hotel, 3000 Paradise Rd. (bet. Desert Inn Rd. & Karen Ave.), 702-732-5111; www.lvhilton.com
"Evocative of the old chophouses" from yesteryear, this "dark" den located east of the Strip in the Hilton serves a "top-flight" cut with "no surprises" and "no disappointments"; the "excellent" staff can't do much about the "uncomfortable seats", and though it can be a "good value", critics conclude "there are better options."

Hugo's Cellar 25 | 21 | 26 | $53
Four Queens Hotel, 202 Fremont St. (Casino Center Blvd.), 702-385-4011; www.fourqueens.com
"If you're looking for bright, new and open, this is not for you", but if you like it "dank and delicious", this "amazing '70s throwback" Downtown is a "gem", even if it's set in the basement of a "grungy casino"; expect "world-class" Continental dining presided over by an "attentive" staff that sees to "all the extras", including a "roving salad cart", "old-fashioned flaming desserts" and a "long-stemmed rose for every lady"; still, some longtimers say an ownership change a couple of years ago "detracted" a bit from the swelegance.

Hush Puppy ▽ 19 | 9 | 17 | $24
1820 N. Nellis Blvd. (Lake Mead Blvd.), 702-438-0005
7185 W. Charleston Blvd. (bet. Buffalo Dr. & Rainbow Blvd.), 702-363-5988
"The all-you-can-eat catfish will cure your Southern nostalgia" at this down-home duo on the East and West Sides where diners in a hurry make "repeat visits" to the drive-up window; sure, they're "dumps", but the "coleslaw is

great" and you can score "outta-sight" deals on shrimp, frogs' legs and snow crab, all of which are "not bad", even if some say an order of the "lousy" namesakes is an ol' miss.

Hyakumi   25 | 19 | 22 | $48

Caesars Palace, 3570 Las Vegas Blvd. S. (Flamingo Rd.), 702-731-7110; www.caesarspalace.com

Get a "quick unagi power boost" before muscling into the madness of Cleopatra's Barge, which rocks beneath this "happening" Japanese where the sushi is "fresh, sweet" and "generous" and the tempura and teppanaki are "excellent"; the "seasoned chefs" "dazzle and delight" with their slice it–and–dice it show, and the rest of the staff is "marvelously attentive", though the "noisy" location above the hydraulized party scene can be a "turnoff."

Il Fornaio   20 | 19 | 18 | $35

Green Valley Ranch, 2300 Paseo Verde Pkwy. (Green Valley Pkwy.), Henderson, 702-492-0054
New York-New York Hotel, 3790 Las Vegas Blvd. S. (Tropicana Ave.), 702-650-6500 ❶
www.ilfornaio.com

Carb-loving clans clamor for the "delicious pasta", claiming "grandfather would love these" "affordable" chain links in Green Valley Ranch and on the Strip, "and grandma would finally get to enjoy dinner with *la famiglia*" if they had a "classic Italian" meal here; at the NY-NY location, you can "sit on the patio and feel like you're in Central Park – well, Central Park with slot machines and fake foliage."

Il Mulino New York   25 | 23 | 23 | $73

Forum Shops at Caesars Palace, 3500 Las Vegas Blvd. S. (Flamingo Rd.), 702-492-6000; www.ilmulinonewyork.com

"Mamma mia!" – Gotham's "home away from home" "lives up to its name" with "delicious, gut-busting" Italian (for "immediate gratification", the antipasto and other freebies are "already there" when you sit down); "the menu is identical to the NYC location" but served in a "much more elegant" space in the Forum Shops where "the tables aren't jammed on top of each other like in Greenwich Village"; no, it's "not inexpensive", but "it's worth every penny."

I Love Sushi NEW   – | – | – | M

11041 S. Eastern Ave. (Aura Dr.), Henderson, 702-990-4055

Raw fish and rice dishes dominate the menu of this bustling sushi palace set in a Henderson strip mall; the rolls have edgy-verging-on-cutesy names (including some that would make your grandma blush) and can be enjoyed either at the bar or in semi-private booths.

India Palace   ▽ 25 | 15 | 20 | $22

505 E. Twain Ave. (bet. Paradise Rd. & Swenson St.), 702-796-4177

"All the food is really nice", but the "lunch buffet is a great deal" for "good variety" at this "favorite Indian restaurant" of "lucky" in-the-know locals; its east-of-the-Strip location is "sketchy", it "looks like a laundromat from the outside" and the interior is "getting long in the tooth", but the "excellent, inexpensive" eats are "worth the visit."

In-N-Out Burger ●✍ 24 | 11 | 18 | $8

4888 Dean Martin Dr. (Tropicana Ave.)
51 N. Nellis Blvd. (Charleston Blvd.)
1960 Rock Springs Dr. (Lake Mead Blvd.)
9240 S. Eastern Ave. (Serene Ave.)
4705 S. Maryland Pkwy. (bet. Flamingo Rd. & Tropicana Ave.)
2900 W. Sahara Ave. (Teddy Dr.)
1051 W. Sunset Rd. (Marks St.), Henderson
800-786-1000
www.in-n-out.com

Even "if you lose your shirt, save enough for" the "best hamburger in the whole dang world" scored from these Southern Californian "legends" where "nothing is frozen" and everything is "fast, cheap" and "outstanding", including the "crisp" hand-cut fries and "awesome shakes", eaten in or taken out via the drive-thru; the only problem with Vegas' "finest hangover fare" and biggest Bang for the Buck is that it "goes down too fast"; in other words, "burp!"

Isla ● 22 | 22 | 20 | $34

Treasure Island Hotel, 3300 Las Vegas Blvd. S.
(Spring Mountain Rd.), 702-894-7349; www.treasureisland.com

"It's nice to see TI update their food" say fans of this "innovative" Mexican yearling by NY chef Richard Sandoval; the "creative" fare pairs well with the "lively" room's "bold colors", not to mention "hundreds of different" pours from the resident Tequila Goddess; the "delightful staff" takes good care, and the "relaxed" room is more than "comfy."

Japengo ☒ 24 | 25 | 23 | $49

Hyatt Regency Lake Las Vegas, 101 Montelago Blvd.
(Lake Las Vegas Pkwy.), Henderson, 702-567-1234;
www.hyatt.com

"What a delight" say the "pretty" patrons hanging out in the "high-end" environs of this "outstanding" Pacific Rim restaurant in the Hyatt Regency Lake Las Vegas; the airy room and waterside terrace match the "spectacular presentations" of "fantastic sushi" and "unusual" chef's specialties, complemented by a "very good wine list"; with "outstanding service" and spacing such that "each table feels very private", it's a "must-do" for "romantic dates" as well as high-rolling "people-watching" "groups."

Japonais NEW – | – | – | E

Mirage Hotel, 3400 Las Vegas Blvd. S. (Spring Mountain Rd.),
702-792-7800; www.mirage.com

One of the newest offerings at the Mirage, this offshoot of the Chicago original offers a fusion of classic Japanese and old-style European cuisine, à la such border-bending dishes as chestnut-encrusted chicken with shiitake rice stuffing and uni hollandaise with satsumaimo pommes frites.

Jasmine 　　　　22　25　22　$59

Bellagio Hotel, 3600 Las Vegas Blvd. S. (Flamingo Rd.), 702-693-8255; www.bellagio.com

"Beauty has a name, and it is Jasmine" say fans of the Bellagio's "posh" Chinese where the designers' "refreshing" use of flowers, chintz and other "light notes" makes for "breathtaking" decor, augmented by "a view of the dancing waters"; dine on "brilliant", "delicately prepared" dishes (both "traditional" and "innovative"), but plan to eat again later, as the "teeny-tiny", "overpriced" portions may leave you "hungry."

Jean Philippe Patisserie 　　25　21　18　$17

Bellagio Hotel, 3600 Las Vegas Blvd. S. (Flamingo Rd.), 702-693-7111; www.bellagio.com

"If it were allowed", "mesmerized" sweet tooths would "bathe in the chocolate fountain" at this "Francophilic" Bellagio patisserie, an "art museum" for "sugar-coated" "masterpieces" where "intensely flavorful, flawlessly executed" edible "dreams" are on exhibit and, of course, for sale – at "reasonable prices"; "you could just pass the time away drooling over gelati, pastries, truffles", "crêpes both sweet and savory" and the "two-story" centerpiece "flowing" with richness.

Jimmy Buffett's 　　　　16　21　16　$25
Margaritaville Cafe ◐

Flamingo Las Vegas, 3555 Las Vegas Blvd. S. (Flamingo Rd.), 702-733-3302; www.margaritavillelasvegas.com

"Nothing says 'restaurant entertainment' like a server who is 'sacrificed' to an indoor volcano, only to emerge in a bikini and slide into an oversized margarita blender" at this perennial Parrot Head "party", a Flamingo-based themester that's "all about life with one simple song" and a lot of booze; "sit in fishing boats", soak up the "continuous Buffett music and videos", live acts and "Hawaiian-shirt" shtick and reel in an "average" cheeseburger in paradise or, for "originality", the conch fritters.

Joël Robuchon 　　　　–　–　–　VE

MGM Grand Hotel, 3799 Las Vegas Blvd. S. (Tropicana Ave.), 702-891-7925; www.mgmgrand.com

Foodies agog at the prospect of the first stateside restaurant from the acclaimed Joël Robuchon aren't likely to be disappointed with the $350, 16-course tasting menu at his New French fete in the MGM Grand; à la carte signatures include scallops cooked in their shells with lemon-and-seaweed butter, Brittany lobster beneath a melting saffron wafer and confit of lamb with semolina couscous, all supported by a 750-bottle wine list and served in an interior lavishly reminiscent of a 1930s Parisian mansion; in other words, ooh-la-la.

Joe's Seafood, Prime Steak & Stone Crab
24 | 21 | 23 | $59

Forum Shops at Caesars Palace, 3500 Las Vegas Blvd. S. (Flamingo Rd.), 702-792-9222; www.leye.com
"Miami surf meets Chicago turf" at this Forum Shops collaboration by the Sunshine State namesake and the Windy City's Lettuce Entertain You; "if you like stone crabs – and who wouldn't? – this is the only game in town" for claws "as good as in Florida", while the "bone-in filet is a wow!"; "smart, trendy" and full of *Sex and the City* types" (who "love the idea of half a piece" of Key lime pie on the menu), it's also "huge and loud, but [that's] what Joe's should be" – other than simply "delicious."

Joyful House Chinese Cuisine ●
▽ 23 | 12 | 15 | $24

4601 Spring Mountain Rd. (bet. Arville St. & Decatur Blvd.), 702-889-8881
"Try ordering from the Chinese specialty list" at this West Side "anti–P.F. Chang's" – it's even "more authentic than the regular menu", which itself features "a number of unique dishes", including "very fresh seafood" ; the "hurried" but "efficient" staff is "reminiscent of New York's" frenetic Chinatown, but "who cares with food this good?"; N.B. cook your own after 10:30 PM, courtesy of the late-night shabu-shabu buffet.

Kathy's Southern Cooking Ⓜ⊄
▽ 26 | 6 | 17 | $18

6407 Mountain Vista St. (Sunset Rd.), Henderson, 702-433-1005
Chef-owner "Mama Kathy" Cook whips up some of the "best fried chicken in town" at this cash-only soul fooder in Green Valley, where the "delicious home cooking" is "put out by people who care"; the service may be "friendly", but be "prepared to wait" for the "yummy" Southern vittles and "homemade desserts" served in a spartan setting where "a little decoration would go a long way."

King's Fish House
21 | 19 | 18 | $32

The District, 2255 Village Walk Dr. (Green Valley Pkwy.), Henderson, 702-835-8900; www.kingsseafood.com
You "can almost smell the Atlantic" at the Henderson branch of this seafood chain where you "can't beat the freshness" of the dozen different types of fish on offer daily; since this "family place" serves "seasonal items, the menu changes constantly" and keeps the "noisy" crowds coming back; for a quieter time, escape to the "wonderful" outdoor patio and enjoy "a nice selection of oysters" while "watching people go by."

Kona Grill   19 20 18 $30
Boca Park, 750 S. Rampart Blvd. (Charleston Blvd.),
702-547-5552; www.konagrill.com
"Hang out with the hip crowd" while sipping and nibbling
"happy-hour specials that can't be beat" at the "inside/
outside bar" at this Pacific Rim–inspired New American in
the Northwest's Boca Park; plenty of partiers dig the
"trendy atmosphere" and "great sushi", even if critics
crab "it's not worth going out of the way for" "hit-or-miss"
fare at just "another 'in' spot that ought to be 'out.'"

Lake Mead Cruises   – – – M
Lake Mead Nat'l Recreation Area, 490B Horsepower Cove (I-93),
Boulder City, 702-293-6180; www.lakemeadcruises.com
The dinner cruises on these paddlewheelers offer "a great
view" of "magnificent Hoover Dam" and "beautiful Lake
Mead" while passengers sample simple American fare
like prime rib, baked chicken and salmon; the April–
October Sunday champagne brunch tour is "fun and filling"
and makes for a "nice day away from Sin City."

La Salsa   16 11 14 $14
Aladdin Resort, 3667 Las Vegas Blvd. S. (Harmon Ave.),
702-892-0645 ☽
Boulevard Mall, 3480 S. Maryland Pkwy. (Twain Ave.),
702-369-1234
Forum Shops at Caesars Palace, 3500 Las Vegas Blvd. S.
(Flamingo Rd.), 702-735-8226
Luxor Hotel, 3900 Las Vegas Blvd. S. (Tropicana Ave.),
702-739-1776
Riviera Hotel, 9000 Las Vegas Blvd. S. (Pebble Rd.),
702-697-4401 ☽
Showcase Mall, 3785 Las Vegas Blvd. S. (Tropicana Ave.),
702-240-6944 ☽
The District, 2265 Village Walk Dr. (Green Valley Pkwy.),
Henderson, 702-263-8233
www.lasalsa.com
"Terrific" salsas made from "very fresh ingredients" are
the trademark of this Mexican chain that's also famed for
"fabulous [yard-long] margaritas" that "come in a variety
of flavors" and are great for washing down "cheap",
"monstrous burritos"; those who bemoan the "drunk,
rowdy crowd" should head for Boulevard Mall (the only
location that doesn't serve booze).

L'Atelier de Joël Robuchon   – – – E
MGM Grand Hotel, 3799 Las Vegas Blvd. S. (Tropicana Ave.),
702-891-7358; www.mgmgrand.com
The more casual of the namesake master chef's two New
French additions to the MGM Grand offers a small number
of tables plus service around a U-shaped counter for the
ultimate open-kitchen experience; specialties include the
legendary truffled mashed potatoes, roasted rack of lamb,

free-range quail stuffed with foie gras and desserts such
as a chartreuse soufflé with pistachio ice cream.

Lawry's The Prime Rib   25 22 24 $48
Hughes Ctr., 4043 Howard Hughes Pkwy. (Flamingo Rd.),
702-893-2223; www.lawrysonline.com
"If you don't love steak, stay away" from this slice of
"prime-rib heaven" east of the Strip; otherwise, "unleash
the carnivore within" and "gorge yourself" on "outstanding"
beef carved tableside by the "old-school staff" in a "digni-
fied", "art deco" space that's "always crowded" "but
worth the wait", even if a handful feels this ritual is "tired."

LE CIRQUE   26 26 25 $88
Bellagio Hotel, 3600 Las Vegas Blvd. S. (Flamingo Rd.),
702-693-8100; www.bellagio.com
"Turn your frown upside down" when you step from the
Bellagio casino into this "elegant" "temple of gastron-
omy", where ringmaster Sirio Maccioni's "synchronized
servers" deliver "superb" New French cuisine and "delectable desserts", albeit at "steep prices"; "lusciously col-
ored" overstuffed chairs and banquettes make the
"intimate" room feel like "sitting inside a jewel box", and a
window table ensures a "great view of the fountains" for
an "elegant" evening; N.B. children under 12 not allowed.

Le Provençal   21 20 19 $35
Paris Las Vegas, 3655 Las Vegas Blvd. S. (bet. Flamingo Rd. &
Harmon Ave.), 702-946-4656; www.parislasvegas.com
At this "well-kept secret" in the Paris, "singing servers"
deliver Italian-French bistro fare like "sublime crêpes"
and bouillabaisse as well as "some of the best pizza in
Vegas"; some feel the "food is good enough without the
show", and others find the songs "fun" and "entertaining",
but everyone agrees the "charming farmhouse" setting is
"excellent for lunch."

Les Artistes Steakhouse   22 22 22 $56
Paris Las Vegas, 3655 Las Vegas Blvd. S. (bet. Flamingo Rd. &
Harmon Ave.), 702-946-4663; www.parislasvegas.com
The "two-level dining room" of this New French beefery in
the Paris is "classy and beautiful" with high ceilings and
Impressionist artwork that create a "romantic" atmosphere in which to enjoy "fantastic bone-in filet" and
"splendid lobster tails"; though a few find it "pricey, pretentious" and "not particularly exceptional", most agree
"it's a safe bet" for "delicious" if "basic steakhouse fare."

LE VILLAGE BUFFET   23 21 18 $27
Paris Las Vegas, 3655 Las Vegas Blvd. S. (bet. Flamingo Rd. &
Harmon Ave.), 702-946-4966; www.parislasvegas.com
A "faux outdoor setting" resembling a "pretty French vil-
lage" in the Paris makes for a "charming" atmosphere in
which to indulge in an "overwhelming array" of "rich"

Gallic "specialties" like "artisanal cheeses", "custom-made crêpes" and "fresh crab legs"; some gourmands grumble about the "long waits on busy days", but most claim this "excellent value" is "*très magnifique!*"

Little Buddha　　　23 25 21 $43

Palms Casino Hotel, 4321 W. Flamingo Rd. (Arville St.),
702-942-7778; www.littlebuddhalasvegas.com
This "sexy" west-of-the-Strip sis to France's Buddha Bar attracts "beautiful people" with a "cool design" featuring a red-hued room lined with statues of the Enlightened One, plus "innovative" Asian fusion dishes; "hoochie mamas" and celebs like "Robin Leach" tolerate "lax" service to get their fill of "fresh sushi", "fab" cocktails and "pounding house" music (which can be "a bit much if you're over 25").

Lombardi's　　　∇ 20 17 18 $32

Desert Passage at Aladdin, 3663 Las Vegas Blvd. S.
(Harmon Ave.), 702-731-1755; www.lombardisrestaurants.com
Those who've stumbled upon this "tried-and-true" Northern Italian in the Desert Passage praise the "ideal location" and "relaxing environment"; savor the "consistently good", "reasonable priced" fare while sitting "on the patio that provides a view" of the strolling musicians and tourists that frequent this section of the mall.

LOTUS OF SIAM　　　28 12 21 $23

Commercial Ctr., 953 E. Sahara Ave. (bet. Maryland Pkwy. &
Paradise Rd.), 702-735-3033; www.lotusofsiamlv.com
"Take a trip off the beaten path" to this "hole-in-the-wall" "hidden treasure" east of the Strip and "don't let the location fool you": it may be in a shopping center, but whatever is "lacking in decor" is made up for with "transcendental" Northern Thai cuisine, like beef that will make you "weep with delight", "staggeringly good tom yum soup" and "ethereal sour sausage"; each "outstanding", "authentic" and yet "inexpensive" dish pairs perfectly with one of the many "amazing Rieslings" on offer.

Lou's Diner ⊉　　　– – – I

431 S. Decatur Blvd. (Alta Dr.), 702-870-1876
You might not think 'diner' when you think 'eggs Benedict', but then this West Sider isn't your average coffee shop, serving family favorites like mom used to make, only better, with friendly service and uncluttered decor; N.B. it's tucked away behind a McDonald's, so keep your eyes open.

Lucille's Smokehouse Bar-B-Que　　21 18 18 $25

The District, 2245 Village Walk Dr. (Green Valley Pkwy.),
Henderson, 702-257-7427; www.lucillesbbq.com
"Bring your appetite" to the District branch of this barbecue chain: though the "portions are large" you'll still want a "second helping" of soul food goodies like "lip-smacking babyback ribs", "tender brisket" and "irresistible" fresh

biscuits – if you can get the "really slow" staff to hustle it for you; N.B. dine on a weeknight and listen to live blues while sipping a mint julep.

Luna Rossa   –   –   –   E

MonteLago Vlg., 10 Via Bel Canto (Lake Las Vegas Pkwy.), 702-568-9921

This Lake Las Vegas Italian fits right in with the theme of MonteLago Village – a re-creation of a quaint Mediterranean town so complete it even has a startlingly similar copy of Florence's famed Ponte Vecchio – serving both traditional and updated dishes in a cozy dining room or on an open-air patio; it's particularly pleasant during one of the resort area's free outdoor jazz concerts.

Lutèce   23 22 23 $78

Venetian Hotel, 3355 Las Vegas Blvd. S. (bet. Flamingo & Spring Mountain Rds.), 702-414-2220; www.arkvegas.com

"Foodies savor the meticulous attention to detail" at this "stylish, minimalist temple of haute cuisine" in the Venetian where the New French tasting menu is especially "wonderful"; although admirers rave over the "beautiful presentations" brought out by "expert servers", the disgruntled grumble about the room's "austerity" and claim that this "way-too-expensive" venue is a "shadow of the [now defunct] New York original."

Luxor Steakhouse   25 22 25 $55

Luxor Hotel, 3900 Las Vegas Blvd. S. (Tropicana Ave.), 702-262-4778; www.luxor.com

"You'll feel like King Tut" when descending into this "dark", "clubby" Luxor surf 'n' turfer, whose "consistently superb" aged prime rib, "top-notch" seafood, "great wine list" and "truly professional" service are "worth every dime"; still, a few find it too "expensive" and "not that exciting."

Maggiano's Little Italy   21 20 20 $33

Fashion Show Mall, 3200 Las Vegas Blvd. S. (Fashion Show Ln.), 702-732-2550; www.maggianos.com

Even for "the city of excess", this "welcome" Italian chain's "heaping" servings are "mind-boggling"; "family-style is a great way to taste everything" on an "excellent-bargain" menu featuring "rich, flavorful sauces over a plethora of pastas and meats"; there are "no surprises", just lots of *delizioso* dishes delivered in a "finely lit", "dark-wood" space that's "as huge as its portions" – "with a great view of the Wynn" on the Strip to boot.

Makino   22 12 16 $25

3965 S. Decatur Blvd. (Flamingo Rd.), 702-889-4477
775 S. Grand Central Pkwy. (Bonneville Ave.), 702-382-8848

"If you're hungry, and you love sushi, this buffet is the deal!" rave fans fishing for all-you-can-eat bargains Downtown and on the West Side; when "loading up on the freshest, tastiest" raw ocean offerings "for the price" (plus "a crab feast at night" and "many hot items"), you'll "be in heaven" – just be warned that it "can get very crowded."

Mama Jo's
▽ 21 | 13 | 18 | $28

3655 S. Durango Dr. (bet. Spring Mountain Rd. & Twain Ave.), 702-869-8099

"Even though no one will want to sit next to you afterwards, the roasted garlic appetizer is a must" at this aptly named "homestyle-away-from-home" Southern Italian on the West Side; they do have a low-carb menu, but it's certainly "not low-calorie", and no matter what you order, given "meatballs the size of baseballs", you're in for "more food than you can handle in one sitting"; it's "not fancy", but it's a "good value" for "standards" "done right all the time."

Marché Bacchus
21 | 21 | 20 | $34

2620 Regatta Dr. (Breakwater Dr.), 702-804-8008; www.marchebacchus.com

"Shhh . . . don't tell anyone about this hidden little gem on a lake" in the Northwest where "a little bit of France" can be had in the "romantic" interior or "delightfully alfresco"; its "eclectic clientele" ask, "what could be better than transporting yourself to a French cafe" with "basic" but "great" fare and "a full-on wine store" from which retail bottles can be purchased "off the shelf" and poured for a $10 corkage fee?

Marc's
▽ 24 | 17 | 22 | $34

7290 W. Lake Mead Blvd. (Tenaya Way), 702-562-1921; www.marcsrestaurant.com

"Ring-a-ding-ding and fly me to the moon and back!" sing natives savoring chicken Sinatra, "loving the lobster cocktail" and "hoping the tourists won't find out about this gem" of an Italian steakhouse in the Northwest part of town; "only locals know how really good" the "homemade ravioli" and "sushi-fresh seafood" are, or for that matter, how "knowledgeable" the staff can be.

MargaritaGrille
▽ 16 | 16 | 19 | $24

Las Vegas Hilton Hotel, 3000 Paradise Rd. (bet. Desert Inn Rd. & Karen Ave.), 702-732-5111; www.lvhilton.com

"As it should, this place has a good margarita", so expect "noisy", "touristy" "fun" at happy hour when you're staying at the Las Vegas Hilton east of the Strip; "you'll need a drink or three" to add some verve to the "ok" Mexican "standards" that are "nothing to sail around the world for."

Market City Caffe
19 | 16 | 18 | $27

Monte Carlo Resort, 3770 Las Vegas Blvd. S. (bet. Harmon & Tropicana Aves.), 702-730-7966; www.dragonnoodleco.com

For "some of the best Italian fare for the price", try this Strip trattoria featuring an all-you-can-eat antipasto bar and "good single-serving pizza"; sure, "service could be

better", and the "small-ish", "quiet setting" is a far cry
from glitz and glamour, but it's "reliable" when you're looking
for a "quick break" from the "wallet crushing."

Marrakech   ▽ 20 | 24 | 21 | $37
3900 Paradise Rd. (bet. Flamingo Rd. & Twain Ave.),
702-737-5611; www.marrakech-vegas.com
"Watching the belly dancers helps with digestion", but
"don't let the bare, undulating torsos distract you from the
fabulous parade" of "tasty" Moroccan dishes brought by
"friendly" servers at this "Marrakech-goes-Marra-kitsch"
den east of the Strip; do let yourself slide into "another
world" where diners "lay on a couch" under the "fabric-
draped tent ceiling" in a "picturesque room with beautiful
carpets" and "feast" their eyes, ears and stomachs.

Mayflower Cuisinier ⊠   25 | 18 | 22 | $36
Sahara Pavilion, 4750 W. Sahara Ave. (Decatur Blvd.),
702-870-8432; www.mayflowercuisinier.com
"Happy" pilgrims "make that arduous trip" to the West
Side to land at this "wonderful" strip-mall "diamond in the
rough" where an "extraordinary French-influenced
Chinese" meal can be found thanks to "great produce as
well as nice spicing" and "beautiful presentations"; the
decor might be "outdated", but the "reasonable" pricing
and "concerned" staff "more than make up for it."

McCormick & Schmick's   21 | 19 | 21 | $43
335 Hughes Center Dr. (Paradise Rd.), 702-836-9000;
www.mccormickandschmicks.com
"It's hard to believe you're in the middle of the desert with
all the fresh fish on the menu" at this "dependably consistent" franchise for seafood east of the Strip; "far more upscale" than most chains and "definitely superior", it's a
"nice place" to "see and be seen" on "a business lunch",
but it can be "crowded" and "loud", especially "during
happy hour" when "the killer $1.95 bar menu" reels 'em in.

MEDICI CAFÉ   26 | 26 | 26 | $51
Ritz-Carlton, Lake Las Vegas, 1610 Lake Las Vegas Pkwy.
(Grand Mediterra Blvd.), 702-567-4700; www.ritz-carlton.com
"Far in the boondocks" of Lake Las Vegas is this "out-of-
the-way gem" where "sublime" New American cuisine
is on offer amid "elegant", silk-and-brocade environs with
a "wonderful view" of the Ritz-Carlton's Florentine gardens; "brunch is delicious", lunch is "fantastic" and dinner is "a special evening every time", thanks to a
"romantic" setting that "provides a serenity that's often
hard to get in Las Vegas."

Melting Pot   18 | 16 | 20 | $39
8704 W. Charleston Blvd. (bet. Durango Dr. & Rampart Blvd.),
702-384-6358

(continued)

(continued)
Melting Pot
8955 S. Eastern Ave. (bet. I-15 & Pebble Rd.), Henderson, 702-944-6358 NEW
www.meltingpot.com
A "cute idea for your teenager's birthday party", a "girls' night out" or a "first date" is this West Side branch of the nationwide chain, a "one-trick pony" for folks who are fond of fondue; all that melted "cholesterol" can be "great fun", but with "just one warming station per table" making dining convenient only "if everyone wants the same thing", some dunksters "wish they didn't have a monopoly" on the "novelty"; N.B. the Green Valley satellite opened post-*Survey*.

Memphis Championship Barbecue | 21 | 17 | 18 | $22 |
2250 E. Warm Springs Rd. (Eastern Ave.), 702-260-6909
1401 S. Rainbow Blvd. (Charleston Blvd.), 702-254-0520
4379 Las Vegas Blvd. N. (Craig Rd.), North Las Vegas, 702-644-0000
www.memphis-bbq.com
"Bring it on!" say surveyors salivating over "melt-in-your-mouth ribs, hot links, pulled pork and brisket" accompanied by two "to-die-for sides", "homemade iced tea in a mason jar" and "service with a smile" at this "real-deal" 'cue trio; "portion control is not on the menu" but "jam-packed" lunchtimes are, so "stay away if you're on a diet" or craving quiet – otherwise, "there's only one word to describe it: mmmmmm!"

MESA GRILL | 24 | 22 | 22 | $54 |
Caesars Palace, 3570 Las Vegas Blvd. S. (Flamingo Rd.), 702-731-7731; www.caesarspalace.com
Sure, "it would be nice if he were present", but even if he's in NYC, this "impressive" Caesars "offshoot" of the TV toque's "ultra-creative" Southwestern flagship is "Bobby Flay's place from the time you enter to leaving"; "beautiful presentations" and "distinctive flavors" "restore your faith in celebrity chefs", and they're backed up by "personable service" in a "stylish" yet "relaxing" space; "if you like a little spice in your meal", this "could become a regular haunt" because it's "flay-bulous!"

Metro Pizza | 22 | 12 | 18 | $16 |
Ellis Island Casino & Brewery, 4178 Koval Ln. (Flamingo Rd.), 702-312-5888 ●⇔
1395 E. Tropicana Ave. (Maryland Pkwy.), 702-736-1955
Renaissance Center W., 4001 S. Decatur Blvd. (Flamingo Rd.), 702-362-7896
www.metropizza.com
"Now we don't need to move back East" raves a "lively crowd" of pieheads relieved to find these "locally owned" "joints" that put out "the best NY-style pizza in town";

"great crusts" topped with "tons" of "strong flavors" in "excellent combinations" make for "some serious 'za", washed down with "very cold beer"; "after a few nights of Strip extravagance, it's so comforting", "Brooklynites" sigh, to eat at a place that "makes me think of home."

MGM Grand Buffet   16 13 13 $23
MGM Grand Hotel, 3799 Las Vegas Blvd. S. (Tropicana Ave.), 702-891-7314; www.mgmgrand.com

For a chow break "when gambling", this "standard buffet" on the Strip is "convenient" for "piles" of "very decent, ordinary food cooked well", but it really "has nothing to make it special"; given decor that "needs to be updated" and a staff that "ignores patrons", "underwhelmed" overeaters grumble that, despite its name, it's "not as grand as it could be."

MICHAEL MINA   27 24 26 $82
Bellagio Hotel, 3600 Las Vegas Blvd. S. (Flamingo Rd.), 702-693-8255; www.michaelmina.net

San Francisco "master chef" Michael Mina feeds fish to the whales (aka "high rollers") at the *Las Vegas Survey*'s top seafooder, an "inspired" spot for "exquisite" eating *à "la mer"* in the Bellagio conservatory; "try the signature lobster" pot pie accompanied by a bottle from the "excellent wine list" and "treat yourself to their caviar service"; the dishes are so "outstanding", the service so "congenial" and the space (with open kitchen) so "chic and cosseting" (if "noisy") that the "sky-high prices" are "worth it."

Michael's   25 22 26 $85
Barbary Coast Hotel, 3595 Las Vegas Blvd. S. (Flamingo Rd.), 702-737-7111; www.barbarycoastcasino.com

"The place to be for old Las Vegas style" is this "coat-and-tie" Continental "hidden away" in the Barbary Coast; your "romantic" meal might include "Châteaubriand tender enough to cut with a fork" and – though it's "not necessary with all the fruit and chocolate brought as a compliment" – cherries jubilee; the "very Victorian" room may need an "upgrade", but along with "impeccable service" and "prices geared toward those comped by the casino", it does allow you to feel like an "1800s railroad baron."

Ming's Table   – – – M
Harrah's Las Vegas, 3475 Las Vegas Blvd. S. (Flamingo Rd.), 702-369-5000; www.harrahs.com

Forget the paper lanterns–and–fortune cookie shtick: the venerable Harrah's Las Vegas has breathed new life into its restaurants of late; this Cantonese spot brings an upscale vibe to the table via an eclectic mix that includes classics like crispy roast duck with plum sauce, traditional dishes such as sliced abalone and contemporary offerings like tempura soft-shell crab, served in a bold, modern setting.

MiraLago
▽ 21 | 23 | 22 | $41

Reflection Bay Golf Club, 75 Montelago Blvd.
(Lake Las Vegas Pkwy.), 702-568-7383; www.lakelasvegas.com
Next to a hole in one, there might be "nothing better than seeing the sun set over Lake Las Vegas" from the patio of this near-"secret" Mediterranean at Reflection Bay Golf Club; abetted by "impeccable service", "the view is worth the cost of the meal", which, "when good, it is very good", albeit "rich", "old-fashioned" and "limited" in choice.

MIX
23 | 27 | 22 | $82

The Hotel at Mandalay Bay, 3950 Las Vegas Blvd. S.,
64th fl. (Mandalay Bay Rd.), 702-632-9500;
www.chinagrillmgt.com
"Dine in an egg-shaped pod" in a room "straight out of a Kubrick film" with "hundreds of glass spheres hanging from the ceiling", a "very hip bar" and "the best view this side of a Vegas showgirl" atop The Hotel at Mandalay Bay; the "outrageously decadent" experience extends to the New French–New American fare, courtesy of über-chef/co-owner Alain Ducasse and chef de cuisine Bruno Davaillon, who "keep your *bouche* amused" throughout; all this and "mind-blowing service" make for a "top-of-the-world" "winner" – at "equally high prices."

MON AMI GABI
23 | 24 | 22 | $42

Paris Las Vegas, 3655 Las Vegas Blvd. S.
(bet. Flamingo Rd. & Harmon Ave.), 702-944-4224;
www.monamigabilasvegas.com
"The desserts will make you melt", and so will "the fountain show" visible from this "charming bistro" with sidewalk seating "spilling out toward the Bellagio lake"; featuring "authentic" French items such as "amazing pommes frites", "great hanger steak", "a very good selection of wines and champagnes" and "lots of drifting cigarette smoke", the "lively", "packed" place is "possibly the only part of the Paris that actually feels like" the namesake city – yet with "better" service.

Montesano's
▽ 19 | 12 | 18 | $18

4235 S. Fort Apache Rd. (bet. Nevso Dr. & Rochelle Ave.),
702-257-3287 NEW
4835 W. Craig Rd. (Decatur Blvd.), 702-656-3708 🗵
3441 W. Sahara Ave. (Valley View Blvd.),
702-876-0348 🗵
www.montesanos.com
"Everything is made from scratch, simply and lovingly" at these "real family-run Italians" where the "pastas are all good" with "interesting combinations of ingredients" and each location boasts a take-out shop for homemade baked goods; just because the "owners are from Arthur Avenue in the Bronx" doesn't mean the eats are all that – some of the "sauces are way too sweet" say connoisseurs.

Morton's, The Steakhouse   25 21 23 $64
400 E. Flamingo Rd. (Paradise Rd.), 702-893-0703;
www.mortons.com
"Morton's lives up to their reputation" at this east-of-the-
Strip branch of the "top-notch" beef chain where the "old-
style" dinner features "wonderful, aged" cuts, "huge
sides" and "desserts to die for", all brought by "efficient
servers"; those looking for a "hipper" vibe find the
"classy" decor too "sober", and unless you "drink
heavily", the "look-at-this-plate-of-raw-meat" "menu on
wheels" is "not that exciting" either.

Mr. Lucky's 24/7 ●   20 17 19 $19
Hard Rock Hotel, 4455 Paradise Rd. (bet. Flamingo Rd. &
Harmon Ave.), 702-693-5592; www.hardrockhotel.com
"It's 3 AM, you've had a lot to drink, you need eggs and a
burger", and you want them served by a "hot pants–clad,
young staff" at "bargain" prices – where do you "drag
your tired butt" but the Hard Rock's "trendy" "all-
nighter"?; given a "high-energy" vibe, "celebrity sight-
ings" and "great" "all-around American junk food", this
"always-happening" coffee shop is the place to "show off
your new tatt" "any time of day."

Neros   – – – VE
Caesars Palace, 3570 Las Vegas Blvd. S. (Flamingo Rd.),
702-731-7110; www.caesarspalace.com
The folks who renovated this chophouse institution in
Caesars Palace didn't fiddle around: the space now sports
an up-to-the-minute, leather-and-wood look highlighted
by an enormous Murano glass chandelier; foodwise, the
menu includes steaks dry-aged for 28 days, funky twists like
foie gras sliders with port-poached rhubarb and preserved
ginger, plus seafood and desserts fit for an emperor.

Nine Fine Irishmen   16 22 18 $29
New York-New York Hotel, 3790 Las Vegas Blvd. S.
(Tropicana Ave.), 702-740-6969; www.ninefineirishmen.com
"Every kind of Irish drink you've ever heard of" can be
downed at this pub in New York-New York where the "authentic" atmosphere features "the finest woods, cubby-
holes for seating, just-right lighting and a noise level that's
deafening"; it's an "affordable" spot for an affable quaff
amid a "high number of expats", who'll tell you that the
"food is bland, just like in Ireland", but it "goes down well"
with "group singing and lots of beer."

N9ne Steakhouse   25 23 22 $64
Palms Casino Hotel, 4321 W. Flamingo Rd. (Arville St.),
702-933-9900; www.n9negroup.com
Call it "celebrityville in Vegas", call it "eye-candy city" –
no matter its moniker, "you'll feel like a movie star" dining
at this "cool, cool, cool" "hot spot" for "the hippest steak"

in town; with "genius" fare, a "friendly staff" and "minimalist design", the Palms Casino's "chic" chophouse lures "loud, young people" for a "high-energy" meal "before hitting the clubs"; both "the hottie in the booth next to you" and the place itself "should be called a Ten."

NOBHILL   26 25 25 $80
MGM Grand Hotel, 3799 Las Vegas Blvd. S. (Tropicana Ave.), 702-891-7337; www.michaelmina.net
"You'd think you're in the city" by the Bay at Michael Mina's "San Francisco treat" in the MGM Grand serving the "talented" toque's "creative" Californian cuisine; carb lovers say the "most delicious things ever tasted" are the complimentary mashed-potato sampler and the "steaming-hot bread fresh from the oven", but Atkins dieters tout the "incredible wine list", "attentive" staff and all-around "posh swankiness."

NOBU ◑   27 22 23 $71
Hard Rock Hotel, 4455 Paradise Rd. (bet. Flamingo Rd. & Harmon Ave.), 702-693-5090; www.nobumatsuhisa.com
"Be adventuresome and trust your waiter – he won't steer you wrong" at this east-of-the-Strip outpost in Nobu Matsuhisa's "unique" Japanese-Peruvian empire, famed for "cutting-edge sushi like you've never had before", "don't-miss miso cod" and other "fabulous fusion" fare; the "tranquil" garden setting is particularly "wonderful" for a "first date", provided you "come with your checkbook" and avoid it on "hotter-than-a-royal-flush" weekends when "noisy crowds" turn it into a sort of "bass-pumping nightclub."

Noodles ◑   20 17 18 $30
Bellagio Hotel, 3600 Las Vegas Blvd. S. (Flamingo Rd.), 702-693-7111; www.bellagio.com
"Bringing welcome variety to the Strip dining scene", this Bellagio eatery offers "every Asian noodle dish you can think of" and "solid weekend dim sum" on a Marco Polo–esque menu that roves the Far East; "simple" and "satisfying", it makes for a "nice little midnight snack", and you can feast your eyes on "numerous different types" of the "addictive" namesake that make up the "peculiar decor."

Noodle Shop ◑   18 13 16 $25
Mandalay Bay Resort, 3950 Las Vegas Blvd. S. (Mandalay Bay Rd.), 702-632-7777; www.mandalaybay.com
"The waits are interminable during busy hours", and "the service is brusque" at what amounts to "basically your typical noodle joint from any Chinatown in America", transported to the casino in Mandalay Bay; nonetheless, you can score a "delicious won ton soup" "fix" on weekends till the wee hour of 3 AM, and "after a long night of losing, nothing tastes better."

Nora's Cuisine ⊠
24 | 15 | 19 | $29

6020 W. Flamingo Rd. (Jones Blvd.), 702-365-6713;
www.norascuisine.com

Nora's Wine Bar & Osteria NEW

1031 S. Rampart Blvd. (W. Charleston Blvd.), 702-940-6672;
www.noraswinebar.com

It's "not a well-kept secret any longer": this "family-
owned" duo are "great little neighborhood Italians" for a
"nice break from the attitude and prices of the Strip";
"dress as you like, rub elbows with locals and feast on
plentiful, well-prepared food" "just like mamma's" – "if
there's a crowd of you, and you want to be noisy, you'll fit
right in"; N.B. the Summerlin branch opened post-*Survey*.

Nove Italiano NEW
– | – | – | E

Palms Casino Hotel, 4321 W. Flamingo Rd., 51st fl. (Arville St.),
702-942-6800; www.n9negroup.com

Talk about a room with a view: the folks behind the Palms'
N9ne Steakhouse have merged a sleek postmodern design
with the traditional cuisine of sunny Italy at this newcomer
atop the resort's Fantasy Tower; there's even a satellite
kitchen in the dining room, so you can watch pasta being
made if the city lights dazzle too much.

ΘKADA
26 | 27 | 24 | $72

Wynn Las Vegas, 3131 Las Vegas Blvd. S. (Desert Inn Rd.),
702-770-9966; www.wynnlasvegas.com

"Another Wynn winner", this Japanese specializes in "excellent teppanyaki" and "must-try robata" cooking, not to
mention "fantastic sushi", served in a "visually stunning"
"Zen garden" featuring a "floating pagoda table" and
"floor-to-ceiling windows" that showcase the hotel's "famous mountain", lake and "lit waterfall"; "first-rate service"
matches the "gorgeous food and decor"; N.B. a post-
Survey chef change may outdate the above Food score.

OLIVES
24 | 23 | 22 | $53

Bellagio Hotel, 3600 Las Vegas Blvd. S. (Flamingo Rd.),
702-693-8255; www.toddenglish.com

The terrace view "overlooking the water show" is "magnificent", though a seat in the "open" interior of Todd
English's "remodeled" Mediterranean is no booby prize; this
Bellagio outpost offers "original tastes, skillfully prepared",
featuring "wonderful appetizers, salads and pizzas", sided
by "delicious olive tapenade", bolstered by a "wicked-good
cocktail" and chased by a "chocolate fallen cake that will
lift anyone's spirits!" – even if the service is "slooow."

Onda
22 | 21 | 22 | $53

Mirage Hotel, 3400 Las Vegas Blvd. S. (Spring Mountain Rd.),
702-791-7223; www.mirage.com

"The cha-chings of the slots start to disappear" as the bar
area's "wonderful piano music" draws you into this "gen-

tle respite" inside the Mirage; "if nothing really jumps out at you" on the "thin" Italian menu, at least everything is "solid", the staff "attentive" and it's "so quiet" in the dining room that you'll "think you're in another world."

Origin India ● NEW   – | – | – | M
4480 Paradise Rd. (Harmon Ave.), 702-734-6342;
www.originindiarestaurant.com
Vegetarians head for this newcomer across from the Hard Rock Hotel that offers a broad variety of vegetable-based dishes from various parts of India as well as a number of meatier selections for carnivores in the crowd.

Ortanique   23 | 21 | 21 | $48
Paris Las Vegas, 3655 Las Vegas Blvd. S. (bet. Flamingo Rd. & Harmon Ave.), 702-946-4346; www.cindyhutsoncuisine.com
"Escape for a delicious meal" to this "hidden" island "treasure" in the Paris where "great chef" Cindy Hutson has tucked this destination in her mini-archipelago of "excellent Caribbean" eateries; with its Eclectic "twists", the "food is original" and "tasty", and the "upbeat", "upscale panache" of the place is aided by tented booths, undersea video projections and "wonderful" live weekend jazz.

Osaka Japanese Bistro ●   23 | 16 | 21 | $36
4205 W. Sahara Ave. (Valley View Blvd.), 702-876-4988
10920 S. Eastern Ave. (Horizon Ridge Pkwy.), Henderson, 702-616-3788
www.lasvegas-sushi.com
"Like Benihana, only better" if simply because it's a Vegas "original", this West Side/Green Valley duo boasts "fluffy, cloudlike tempura", "fresh, fresh, fresh sushi" and other "excellent" Japanese specialties; for a "great time", try the "lively" teppanyaki rooms where the "entertaining chefs" are "very good at throwing food in the air"; N.B. it's unaffiliated with Osaka Japanese Cuisine.

Osaka Japanese Cuisine ●   ▽ 24 | 20 | 25 | $40
7511 W. Lake Mead Blvd. (bet. Buffalo Dr. & Tenaya Way), 702-869-9494
"Excellent sushi" is carved by "the fastest knives" in the desert at this "favorite neighborhood Japanese" in the Northwest offering "good happy-hour deals" on raw fish, and "great hibachi dining too"; the "nice-looking" staff's "personalized service" somewhat makes up for a menu and an entertainer "slightly lacking in selection" – "there is a guy on a piano that only knows a couple songs, and he keeps playing them again and again, not softly."

Osteria del Circo   25 | 25 | 23 | $61
Bellagio Hotel, 3600 Las Vegas Blvd. S. (Flamingo Rd.), 702-693-8150; www.bellagio.com
The Maccionis' "'discount'" eatery in the Bellagio delivers "all the pomp and circumstance you expect from a high-

caliber" restaurant "without the fuss" and with "less expense than its big brother", Le Cirque; the "inventive, savory" Tuscan cuisine is to be "toothed with a maximum joy", but the real "show" is in the "buoyant atmosphere", thanks to the "colorful, circus"-like decor and a fountain view from "coveted tables ringside to the floor-to-ceiling windows"; now someone should tell the staff in this "fantasy menagerie" to lose their "New York attitude."

Outback Steakhouse   18 | 14 | 18 | $29
Casino Royale Hotel, 3411 Las Vegas Blvd. S. (Flamingo Rd.), 702-251-7770 ◐
7380 Las Vegas Blvd. S. (Warm Springs Rd.), 702-643-3148 NEW
1950 N. Rainbow Blvd. (Lake Mead Blvd.), 702-647-1035
4141 S. Pecos Rd. (Flamingo Rd.), 702-898-3801
3685 W. Flamingo Rd. (Valley View Blvd.), 702-253-1020
8671 W. Sahara Ave. (Durango Dr.), 702-228-1088
4423 E. Sunset Rd. (Arville St.), Henderson, 702-451-7808
2625 W. Craig Rd. (Fuselier Dr.), North Las Vegas, 702-647-4152
www.outback.com
A "fair dinkum" "Aussie contribution to the USA", this "reliable steakhouse" chain serves meals that don't cost "an arm and a leg"; it's "not for business", it's "not for romance", but is "good for families" who "want to eat something familiar and save money for the casinos."

Pahrump Valley Winery   ▽ 20 | 20 | 21 | $31
3810 Winery Rd. (east of Hwy. 160), Pahrump, 775-727-6900; www.pahrumpwinery.com
"Wine in the desert?" – yes, indeed, at this "charming" "oasis" that's worth the trip out to Pahrump, an area that's otherwise "full of below-average places that cater to cowboys"; "delightful, delicious" and "a drive" to get to, the "cozy, quiet" dining room serves "creative" Continental cuisine in the middle of Nevada's only vineyard; for a real "experience", take a helicopter there for "Sunday lunch."

PALM   25 | 19 | 23 | $60
Forum Shops at Caesars Palace, 3500 Las Vegas Blvd. S. (Flamingo Rd.), 702-732-7256; www.thepalm.com
"Testosterone-addled" "Palmophiles" patronize this surf 'n' turfer in the Forum Shops "ready to get stuffed" on filets "the size of a roast" and lobsters so "big", "no one in their right mind or stomach would try and finish" one; the atmosphere is all "oak and alcohol and NY-style loudness" (some of the latter in the form of the waiters' "sarcastic banter"), but the "food still rocks" and is a relative "bargain" during lunch.

Pampas Churrascaria NEW   – | – | – | E
Desert Passage at Aladdin, 3663 Las Vegas Blvd. S. (Harmon Ave.), 702-737-4748; www.pampasusa.com
Meat, meat and more meat is the name of the game at this airy newcomer in the Aladdin's Desert Passage that takes

its name from the high-plains grasslands of South America; in the finest gaucho tradition, servers bear skewer after skewer of beef spit-roasted over a brick rodizio, along with traditional sides and a selection of cold dishes.

PAMPLEMOUSSE Ⓜ 26 23 25 $52
*400 E. Sahara Ave. (bet. Joe W. Brown Dr. & Paradise Rd.),
702-733-2066; www.pamplemousserestaurant.com*
"Named by Bobby Darin", this traditional French "gem" once favored by the "Rat Pack" is an "oldie but still a goodie" thanks to chef-owner George LaForge's "classic", "quirky menu (they recite it to you)" and the "romantic shanty" setting east of the Strip; the "fabulous waiters" ply you with "remarkable crudités", followed by an "outstanding" meal.

Panevino Ristorante & 20 25 21 $45
Gourmet Deli
*246 Via Antonio Ave. (Sunset Rd.), 702-222-2400;
www.panevinolasvegas.com*
Natives pop by this south-of-the-Strip Italian's "wonderful deli" for lunch and return in the evening to the "stunning" environs of the "terrific retro-populuxe" dining room to "have dinner and watch the planes take off and land at the airport"; "a nice place to go in an area that needs restaurants", it serves "great", "rustic" cuisine, including pizza from a wood-burning oven and salads so "super-fresh", they "taste like they went out back and picked them."

Paradise Buffet & Cafe 19 16 18 $15
*Fremont Hotel, 200 Fremont St. (Casino Center Blvd.),
702-385-3232; www.fremontcasino.com*
Yes, it feeds the "can't-leave-without-one-more-dessert crowd", but this all-you-can-eat Downtown Eclectic "also offers the option of ordering off the menu", which is "great when you're traveling with others who might not want to do another buffet"; still, the fare is generally "unimaginative", and the faux rainforest decor irks folks who "don't like plants hanging over their table and in their food."

Paradise Garden Buffet 15 15 15 $19
*Flamingo Las Vegas, 3555 Las Vegas Blvd. S. (Flamingo Rd.),
702-733-3282; www.flamingolasvegas.com*
"Enjoy the ducks" – not the ones on your plate, but the feathered fellows palling around with the flamingos and penguins in the "wildlife habitat" by the windows of this Eclectic buffet on the Strip; unfortunately, "watching the birds is more interesting" than eating the "institutional" grub replenished by a "grumpy" staff.

Pasta Mia West ▽ 22 13 19 $25
*Flamingo & Arville Plaza, 4455 W. Flamingo Rd. (Arville St.),
702-251-8871; www.pastamiawest1.com*
The "wonderful aroma of sautéed and roasted garlic" wafts through this "Vegas favorite" for "huge" portions of

"outstanding", "authentic Italian" entrees that "come with salad", a side of "superb pasta" and "terrific, homemade" bread; the West Side space is "comfortable", "homey" and filled with "locals" hip to its "reasonable prices."

Pasta Shop & Ristorante   ∇ 27 | 14 | 25 | $26
Ocotilla Plaza, 2495 E. Tropicana Ave. (Eastern Ave.), 702-451-1893; www.pastashop.com
Chef/co-owner David Alenik "loves his work, and it shows" in his "hands-on expertise" with "imaginative specials", "tasty" sauces and the "freshest pasta in Vegas" at this "excellent" "neighborhood Italian" on the East Side; his "friendly" brother, Glen, is "eager to wait on you", "welcoming you by name and making you feel at home" – no wonder the "small" place gets so "crowded."

Paymon's Mediterranean Café ● 21 | 17 | 18 | $21
Tiffany Sq. Shopping Plaza, 4147 S. Maryland Pkwy. (Flamingo Rd.), 702-731-6030
8380 W. Sahara Ave. (Durango Dr.), 702-731-6030
www.paymons.com
"Grown more popular" and expanded to two locations "without sacrificing quality", this Med-Mideast pair in the University District and on the West Side proves itself to "authentic foodies" with a "wide variety" of "well-made, unusual flavors", taken in the cafe or the "adjoining hookah lounge"; the "low prices please even the family scrooges", and "Maryland Parkway has an attached market."

Pearl   24 | 23 | 24 | $57
MGM Grand Hotel, 3799 Las Vegas Blvd. S. (Tropicana Ave.), 702-891-7380; www.mgmgrand.com
"Each dish is a work of art", and the "hip" ambiance "fits the cuisine" at this French-influenced Chinese in the MGM Grand; the "inventive", "gourmet" offerings include a "fantastic tasting menu" and some of the "freshest seafood in LV", preferred by "expert" servers amid "contemporary" decor that manages to be both "trendy" and "relaxing."

Penazzi NEW   – | – | – | M
Harrah's Las Vegas, 3475 Las Vegas Blvd. S. (Flamingo Rd.), 702-369-5084; www.harrahs.com
This new, breath-of-fresh-air trattoria at Harrah's purveys both familiar dishes as well as innovative recipes from the owner's family that have been updated into a kind of intra-Italy fusion; the concept is reflected in decor that lies somewhere between sleek and funky.

P.F. Chang's China Bistro   21 | 19 | 19 | $30
Aladdin Resort, 3667 Las Vegas Blvd. S. (Harmon Ave.), 702-836-0955 ●
4165 Paradise Rd. (Flamingo Rd.), 702-792-2207
1095 S. Rampart Blvd. (Charleston Blvd.), 702-968-8885
(continued)

(continued)
P.F. Chang's China Bistro
101 S. Green Valley Pkwy. (I-215), Henderson, 702-361-3065
www.pfchangs.com
"In the middle of gambling, shopping and carousing", "you can't go wrong" at one of the town's four Chinese brothers from this extended family of "perennial favorites" where "big portions, bold flavors", "reasonable prices" and "lots of action" at the "well-stocked bars" make them "fun places to meet and eat"; of course, "there's not one Asian face" amid the "energetic staff" or the "yuppie" crowd – "so why would you expect the food to be authentic?"

PICASSO　　　　　　27 | 28 | 27 | $102
Bellagio Hotel, 3600 Las Vegas Blvd. S. (Flamingo Rd.),
702-693-8255; www.bellagio.com
Just like the "beautiful" namesake originals on the wall, chef Julian Serrano's "exquisite" Spanish-inflected New French dishes are "meticulously honed" "masterpieces" at this "MoMA-meets-Bacchus" "splurge" in the Bellagio (voted tops for Decor and Service as well as Most Popular in Las Vegas); other enticements include "perfect wines", "gorgeous flowers", "a view of the dancing fountains" and a "gracious" staff; of course it's "expensive", but "it still costs less than 15 minutes at blackjack"; N.B. closed Tuesdays.

Piero's Trattoria　　　　　▽ 22 | 18 | 21 | $43
Hughes Ctr., 325 Hughes Center Dr. (Flamingo Rd.), 702-892-9955
"Great pastas, steaks, veal dishes" and pizzas are "done with *amore*" at this "friendly", casual Italian owned by Evan Glusman, son of fabled Piero's Italian Cuisine owner Freddy; it's "not quite as good as the original" and its east-of-Strip location is "so-so", but if "the 'in' crowd" goes elsewhere for dinner, at lunch they pack the place, making the power "scene" here "a hit" "at half the cost" of other joints.

Ping Pang Pong ●　　　　▽ 23 | 9 | 14 | $25
Gold Coast Hotel, 4000 W. Flamingo Rd. (bet. Valley View Blvd. & Wynn Rd.), 702-367-7111; www.goldcoastcasino.com
"The won ton soup is won-derful, the walnut prawns are hall of fame" and all of the "creative Chinese" dishes are "not to be expected in such simple" "cafeteria decor", but here they are, at this "real surprise" on the West Side; open till 2:45 AM, it's "good for a late-night snack", if you can deal with the staff – though "the food belies the location", the service does not: "either the waiters won't leave you alone, or they won't come back."

Pink Taco　　　　　　19 | 18 | 17 | $24
Hard Rock Hotel, 4455 Paradise Rd. (bet. Flamingo Rd. & Harmon Ave.), 702-693-5525; www.hardrockhotel.com
Your "perfect hangover cure"?: "tequila and tacos" "served alongside [and by] hard, beautiful bodies" at this

"kick-ass Mexican" in the Hard Rock where the "intriguing decor" includes a "nice view of the pool" "if you sit outside"; they might be "more interested in selling alcohol than in culinary efforts" at this "meat market", but the "solid" fare is still "better than the locker room–inspired name."

Pinot Brasserie   20 19 19 $50
Venetian Hotel, 3355 Las Vegas Blvd. S. (bet. Flamingo & Spring Mountain Rds.), 702-414-8888; www.patinagroup.com
"Escape from the ringing slots" to "the Champs-Elysées" inside Joachim Splichal's French bistro at the Venetian where "authenticity" abounds in the "well-executed" fare, the "romantic" room and the staff's "snobby attitude"; still, though this spot is "cute" for a "moderately priced" "afternoon snack", "the California outposts" in the "celeb chef's" Patina group "are decidedly better."

Planet Hollywood   11 18 14 $26
Forum Shops at Caesars Palace, 3500 Las Vegas Blvd. S. (Flamingo Rd.), 702-791-7827; www.planethollywood.com
"The family was shopping, the kids got hungry" and you needed "entertainment for young ones" – all reason enough to stop for American "pub grub" at this "movie memorabilia"–mobbed themester in the Forum Shops; foes fret about fare "lacking flavor" and "too commercial" decor, marveling "people still inhabit this Planet?"

Postrio   23 22 22 $56
Venetian Hotel, 3355 Las Vegas Blvd. S. (bet. Flamingo & Spring Mountain Rds.), 702-796-1110; www.wolfgangpuck.com
Spinning off the "top of the Puck line", über-chef Wolfgang goes for a "serious contender" at this New American–Mediterranean in the Venetian, where the "warm", "bordello-red decor" is almost as "delicious" as the "fabulous" fare ferried by the "excellent" staff; some diners are "disappointed" in dishes that "don't always live up to their ambitions", but even they revel in the 'outside' seating for "serenading gondoliers" and "people-watching in Venice", "authentic-fabricated Vegas"–style.

PRIME STEAKHOUSE   27 27 26 $83
Bellagio Hotel, 3600 Las Vegas Blvd. S. (Flamingo Rd.), 702-693-8255; www.bellagio.com
"Sink into the lavish seats" and "begin an evening of delight" at the town's No. 1 steakhouse where Jean-Georges Vongerichten's "pampering" staff serves "heaven on a plate (and in a glass)"; "if the Rat Pack were still around, they'd congregate here" for "marvelous" meat, "martini-centric drinks", "theatrical decor" and "fantastic" fountain views, "all of which scream 'ring-a-ding Vegas'"; just "know that you'll be spending a ton" and you'll "want to dress up" to dine among the "famous" folk.

Pullman Grille Ⓜ   20 | 23 | 19 | $33 |
Main Street Station Hotel, 200 N. Main St. (Ogden Ave.),
702-387-1896; www.mainstreetcasino.com
This "true find" Downtown in the Main Street Station is a
"bit out of the way" but "worth getting on board" to enjoy
"excellent" chophouse fare while "soaking up the atmosphere" of a "romantic Victorian" room that's "big on
wood" and "antique furnishings"; polish off the evening
with "after-dinner cigars and drinks" in the "actual rail car
that belonged to Louisa May Alcott."

Quark's   16 | 24 | 17 | $24 |
Las Vegas Hilton Hotel, 3000 Paradise Rd. (bet. Desert Inn Rd. &
Karen Ave.), 702-697-8725; www.startrekexp.com
Sci-fi "fanatics" scream "beam me up, Scotty" at this
"intergalactic" "hoot" east of the Strip populated by
staffers serving "rather ordinary" American eats done up
as "Tribble medallions" and washed down with "dyed
beer" "named Romulan Ale"; it's a "must-see if you're
a Trekkie" and naturally a "hit with the kids", but you otherwise might decide to "never go again" "'where no man
has gone before.'"

Raffles Cafe ◑   18 | 15 | 14 | $23 |
Mandalay Bay Resort, 3950 Las Vegas Blvd. S.
(Mandalay Bay Rd.), 702-632-7406; www.mandalaybay.com
"Far above the jingle" of the Mandalay Bay casino is this
"solid" 24/7 coffee shop, a "benchmark" for "better-than-
you'd-expect" Traditional American fare fit for "late-night
cravings and hangover breakfasts"; "good-sized portions"
make it a "terrific spot anytime", unless you stop by when
"service is painfully slow."

Rainforest Cafe ◑   14 | 22 | 15 | $25 |
MGM Grand Hotel, 3799 Las Vegas Blvd. S. (Tropicana Ave.),
702-891-8580; www.rainforestcafe.com
"Complete with rain", "bird sounds" and animatronic "animals everywhere", this MGM Grand American toes the
line between "cheesy" and "brings-the-kid-out-in-anyone"
"cool" with a tropical setting that some suspect is "meant
to camouflage" its "barely adequate" eats; not just that,
but "tons of children hyped up on sugar" plus "nonexistent"
service make this joint a "jungle within a jungle."

Range Steakhouse   21 | 21 | 23 | $54 |
Harrah's Las Vegas, 3475 Las Vegas Blvd. S. (Flamingo Rd.),
702-369-5000; www.harrahs.com
With "floor-to-ceiling windows" offering a "commanding
view of the Strip", this Harrah's surf 'n' turf is a "quiet
place" to watch "the bustle" while attended to by a "super" staff; although some say the "standard steakhouse
fare" "seems as dated" as the decor, it remains a "nice"
choice "for before or after a show."

r bar cafe   ▽ 21 | 20 | 23 | $48
Mandalay Place, 3950 Las Vegas Blvd. S. (Mandalay Bay Rd.), 702-632-9300
You "better like fish as there's little else on the menu" at this casual downstairs counterpart to Mandalay Place's so-phisticated restaurant rm; erstwhile NY chef Rick Moonen shows off his flair with seafood at the raw bar and on a menu of "simple", "fresh" fin fare (think "flavorful" chow-ders and hot seafood salads) all served by a "very helpful" staff in an open, comfortable setting.

Red 8 Asian Bistro   23 | 23 | 20 | $41
Wynn Las Vegas, 3131 Las Vegas Blvd. S. (Desert Inn Rd.), 702-770-9966; www.wynnlasvegas.com
This "authentic" Southeast Asian noodle kitchen in the Wynn Las Vegas is "worth seeking out" for "excellent" dim sum and a "wide selection" of dishes that fuse flavors from the chef's native Malaysia with those of Thailand, Singapore and Canton; a "stylish, modern" setting "lush" with color distracts diners from sometimes "unavailable" service and "pricey" tabs.

Red, White and Blue   16 | 12 | 15 | $26
Mandalay Bay Resort, 3950 Las Vegas Blvd. S. (Mandalay Bay Rd.), 702-632-7405; www.chinagrillmgt.com
For a "reasonably priced" "change from buffet food", head to Mandalay Bay's "casual" "three-in-one" Traditional American, where the space and menu are sorted by the colors on Old Glory: 'red' for regional cuisine in the bistro, 'white' for desserts from the bakery and 'blue' for burgers and sandwiches in the deli; though the food's "nothing to wave a flag about", a "broad" selection and "friendly service" make it "good for a quick bite."

Redwood Bar & Grill   22 | 20 | 22 | $40
California Hotel, 12 E. Ogden Ave. (Main St.), 702-385-1222; www.thecal.com
A "hidden treasure" Downtown, this surf 'n' turfer parked in an "old-time casino" will "take you back" to Vegas' hey-day with "professional service" and a "warm, relaxing" setting that's a "change from the hectic pace" of the Strip; nightly live piano music is a "nice touch" as are "value-for-the-dollar" entrees, including a $19.95 porterhouse special that's "not on the menu."

Rincon Criollo Ⓜ   – | – | – | I
1145 Las Vegas Blvd. S. (Charleston Blvd.), 702-388-1906
When it comes to hole-in-the-wall ethnic spots, this Downtown Cuban in the shadow of the Stratosphere de-fines the genre with carefully prepared, country-style fare that seems all the more authentic served in a no-frills storefront complete with paper place mats bearing maps of the old country.

| | 20 | 22 | 20 | $59 |

rm
*Mandalay Place, 3930 Las Vegas Blvd. S. (Mandalay Bay Rd.),
702-632-9300; www.mandalaybay.com*
Chef-owner Rick Moonen closed up shop in NYC and
sailed to Mandalay Bay to open this "elegant" seafooder
set in a "lovely" polished wood–and-glass "interior that
looks like a ship", albeit one with a two-story exhibition
kitchen; an "excellent tasting menu" encourages diners to
"try a lot" of fin fare (from Pacific halibut to arctic char),
but critics carp that "unimaginative" food, plus service
that's merely "good" don't match the "outrageous prices";
N.B. downstairs is its more casual cousin, r bar cafe.

| | 15 | 17 | 16 | $19 |

Roadrunner ⏺
5990 Centennial Pkwy. (Azure Rd.), 702-309-6015 NEW
*6910 E. Lake Mead Blvd. (Hollywood Blvd.), 702-459-1889
921 N. Buffalo Dr. (bet. Vegas Dr. & Washington Ave.),
702-242-2822
9820 W. Flamingo Rd. (Grand Canyon Dr.), 702-243-5329
Albertson's Shopping Ctr., 754 S. Boulder Hwy. (Major Ave.),
Henderson, 702-566-9999
2430 E. Pebble Rd. (Myrtle Beach Dr.), 702-948-8282
www.roadrunnerlasvegas.com*
There's "something for everyone" at these "Western-
style" roadhouses serving "standard pub stuff",
from "great cornbread" to "nachos large enough to feed a
Mexican army"; "great drinking hangouts" for "boys
watching sports", these joints remain "busy" with dudes
huddling around the patio fire pits at the Flamingo and
Pebble Road offshoots.

| | 19 | 17 | 18 | $25 |

Romano's Macaroni Grill
*2001 N. Rainbow Blvd. (Lake Mead Blvd.), 702-648-6688
2400 W. Sahara Ave. (Rancho Dr.), 702-248-9500
573 N. Stephanie St. (bet. Sunset & Warm Springs Rds.),
Henderson, 702-433-2788
www.macaronigrill.com*
At these "consistent" links in a national chain, "you always
know what you're getting": "basic Italian without much
fanfare" in a "noisy", "step-above-standard" setting; sure,
they're "nothing fancy", but "good size portions",
"reasonable prices" and complimentary crayons for the
kiddies make them "great family places."

| | 28 | 21 | 26 | $52 |

ROSEMARY'S
*W. Sahara Promenade, 8125 W. Sahara Ave. (bet. Buffalo Dr. &
Cimarron Rd.), 702-869-2251; www.rosemarysrestaurant.com*
Tucked "way off the Strip" on the West Side, this "not-to-
be-missed" New American from chef-owners Michael
and Wendy Jordan may be Las Vegas' "ultimate epicurean
event", a "hidden treasure" that's toppled Nobu to become
No. 1 for Food in the *Las Vegas Survey*; "fabulous tastes
and flavors" are served in a "pretty" space that "belies its

strip-mall location", while "excellent prix fixes" and "exceptional" service that "goes above and beyond expectations" make it "worth every penny of the cab ride."

Rosewood Grille & Lobster House ◖

| 19 | 16 | 19 | $70 |

3763 Las Vegas Blvd. S. (bet. Harmon & Tropicana Aves.), 702-792-6719

"Mouthwatering" steaks and "lobsters as big as your head" will "spoil you" at this "above-average" surf 'n' turfer on the Strip that's "a tradition for many"; still, those who say the "formula still works" should consider service that seesaws from "steady" to "unbearable", and prices so "devastating" you'll need to "take out a second mortgage on your house."

Roxy's Diner

| ▽ | 15 | 17 | 19 | $17 |

Stratosphere Hotel, 2000 Las Vegas Blvd. S. (north of Sahara Ave.), 702-383-4834; www.stratospherehotel.com

"Take a trip back in time to the '50s" at the Stratosphere's "family"-friendly "faux-diner" that "comes complete with soda fountain and singing waiters"; the "ordinary" eats like sliders and chicken-fried steak are "surprisingly good", and if the "music's way too loud" for conversation, at least the "song-and-dance" staff is "exceptionally talented."

Roy's

| 25 | 22 | 23 | $50 |

620 E. Flamingo Rd. (Palo Verdes St.), 702-691-2053
8701 W. Charleston Blvd. (bet. Durango Dr. & Rampart Blvd.), 702-838-3620
www.roysrestaurant.com

"Roy Yamaguchi groupies" say "mahalo for bringing the islands to the desert" at these east-of-the-Strip and West Side "tropical delights" where "fresh", "creative combinations" make for "out-of-this-world" Hawaii Regional dishes (think "misoyaki butterfish that's the stuff of food dreams"); "camera-worthy" presentations, "attentive service" and an "aloha" ambiance mean this is "not your normal chain."

Rubio's Fresh Mexican Grill

| 17 | 12 | 15 | $11 |

Red Rock Casino, 11011 W. Charleston Blvd. (Hwy. 215), 702-254-7470 NEW
Trails Village Ctr., 1910 Village Center Circle (Town Center Dr.), 702-838-1001
7290 W. Lake Mead Blvd. (Tenaya Way), 702-233-0050
9310 W. Sahara Ave. (Fort Apache Rd.), 702-804-5860
Pebble Mkt., 1500 N. Green Valley Pkwy. (Pebble Rd.), Henderson, 702-270-6097
www.rubios.com

A "special trip from the Strip" to one of these "semi-fast-food" chain Mexicans is "worth the drive" for "fresh", "filling" fare including what some amigos swear are the "best fish tacos north of Baja"; they're "good for a quick meal", but some say "you get what you pay for": "ok, but not great" dining.

Ruth's Chris Steak House   24 | 20 | 22 | $57 |
Cameron Corner Shopping Ctr., 4561 W. Flamingo Rd.
(bet. Arville St. & Decatur Blvd.), 702-248-7011 ●
Citibank Park Plaza, 3900 Paradise Rd. (bet. Flamingo Rd. &
Twain Ave.), 702-791-7011
www.ruthschris.com
"Always winners" for "top-notch, sizzling steaks" broiled in butter, along with "huge portions" of "extra-tasty sides" and "very good seafood", these chophouse links east of the Strip and on the West Side "will make you forgive yourself for eating at a chain"; even so, the skeptical suggest that "service needs to improve" to match the "ouch"-inducing prices; P.S. the Flamingo Road outpost stays open till 3 AM.

Salt Lick Bar-BQ NEW   – | – | – | I |
Red Rock Casino, 11011 W. Charleston Blvd. (Hwy. 215),
702-797-7576; www.redrocklasvegas.com
Spun off from the bare-bones original in Driftwood, Texas, this new Red Rock Casino BBQ specialist is considerably more upscale than its parent, with a carefully designed wood-and-rock interior; its smoked meats have the same earthy flavor, created by long hours in close proximity to burning wood.

Samba Brazilian Steakhouse   20 | 18 | 21 | $44 |
Mirage Hotel, 3400 Las Vegas Blvd. S. (Spring Mountain Rd.),
702-791-7337; www.mirage.com
"It's key to understand that the red side of the button means 'stop!'" at this Brazilian flesh "fiesta" in the Mirage where the waiters "keep coming" with "tasty all-you-can-eat" carnivorous cuts on "big swords"; the rodizio's "meaty menu pairs well with the sweet, strong drinks", "plentiful" sides and an "endless salad bowl", all of which "guarantee you get your money's worth"; though some find it a "disappointment", beef "gluttons" find themselves "too stuffed to move."

Sammy's Woodfired Pizza   20 | 15 | 17 | $22 |
6500 W. Sahara Ave. (Torrey Pines Dr.), 702-227-6000
4300 E. Sunset Rd. (Green Valley Pkwy.), Henderson,
702-450-6664
www.sammyspizza.com
"Not a rip-off of California Pizza Kitchen but an homage", the Green Valley and West Side branches of the La Jolla original turn out "decent" SoCal thin crusts with "traditional toppings as well as innovative ones", plus "can't-be-beat salads" and such; the "huge portions" are an "excellent value", and when you're urged to "leave room for the aptly named Messy Sundae", you can bet that "kids are welcome."

Sam Woo BBQ ☞ 20 | 8 | 10 | $17 |
Chinatown Plaza, 4215 Spring Mountain Rd. (bet. Arville St. & Wynn Rd.), 702-368-7628
"It isn't fusion, it isn't New Age, it isn't Americanized" – "in case you couldn't tell by the 95 percent Asian clientele, it is where you go for real Chinese" dished up "fast", "cheap" and "family-style"; its West Side setting is "nothing fancy", and you might want to "BYOT (bring your own translator)" to get service from the "inattentive staff", but if you can deal with the fact that "the ducks still have heads and the chicken still have feet", it's an "adventure."

Sapporo NEW – | – | – | M |
9719 W. Flamingo Rd. (Grand Canyon Dr.), 702-216-3080
Just like the Scottsdale, AZ, original, this West Side Japanese offers Pacific Rim cuisine as well as more traditional sushi and teppanyaki dishes; it's set in a darkly attractive postmodern room that's lightened by bright blue accents and also features an outdoor patio.

Seablue 24 | 22 | 23 | $63 |
MGM Grand Hotel, 3799 Las Vegas Blvd. S. (Tropicana Ave.), 702-891-3486; www.michaelmina.net
The "knowledgeable servers are eager to describe the ultrafresh seafood preparations" on Michael Mina's "innovative" (but "not overly elaborate") menu at this "global" oceanic "experience" in the MGM Grand where other list "twists" include a "great build-your-own salad" and "melt-in-your-mouth Kobe rib-eye"; given prices that are "high but not off the charts" and "hip" decor including a "cool fish tank", "you won't feel blue" here.

Second Street Grill ∇ 24 | 21 | 23 | $39 |
Fremont Hotel, 200 Fremont St. (Casino Center Blvd.), 702-385-6277; www.fremontcasino.com
"Creative cuisine shines" at this "bargain" for "high-end dining in a surprising location" "in the middle of the Fremont casino floor" Downtown; a "best-kept secret" of those in-the-know, it's a "real treat" for "outstanding" Pacific Rim plates proffered in "intimate" digs with "art deco flair"; N.B. closed on Tuesday and Wednesday.

Sen of Japan NEW – | – | – | M |
8480 W. Desert Inn Rd. (Durango Dr.), 702-871-7781; www.senofjapan.com
With sushi bars becoming as popular as dice in Las Vegas, this new arrival in a West Side strip center distinguishes itself from the pack thanks to a chef formerly at Nobu in the Hard Rock Hotel; his traditional and offbeat interpretations of the genre are taking things to a level not usually experienced in the suburbs.

Sensi
| – | – | – | E |

Bellagio Hotel, 3600 Las Vegas Blvd. S. (Flamingo Rd.),
702-693-8800; www.bellagio.com
This sleek stone-and-wood wonder (with waterfalls for accents) fits perfectly into the Bellagio's spa tower, where you can watch the chefs work out in the central kitchen; top toque Martin Heierling's Asian-Italian seafood menu includes an impressive bento box and a smashing twist on traditional fish 'n' chips, washed down with homemade ginger ale to take the edge off a sultry day.

Shanghai Lilly
| 24 | 24 | 23 | $49 |

Mandalay Bay Resort, 3950 Las Vegas Blvd. S.
(Mandalay Bay Rd.), 702-632-7409; www.mandalaybay.com
"Ask for one of the booths: you'll feel like royalty behind the billowing curtains" sampling a "fabulous selection of elegant" Cantonese and Szechuan cuisine at this Mandalay Bay "gem"; in fact, the "sexy" setting is so "inviting" and the servers so "nice", you might not ever want to leave, so it's a good thing you "could eat here for a month and never have the same dish"; the cuisine may be "all recognizable, but the taste is extraordinary."

Shibuya
| – | – | – | VE |

MGM Grand Hotel, 3799 Las Vegas Blvd. S. (Tropicana Ave.),
702-891-3110; www.mgmgrand.com
Artfully decked out in urban-minimalist decor that reflects the Tokyo district for which it is named, this upscale Japanese in the MGM Grand offers top-quality sushi at its 50-ft. bar, plus teppanyaki, tempura and an intoxicating array of sakes; less-standard offerings run from the cold side (Kumamoto oysters with green-apple ponzu) to the hot (chicken with ginger-yam puree).

Shintaro
| 26 | 25 | 23 | $68 |

Bellagio Hotel, 3600 Las Vegas Blvd. S. (Flamingo Rd.),
702-693-8255; www.bellagio.com
Whether you "watch the fountain show" at a window seat, the "entertaining chefs" at the teppanyaki tables or the "relaxing jellyfish" in the "tanks at the sushi bar", you're in for "excellent, high-end" Japanese dining at this Bellagio destination; aided by "superb service", it's "perfect" for a "celebration with a small group", even if it's "expensive."

Simon Kitchen & Bar
| 23 | 20 | 21 | $52 |

Hard Rock Hotel, 4455 Paradise Rd. (bet. Flamingo Rd. &
Harmon Ave.), 702-693-5000; www.hardrockhotel.com
"Those pretty hardbodies flitting by on the way to the pool as you enter" this "super-hip" Hard Rock spot may not know "it's a sin not to try the desserts" (including "to-die-for cotton candy") conjured by "whimsical" pastry chef Justin Nielson – that is, after first sampling "rising star" Kerry Simon's "marvelous" American-Eclectic dishes; the

"MTV crowd" makes this "friendly" joint "happening", "hot" and "noisy."

Sir Galahad's
19 17 19 $39

Excalibur Hotel, 3850 Las Vegas Blvd. S. (Tropicana Ave.), 702-597-7448; www.excalibur.com

"If the kids dragged you to Excalibur", you might as well dine like "tourist" royalty on a "mountain of succulent prime rib" "wheeled on a big silver cart" and "carved tableside" in this "dark castle" of a cow palace on the Strip; even commoners "without the bankroll of a king" can feast at this "great value", though some would like to overthrow the "pedestrian" provender and "dated" decor.

Smith & Wollensky ●
23 19 22 $62

3767 Las Vegas Blvd. S. (bet. Harmon & Tropicana Aves.), 702-862-4100; www.smithandwollensky.com

Dudes attending "bachelor parties" in the "kitchen's great glass-walled" chef's table say it's "worth a few chips" to "sit at the bar and enjoy a cigar after a fabulous filet and Caesar salad" at this "classic" chophouse chainster that might be Stripside but "looks, feels and acts like NY"; "Tyrannosaurus rex would have loved" the "big, big" beef servings and "giant martinis", and maybe the staff wouldn't be as "pushy" with the dino as they can be with diners.

Social House NEW
– – – E

Treasure Island Hotel, 3300 Las Vegas Blvd. S. (Buccaneer Blvd.), 702-894-7223; www.socialhouselv.com

Tranquility rules at this Pan-Asian monument to movers and shakers (especially those of the celebrity persuasion) at Treasure Island, featuring an open wood-and-steel design courtesy of NYC's avant-garde design team AvroKO; late-night, the dining tables are hydraulically lowered to cocktail level and the whole place becomes a party spot with a live DJ just steps from the sushi bar.

Sonoma Cellar Steakhouse
▽ 26 24 23 $52

Sunset Station Hotel, 1301 W. Sunset Rd. (Stephanie St.), Henderson, 702-547-7777; www.stationcasinos.com

Managing to be "classy without being pretentious", this Sunset Station steakhouse is a "great place to impress a date" in the Henderson area ("who would have imagined?"); locals say the "living-room atmosphere" is "romantic", the service "friendly", the cooking "excellent" and the wine list "outstanding."

SPAGO
23 19 21 $48

Forum Shops at Caesars Palace, 3500 Las Vegas Blvd. S. (Flamingo Rd.), 702-369-0360; www.wolfgangpuck.com

Amid the "fancy chefs and restaurants arriving in Vegas by the trainful" lately, this teenaged "Wolfgang wonder" in the Forum Shops remains a "sure bet" for New American cuisine on a "high, yet highly accessible, plane"; "it's

Puck, so what else do you expect?" ask acolytes, who also appreciate the "knowledgeable staff" and "people-watching" patio; though the decor is "starting to look a bit dated", "the menu changes [daily], so repeat visits mean trying new things", which "delights" diversity-seekers.

Spice Market Buffet 22 16 17 $25
Aladdin Resort, 3667 Las Vegas Blvd. S. (Harmon Ave.), 702-785-9005; www.aladdincasino.com
There's "more variety than a Vegas talent show" at this "sumptuous feast" in the Aladdin, where "samplings from around the world" include a "wonderful Middle Eastern selection", all for a price so "reasonable" that "you'll be refilling that plate until you feel like you're going to explode."

Spiedini 24 22 21 $38
JW Marriott, 221 N. Rampart Blvd. (Summerlin Pkwy.), 702-869-8500; www.spiedini.com
"Well-known local chef" Gustav Mauler does a "nice job" at this Summerlin "treat" where the "excellent Italian" fare includes "great spit-roasted dishes" "served quickly and piping hot", and even better, at "non-Strip prices"; "ask to sit on the patio" and enjoy a bottle from the "impressive" wine list.

Stack NEW – – – E
Mirage Hotel, 3400 Las Vegas Blvd. S. (Spring Mountain Rd.), 702-792-7800; www.stacklasvegas.com
At heart a steakhouse, this Strip newcomer in the Mirage takes things a step further by offering a variety of share-and-share-alike small-plates options; its walls are made of stacked layers of wood evoking Red Rock Canyon, and the signature dish echoes this design via a small steamer filled with hot rocks atop, which patrons cook thin slices of beef.

Stage Deli 20 10 14 $20
Forum Shops at Caesars Palace, 3500 Las Vegas Blvd. S. (Flamingo Rd.), 702-893-4045; www.arkvegas.com
MGM Grand Hotel, 3799 Las Vegas Blvd. S. (Tropicana Ave.), 702-891-3373; www.mgmgrand.com ●
For "corned beef and pastrami heaped to the sky" (and "fabulous pickles") "without having to hail a cab to New York", go for a "gut-busting good" sandwich at this "true" deli duo in "cafeterialike" settings in the Forum Shops and the MGM Grand; the "quick, casual meals" come with an authentically "saucy" "attitude", yet some Gothamites still grumble "there's nothing like the real thing, baby."

STEAK HOUSE 26 21 24 $47
Circus Circus Hotel, 2880 Las Vegas Blvd. S. (Circus Circus Dr.), 702-794-3767; www.circuscircus.com
"Fred and Barney" could order a couple of "dead-bang-perfect" brontosaurus-sized steaks and "kick it old-school"-style at this "dark-wood-and-leather" steakhouse

in Circus Circus, where the "excellent" cuts come with "soup or salad and sides included" (and offset by a rather limited wine list), at "amazingly" prehistoric prices; all this and one of "the best Sunday brunches out there" lure "real-deal" hunters to venture "past the kiddies and clowns" in the "bizarre hotel" to get in.

Steak House, The   25 20 22 $56
Treasure Island Hotel, 3300 Las Vegas Blvd. S.
(Spring Mountain Rd.), 702-894-7351; www.treasureisland.com
"Better than you'd expect" "without all the hoopla of the brand-name-chef steakeries elsewhere on the Strip", this Treasure Islander serves up "fantastic" filets and other "traditional" fare in "understated" yet "inviting" digs; it's "not necessarily intimate", and it can be "a bit noisy", but the "excellent service" helps make it "worth every penny."

Steakhouse46   22 21 23 $49
Flamingo Las Vegas, 3555 Las Vegas Blvd. S. (Flamingo Rd.),
702-733-3502; www.flamingolasvegas.com
Take a "giant step back in time" inside this Flamingo chophouse where they've changed the name (fka Conrad's) but nothing else; the "old-school decor", abetted by a "competent staff", make for a "peaceful" place in which to enjoy a "solid", "hearty meal" with "a fine glass of wine or a fancy cocktail"; just remember to "leave a seat open for Bugsy."

STERLING BRUNCH Ⓜ   26 19 23 $60
Bally's Las Vegas Hotel, 3645 Las Vegas Blvd. S. (Flamingo Rd.),
702-739-4111; www.ballyslasvegas.com
Yes, it's only open on Sundays (9:30 AM–2:30 PM), but for a "delightful experience" fueled by "free-flowing Perrier Jouët", this Bally's American brunch is "absolutely grand"; "feel free to pile your plate five deep with grilled lobster and top them off with good-quality American sturgeon caviar", finishing your meal with a "decadent dessert"; just remember to reserve in advance, "bring a credit card with a large limit" and be prepared to deal with "crowds."

StripSteak NEW   – – – E
Mandalay Bay Resort, 3950 Las Vegas Blvd. S.
(Mandalay Bay Rd.), 702-632-7414; www.mandalaybay.com
Chef Michael Mina – primarily known for his seafood, showcased at several Vegas venues – has unveiled his first steakhouse, this glass-fronted meat eaters' dream between the Restaurant Row and events center at Mandalay Bay; look for Angus and Wagyu cuts prepared on a pair of 12-ft. grills, compartmented to allow for the use of various types of burning wood.

Stuart Anderson's Black Angus   16 15 17 $25
5125 W. Sahara Ave. (Decatur Blvd.), 702-251-9300
(continued)

(continued)

Stuart Anderson's Black Angus
*Mall at Galleria, 651 Mall Ring Circle (bet. N. Stephanie St. &
W. Sunset Rd.), Henderson, 702-451-9300*
www.stuartandersons.com
The Henderson and West Side locations of this "long-
standing poor man's" beef chain "can be acceptable at
times" – particularly "if you use the coupon" in the local
paper for an all-inclusive "bargain lunch"; still, given meat
"not cooked to order" consistently, "one has to wonder,
with all the great steakhouses in town, why go here?"

Sushi Avenue   – – – M
4145 Grand Canyon Dr. (Flamingo Rd.), 702-368-4336
This Southwestern suburban Japanese offers steaks
prepared at its teppan tables as well as tempura, teri-
aki and katsu, but you'd be remiss to bypass the innovative interpretations of the namesake specialty,
whose clever monikers never overshadow the creativity of its sushi chefs.

Sushi Roku   25 23 21 $51
*Forum Shops at Caesars Palace, 3500 Las Vegas Blvd. S.
(Flamingo Rd.), 702-733-7373; www.innovativedining.com*
This LA import delivers "amazing sushi" in the Forum
Shops at Caesars, where you can "back away" from the
mall mania and "drop your jaw" at one of "the most fabulous views of the Strip"; rolls and slices ranging from the
"typical to the innovative" pair well with "potent specialty
cocktails" for a "delicious", "relaxing" break from the
"busy" stores, even if the "slow" service "leaves something to be desired."

Swish NEW   – – – M
*Sahara Hart Plaza, 7875 W. Sahara Ave. (Buffalo Dr.),
702-870-7947*
This shabu-shabu specialist on the West Side offers do-it-
yourself types the opportunity to suspend paper-thin
meats, vegetables and seafood in a bubbling broth, then
dunk them into a full-flavored sauce; since each patron
has their own boiling pot, there are no fork feuds as there
can be in fondue.

Swiss Cafe Restaurant ⊠   ∇ 21 19 22 $29
*3175 E. Tropicana Ave. (bet. McLeod & Pecos Rds.),
702-454-2270*
Mary and chef Wolfgang Haubold are "still making it work
after all these years" at their thirtysomething Alpine-oriented
Continental on the East Side; it's "hidden" in a "strip mall",
so "you have to know it's there", but once you find it, don't
be fooled by its "most unusual" "Swiss/German-time-
warp" decor – there's "no oompah-pah here, just good
spaetzle" and "terrific goulash."

SW STEAKHOUSE   26 | 26 | 25 | $74

*Wynn Las Vegas, 3131 Las Vegas Blvd. S. (Desert Inn Rd.),
702-770-9966; www.wynnlasvegas.com*

Surveyors savor "steak you can cut with a fork" at this
"fabulous" chophouse in the Wynn, where the room is as
"breathtaking" as the fare, featuring a patio overlooking
the "lake and forest with a water show at night"; "sensa-
tional service" and a "reasonable wine list" help make this
an "excellent" addition to the high-rolling scene; N.B. the
post-*Survey* departure of chef Eric Klein may outdate
the Food score.

Tableau   ▽ 26 | 26 | 26 | $71

*Wynn Las Vegas, 3131 Las Vegas Blvd. S. (Desert Inn Rd.),
702-770-9966; www.wynnlasvegas.com*

The "wonderfully attentive staff" may suggest you
"choose the chef's tasting menu" "with the wine pairing"
at this "phenomenal" Med-influenced New American
"hidden" in the "beautiful atrium" of the Wynn's south
tower; those who worry that this "great sleeper" might
be "getting lost in the crowd" should note standout
touches like the "cute copper saucepans that hold the
bread" and – a rarity among "exclusive" Vegas spots – a
vegetarian tasting menu.

Tamba Indian Cuisine   – | – | – | M

*Hawaiian Mktpl., 3743 Las Vegas Blvd. S. (Harmon Ave.),
702-798-7889*

An Indian restaurant in a Hawaiian marketplace may seem
odd, but is par for the course in Vegas; naturally, this Strip
subcontinental serves dinner, but it's especially popular
for the economical $11.95 lunch buffet, served in a high-
ceilinged room or on a terrace overlooking a plaza area.

Tao ◑   – | – | – | M

*Venetian Hotel, 3355 Las Vegas Blvd. S. (bet. Flamingo &
Spring Mountain Rds.), 702-388-8588; www.taorestaurant.com*

New York meets Las Vegas at this Pan-Asian import oozing
Manhattan style from the circular portal lined with tubs of
floating rose petals to the candlelit interior with its statues
of Buddha; supplicants sample sushi, Kobe shabu-shabu,
Thai fish hot pot and the 'Harmonized Vegetable Feast for
the Minor Gods' until later in the evening when the place
transcends dining and reaches nightlife nirvana.

Taqueria Canonita   21 | 20 | 19 | $29

*Venetian Hotel, 3355 Las Vegas Blvd. S. (bet. Flamingo &
Spring Mountain Rds.), 702-414-3773; www.venetian.com*

"Mexican food on the canals of Venice?" – the "mis-
matched cultural cues" might leave you "not sure whether
to order a margarita or Chianti" at this Venetian cantina,
but it works well for a "quick", "informal" lunch; "unwind"
while "singing gondoliers" float by, and enjoy this

"strange" but "welcome respite from the high-priced restaurants of the Strip."

T-Bones Chophouse NEW   - | - | - | E

Red Rock Casino, 11011 W. Charleston Blvd. (Hwy. 215), 702-797-7576; www.stationcasinos.com

No Las Vegas casino-hotel property would be complete without a steakhouse, and this new meat market in the Red Rock Casino is a glitzy, rock-and-crystal-heavy affair; a patio overlooking the pool is just the ticket for those who prefer to dine alfresco and smoke a stogie while they're at it.

Tenaya Creek   ▽ 17 | 19 | 17 | $25
Restaurant & Brewery ◑

3101 N. Tenaya Way (Cheyenne Ave.), 702-362-7335; www.tenayacreekbrewery.com

An "awesome beer selection" has the "bar packed three deep" at this Northwest microbrewery, but "walk through to the restaurant" where the Traditional American fare can be as "great" as the "fabulous" suds; others who knew it when opine that the "food went south after they added the pool tables", making it more of a "typical sports bar."

T.G.I. Friday's ◑   14 | 13 | 15 | $21

1800 E. Flamingo Rd. (Spencer St.), 702-732-9905
Orleans Hotel, 4500 W. Tropicana Ave. (Arville St.), 702-873-1801 NEW
4570 W. Sahara Ave. (bet. Arville St. & Decatur Blvd.), 702-889-1866
4330 E. Sunset Rd. (Green Valley Pkwy.), Henderson, 702-990-8443
www.tgifridays.com

Hooch hounds have it that the "Jack Daniel's flavoring is very good on the steaks and ribs", and it ain't bad in the glass either at this "after-work" "meat market" quartet that's part of the chain of "assembly-line" American eateries; "if you're not adventurous or maybe lazy" or "drunk", "this will work", although "you can do better."

Thai Spice ☒   ▽ 27 | 20 | 20 | $23

Flamingo & Arville Plaza, 4433 W. Flamingo Rd. (Arville St.), 702-362-5308

"Thoughtful" servers "give you a choice of how hot you want your meal on a scale of one to 10" at this West Side Thai that's "absolutely loved" by locals; at this location for 16 years, it's "still packing them in" for the "great house specialty mint leaf chicken" and one of the "best lunch deals" "under $10" in town.

Tillerman, The   21 | 20 | 20 | $46

2245 E. Flamingo Rd. (west of Eastern Ave.), 702-731-4036; www.tillerman.com

"Lots of locals" will tell you that a "nice place to go off the Strip" is this "old-time" "standby", a "solid performer" for "great fish" and meat "grilled over hardwood"; the "friendly", "professional waiters" make this East Side steak-and-seafood house "very comfortable", and the "trees growing through the middle" of the interior add to the "tranquil" ambiance.

Tinoco's Bistro Ⓢ   ▽ 21   17   19 $31

103 E. Charleston Blvd. (Casino Center Blvd.), 702-464-5008
A "Las Vegas restaurant that doesn't feel like it", this "bohemian" Italian-tinged Continental in Downtown's Arts District emits a "cozy vibe" for "low-key" dining featuring signatures like "Chilean sea bass with an excellent curry lobster sauce"; still, some call the operation "slipshod at best", with "just ok" fare and a room that "could use some major help in the design department."

Tintoretto Bakery & Cafe ◑   21   18   18 $18

Venetian Hotel, 3355 Las Vegas Blvd. S. (bet. Flamingo & Spring Mountain Rds.), 702-414-3400; www.venetian.com
For a "first choice for breakfast" in the "real" Italian style, check out this "charming" bakery in the Venetian where the "best espresso and cappuccino" is paired with "amazing pastries and decent breads"; at lunchtime, enjoy lasagna or a "creative sandwich" while "watching the gondoliers march by on their way to the canal" and, 'round midnight, "pick up a sweet on the way to your room."

Toby Keith's
I Love This Bar & Grill ◑   – – – M

Harrah's Las Vegas, 3475 Las Vegas Blvd. S. (Flamingo Rd.), 702-369-5000; www.harrahs.com
Folks hankering for gen-u-wine Southern cooking like this Harrah's eatery from the eponymous country crooner, serving chicken-fried steak, barbecue, meatloaf and even a fried bologna sandwich; once your belly's full you can two-step to live C&W tunes in a honky-tonk that's so red-white-and-blue that you'll feel like you're in Oklahoma.

Todai   17   12   14 $29

Desert Passage at Aladdin, 3663 Las Vegas Blvd. S. (Harmon Ave.), 702-892-0021; www.todai.com
"All-you-can-eat buffets are common in this town, but there aren't many Asian ones", so if you're hankering to pig out "without spending a fortune", this "cafeteria-style" chainster offering "sushi galore" is your "economy" ticket when hoofing the Desert Passage; "it's great for kids" – "and people with no taste buds" crab critics of the "average" cooking.

Todd's Unique Dining Ⓢ   26   18   26 $39

4350 E. Sunset Rd. (bet. Green Valley Pkwy. & W. Sunset Rd.), Henderson, 702-259-8633; www.toddsunique.com
"Finally, fabulous food that doesn't cost an arm and a leg or involve a smoke-filled room" sigh Henderson's hungry

who hail this "winner" in a "quiet mall"; chef-owner Todd Clore brings the Eclectic sensibilities he honed at the Sterling Brunch to a daily changing menu including "innovations" like goat-cheese won tons with raspberry-basil sauce; "also high on the list" of its "charms" are the "reasonably priced wines" and "personal service", while the "only negative" is the "lousy decor."

Togoshi Ramen ⊅
| – | – | – | I |

Twain Ctr., 855 E. Twain Ave. (Swenson St.), 702-737-7003

"Prepare to be adventurous" at this "hole-in-the-wall" ramen house in the Twain Center east of the Strip; "Japanese people" who frequent it to slurp up traditional bowls of noodles (there's "no sushi" here) say it's not for romance, pampering service or trendy crowds – it's "just for the food."

Tokyo Restaurant
| – | – | – | M |

Commercial Ctr., 953 E. Sahara Ave. (bet. Maryland Pkwy. & Paradise Rd.), 702-735-7070

Sure, it's in a commercial center east of the Strip, but if you like "traditional" Land-of-the-Rising-Sun-style dining, plus "great service", insiders say "this is the spot"; the decor, complete with a private tatami room, "makes you feel like you are eating in Japan", and the sushi is "decent"; N.B. reservations are required.

Tony Roma's
| 18 | 13 | 17 | $27 |

620 E. Sahara Ave. (bet. Maryland Pkwy. & Paradise Rd.), 702-733-9914
Fremont Hotel, 200 Fremont St. (Casino Center Blvd.), 702-385-3232
2040 N. Rainbow Blvd. (Lake Mead Blvd.), 702-638-2100
555 N. Stephanie St. (Sunset Rd.), Henderson, 702-436-2227
www.tonyromas.com

The mood is "down to earth", but the "ribs are out of this world" at these links of the national barbecue chain offering "good" babybacks, "decent sides" and a "great-tasting", "greasy mess of an onion loaf"; the approval isn't universal, however: "indifferent service" and "high-school canteen" decor have critics shrugging "there are better BBQ places in the city."

Top of the World
| 21 | 25 | 22 | $60 |

Stratosphere Hotel, 2000 Las Vegas Blvd. S., 106th fl. (north of Sahara Ave.), 702-380-7711; www.stratospherehotel.com

"Go at dusk to watch the sun set and the neon wake up" at this "first-night stop" in Sin City, a revolving restaurant 800 feet up in the Stratosphere where the "incredible" "bird's-eye view" allows you to "see where you want to go during the rest of your stay"; despite its "touristy nature", the New American fare is "surprisingly above par", but the "height" of the tab can make you as "dizzy" as the "rotational sightseeing trip" might.

Trattoria del Lupo

| 20 | 17 | 19 | $47 |

Mandalay Bay Resort, 3950 Las Vegas Blvd. S.
(Mandalay Bay Rd.), 702-632-7410; www.wolfgangpuck.com

"Pizza, red wine and watching the talent hit the Mandalay Bay clubs" are three reasons to pop into this "solid" Wolfgang Puckster where "a touch of American style and flavor" stoke the wood-burning flame, adding "tantalizing tastes" to an otherwise "ordinary Italian" menu; the "noisy" setting may "feel like you're eating in a mall", but at least this is "one of the most reasonably priced eateries" in the hotel.

Tremezzo

| 22 | 20 | 20 | $49 |

Aladdin Resort, 3667 Las Vegas Blvd. S. (Harmon Ave.),
702-785-9013; www.aladdincasino.com

A low-key location in the Aladdin might mean that even the "concierge hasn't heard of it", but this "unknown" Italian is "surprisingly good" with "reasonably priced", sometimes "super" dishes, best enjoyed at a "window table with a Bellagio fountain view"; but detractors declare the dishes "a bit lackluster", the decor "old-fashioned" and the service "slow."

Triple George Grill NEW

| – | – | – | M |

201 N. Third St. (Ogden Ave.), 702-384-2761;
www.triplegeorgegrill.com

Bringing new life to a moribund part of Las Vegas, this Downtown interpretation of a classic San Francisco seafood house is done up with enough dark wood, tiny octagonal tiles and floor-to-ceiling booths to evoke a pre-neon era; N.B. there's valet parking at the curb, or you can validate for the Lady Luck's garage.

Triple 7 Restaurant & Brewery ●

| 21 | 19 | 18 | $20 |

Main Street Station Hotel, 200 N. Main St. (Ogden Ave.),
702-387-1896; www.mainstreetcasino.com

Those who "want to watch a game" while they eat say that Main Street Station's "great microbrewery" is "probably your best bet for Downtown"; sure, the American menu (plus sushi) is your "typical pub stuff" and the vibe is standard "sports bar", but some "hot, hot wings" and a "nice sampler" of "handcrafted suds" are just the ticket if you're "looking to fill your inner grease receptical" and "stagger home" afterwards.

Valentino

| 24 | 22 | 23 | $72 |

Venetian Hotel, 3355 Las Vegas Blvd. S. (bet. Flamingo &
Spring Mountain Rds.), 702-414-3000; www.welovewine.com

This is "food to live for" laud loyalists of Piero Selvaggio's "sleek" Italian in the Venetian where chef Luciano Pellegrini's "fantastic" "twists on the expected" and a "mind-boggling" wine list the "size of a phone book" add up to a much-appreciated sibling of the Santa Monica

flagship; still, those put off by the "pretentious" service
and "noisy grill" insist there are "better places in town for
this kind of cash."

Ventano
20 | 21 | 19 | $35

*191 S. Arroyo Grande Blvd. (Horizon Ridge Pkwy.),
Henderson, 702-944-4848*

You'll be "sitting on top of the hill" at chef-owner Arnauld
Briand's Henderson Northern Italian with such "spectacular
views" of the valley through its "wall of windows" that the
"food seems even better than it is"; but a few feel that's the
problem: it "never lives up to its reputation" (or its location),
and "sometimes the service takes away from what could
otherwise be a great experience."

VERANDAH
24 | 25 | 26 | $47

*Four Seasons Hotel, 3960 Las Vegas Blvd. S. (Four Seasons Dr.),
702-632-5121; www.fourseasons.com*

Even if you have a bad day at the tables, you'll "feel like a
winner again" when you head to the Four Seasons inside
the Mandalay Bay complex where this "casually elegant"
"oasis" delivers a dose of "uncommon tastefulness" "away
from the clanging of the slots"; with a "quietly attentive
staff", peaceful, poolside dining and an "outstanding"
New American menu, it's "wonderful from start to finish."

Viaggio
20 | 21 | 18 | $36

*11261 S. Eastern Ave. (Pecos Ridge Pkwy.), Henderson,
702-492-6900; www.viaggio.net*

The "view of Vegas is amazing" say fans of this colorful
Henderson Italian with a "friendly staff", a "great wine selection" and a "hip downstairs bar"; however, unhappy
travelers, citing the "very ordinary" fare and "disappointing
service", aren't having a *buon viaggio* here.

Vic & Anthony's Steakhouse NEW
– | – | – | E

*Golden Nugget Hotel, 129 Fremont St. (Main St.), 702-386-8399;
www.goldennugget.com*

Spun off from the original in Houston, this clubby new
Downtown steakhouse in the Golden Nugget features
dark-wood paneling, etched glass and a terraced floor
plan; look for USDA Prime chops in all the classic cuts for
the usual big bucks.

Victorian Room ●
∇ 18 | 15 | 17 | $23

*Barbary Coast Hotel, 3595 Las Vegas Blvd. S. (Flamingo Rd.),
702-737-7111; www.barbarycoastcasino.com*

"Early-risers or night owls" head to this "packed" 24/7
Chinese-American diner in the Barbary Coast for a "taste
of old Vegas" complete with "great grub", "bargain"
prices, "cat-house" decor and "sympathetic waitresses"
telling "stories from the Rat Pack days"; still, some snap
the "long wait for a table" is endurable only if you're "com-
pletely starving or taste-challenged."

Village Seafood Buffet   21 | 14 | 16 | $37
*Rio All-Suite Hotel, 3700 W. Flamingo Rd. (bet. I-15 &
Valley View Blvd.), 702-777-7943; www.playrio.com*
When you want "fish up to your gills" but have "trouble
committing to one type", drop anchor at this French-
inspired seafood buffet in the Rio All-Suite where "you
have to take a number to get in line" and then endure
"fast-food decor" and a "frenetic" ambiance; though
many claim it "never fails to satisfy", critics carp that
"mangled crab legs and microscopic lobster tails do not a
great buffet make."

Viva Mercado's   ▽ 23 | 14 | 21 | $21
*6182 W. Flamingo Rd. (Jones Blvd.), 702-871-8826;
www.vivamercadoslv.com*
It's "absolutely worth the trip off the Strip" for "authentic
Mexican" food (fried in canola oil, not lard) at this "usually
crowded", family-owned eatery where the "pride in the
product shows"; "they know how to make salsa spicy" and
there are lots of varieties here, along with 52 types of tequila,
"wonderful service" and a casual setting.

VooDoo Cafe   19 | 23 | 19 | $45
*Rio All-Suite Hotel, 3700 W. Flamingo Rd., 50th fl. (bet. I-15 &
Valley View Blvd.), 702-247-7800; www.playrio.com*
"A window table is not for those afraid of heights" at this
aerie atop the Rio where the "pretty good twists on
N'Awlins cuisine" are abetted by a "top-notch" club upstairs
for after dinner; a few put a hex on the "poor service",
however, concluding it's best for "excellent specialty
drinks" with "out-of-towners" who can have their "picture
taken from the terrace."

'wichcraft   20 | 12 | 16 | $18
*MGM Grand Hotel, 3799 Las Vegas Blvd. S. (Tropicana Ave.),
702-891-3166; www.mgmgrand.com*
If you're hankering for an "out-of-the-ordinary" sandwich
"on the fly", this "fast and fabulous" offshoot of Tom
Colicchio's NYC original in the MGM Grand earns an "A+"
from "budget gourmets" for its "innovative" options and
"modern" look; to the few who say "no big deal", others
retort it's "no big price, either."

Wing Lei   ▽ 22 | 24 | 23 | $69
*Wynn Las Vegas, 3131 Las Vegas Blvd. S. (Desert Inn Rd.),
702-770-9966; www.wynnlasvegas.com*
"Fabulous table settings" set the stage for "elegant but
small presentations" of "classic" preparations at this
high-end Chinese in the Wynn; with a tiger-marble bar,
dragon-scale upholstery and a view of an enormous
Botero surrounded by hundred-year-old pomegranate
trees, the room is as "over the top" as the "wonderful"
menu, which "calls for multiple visits"; but dissenters say

"some dishes are sublime, and others are as pedestrian as a local buffet."

Wolfgang Puck Bar & Grill　21 | 17 | 20 | $38 |
MGM Grand Hotel, 3799 Las Vegas Blvd. S. (Tropicana Ave.), 702-891-3000; www.wolfgangpuck.com

Since when can you eat at a bar and grill and claim "every bite is an experience"? – since Wolfgang Puck "reinvented" his "backyard-y" MGM Grand New American with "delicious" twists on "comfort food as the guiding principle"; it's "in the center of the casino", so you might "have to struggle to hear your companion when granny hits the slots."

Yolie's Brazilian Steakhouse　21 | 17 | 21 | $38 |
Citibank Park Plaza, 3900 Paradise Rd. (bet. Flamingo Rd. & Twain Ave.), 702-794-0700

"Not for the faint of heart" or "stomach", this Brazilian "house o' meat" east of the Strip is a "great concept", if you're angling to "eat until you explode"; the "kind servers" "keep coming and coming" with "various flame-broiled meats" and "great caipirinhas", so "bring your appetite" and "your conventioneer's badge, and you'll fit right in" at this "tourist" "fleshfest."

Zeffirino ◑　22 | 22 | 20 | $56 |
Venetian Hotel, 3355 Las Vegas Blvd. S. (bet. Flamingo & Spring Mountain Rds.), 702-414-3500; www.zeffirinolasvegas.com

With a "fabulous view" from the patio "overlooking the Grand Canal and gondoliers", "you may as well be in Italy" at this "romantic Northern Italian" in the Venetian offering "excellent" dishes that reflect the chef's Genoese heritage; though "wandering musicians" add ambiance as you "watch the boats go by", less "inconsistent" service and "larger portions would be nice for the price."

Z'Tejas Grill　19 | 16 | 18 | $28 |
9560 W. Sahara Ave. (Fort Apache Rd.), 702-638-0610; www.ztejas.com

The "ancho-fudge pie has a wonderful kick", and if dessert is that "spicy", you should try the rest of the menu at this Southwestern chainster in Summerlin; the "flavors are well blended" suggesting the "creative flair" in the kitchen, and at the bar, the "great margaritas" are as "reasonably priced" as the rest of the menu.

Restaurant Indexes

CUISINES
LOCATIONS
SPECIAL FEATURES

CUISINES

American (New)
Aureole
Bistro Zinc
Bradley Ogden
Café Bellagio
Cafe Tajine
Canyon Ranch
Kona Grill
Medici Café
Mix
Postrio
Rosemary's
Simon Kitchen
Spago
Tableau
Top of the World
Verandah
Wolfgang Puck

American (Traditional)
All-American B&G
America
Applebee's
Big Dog's
Buffet (Golden Nugget)
Cafe, The
Cafe Lago
Caribe Café
Center Stage
Cheesecake Factory
Chicago Brewing
Chili's G&B
Egg & I
Fix
Hard Rock Cafe
Harley-Davidson
Hash House
Hilltop House
Lake Mead Cruises
Lou's Diner
MGM Grand Buffet
Mr. Lucky's 24/7
Planet Hollywood
Quark's
Raffles Cafe
Rainforest Cafe
Red, White & Blue

Sterling Brunch
Tenaya Creek
TGI Friday's
Triple 7
Victorian Room

Asian
Café Wasabi
China Grill
Chinois
Fusia
Little Buddha
Sensi

Bakeries
Il Fornaio
Tintoretto Bakery

Barbecue
Famous Dave's
Lucille's BBQ
Memphis BBQ
Salt Lick Bar-BQ
Tony Roma's

Brazilian
Pampas Churrascaria
Samba Brazilian
Yolie's Brazilian

British
Crown & Anchor

Cajun
Big Al's Oyster
Emeril's
VooDoo Cafe

Californian
Nobhill

Caribbean
Ortanique

Chinese
(* dim sum specialist)
Ah Sin*
Amlee Gourmet

Cathay House*
Chang's
Chin Chin*
Dragon Noodle
Empress Court*
Fin
Full Ho
Jasmine
Joyful House
Mayflower Cuisinier
Ming's Table
Noodle Shop
Pearl
P.F. Chang's
Ping Pang Pong
Sam Woo BBQ
Shanghai Lilly
Victorian Room
Wing Lei

Coffee Shops/Diners
Café Bellagio
Caribe Café
Coco's
Coffee Pub
Mr. Lucky's 24/7
Raffles Cafe
Roxy's Diner

Continental
Hugo's Cellar
Michael's
Pahrump Valley
Swiss Cafe
Tinoco's Bistro

Creole
Big Al's Oyster
Commander's Palace
Emeril's
VooDoo Cafe

Cuban
Florida Cafe
Rincon Criollo

Delis
Cafe Heidelberg
Canter's Deli

Carnegie Deli
Stage Deli

Dessert
Cheesecake Factory
Chocolate Swan
Ethel's Chocolate Lounge
Giorgio Caffè
Jean Philippe
Red, White & Blue
Tintoretto Bakery

Eclectic
Bay Side Buffet
Bellagio Buffet
Big Kit. Buffet
Black Mtn. Grill
Buffet (Hilton)
Cafe Lago
Carnival World
Carson St. Cafe
Courtyard Buffet
Cravings
Elephant Bar
Feast, The
Feast Around World
Festival Buffet
Firelight Buffet
Flavors Buffet
French Mkt. Buffet
Garden Court
Grand Lux Cafe
Ortanique
Paradise Buffet
Paradise Garden
Simon Kitchen
Spice Mkt. Buffet
Todd's Unique Dining

Ethiopian
Cottage Café

Floribbean
Jimmy Buffett's

Fondue
Melting Pot

French
Alex
André's

Eiffel Tower
Le Village Buffet
Pamplemousse

French (Bistro)
Bouchon
Le Provençal
Marché Bacchus
Mon Ami Gabi
Pinot Brasserie

French (New)
Alizé
Daniel Boulud
Drai's
Fleur de Lys
Guy Savoy
Joël Robuchon
L'Atelier/Joël Robuchon
Le Cirque
Les Artistes Steak
Lutèce
Mix
Picasso

German
Cafe Heidelberg

Hamburgers
All-American B&G
Big Dog's
Burger Bar
Fatburger
Hard Rock Cafe
In-N-Out Burger
Quark's

Hawaiian
808

Hawaii Regional
Roy's

Health Food
Canyon Ranch

Indian
Gandhi India
Gaylord's

India Palace
Origin India
Tamba

Irish
Auld Dubliner
Nine Fine Irishmen

Italian
(N=Northern; S=Southern)
al Dente (N)
Andiamo (N)
Anna Bella
Antonio's
Bartolotta
Battista's
Bella Luna
Bertolini's
Bootlegger Bistro (S)
Canaletto (N)
Carluccio's
Center Stage
Chianti Café
Chicago Joe's
Enrico's
Fellini's
Ferraro's
Fiamma Trattoria
Fiore Steak (N)
Francesco's
Gaetano's (N)
Giorgio Caffè
Il Fornaio
Il Mulino NY
Le Provençal
Lombardi's (N)
Luna Rossa
Maggiano's
Mama Jo's (S)
Marc's
Market City
Montesano's
Nora's
Nove Italiano
Onda
Osteria del Circo (N)
Panevino

Pasta Mia (N)
Pasta Shop
Penazzi
Piero's Trattoria (N)
Romano's Macaroni
Sensi
Spiedini
Tintoretto Bakery
Trattoria del Lupo
Tremezzo (N)
Valentino
Ventano (N)
Viaggio
Zeffirino (N)

Japanese
(* sushi specialist)
Ah Sin*
Benihana
Hamada*
Hyakumi*
I Love Sushi*
Japengo*
Japonais
Makino*
Nobu*
Okada*
Osaka Bistro*
Osaka Cuisine*
Sapporo*
Sen of Japan*
Shibuya*
Shintaro*
Sushi Avenue*
Sushi Roku*
Swish
Todai*
Togoshi Ramen
Tokyo*

Mediterranean
Alex
Andiamo
Chandelier
Grape St. Cafe
MiraLago
Olives

Paymon's Med. Café
Postrio

Mexican
Agave
Baja Fresh
Bamboleo
Border Grill
Chevys Fresh Mex
Chipotle
Diego
Doña Maria
Don Miguel's
El Jefe's Mexican
El Sombrero Café
Garduño's
Guadalajara B&G
Isla
La Salsa
MargaritaGrille
Pink Taco
Rubio's Mexican
Taqueria Canonita
Viva Mercado's

Middle Eastern
Paymon's Med. Café
Spice Mkt. Buffet

Moroccan
Marrakech

Noodle Shops
Noodles
Noodle Shop
Togoshi Ramen

Pacific Rim
Café Wasabi
Japengo
Sapporo
Second St. Grill

Pan-Asian
Ah Sin
Hannah's
Social House
Tao

Peruvian
Nobu

Pizza
Bella Luna
Bootlegger Bistro
California Pizza
Canaletto
Le Provençal
Metro Pizza
Sammy's Pizza
Trattoria del Lupo

Pub Food
Auld Dubliner
Chicago Brewing
Crown & Anchor
Nine Fine Irishmen

Russian
Eliseevsky

Sandwiches
Canter's Deli
Capriotti's
Carnegie Deli
Stage Deli
'wichcraft

Seafood
AquaKnox
Bartolotta
Bay Side Buffet
Bella Luna
Big Al's Oyster
Billy Bob's
Bonefish Grill
Broiler
Buzio's
Canal Street
Como's
Costa del Sol
Craftsteak
Dan Marino's
808
Emeril's
Empress Court
Fin

Hilton Steak
Hush Puppy
Joe's Sea/Steak
Joyful House
King's Fish House
Luxor Steak
Makino
McCormick & Schmick
Michael Mina
Morton's Steak
Nobhill
Palm
Paradise Buffet
Ping Pang Pong
Range Steak
r bar cafe
Redwood B&G
rm
Rosewood Grille
Seablue
Sensi
Tillerman
Triple George Grill
Village Seafood

Small Plates
(See also Spanish/Tapas)
Rosemary's (New American)
Stack (Steakhouse)

Soul Food
Kathy's Southern
Lucille's BBQ

Southeast Asian
Red 8 Asian Bistro

Southern
Hush Puppy
Kathy's Southern
Toby Keith's B&G

Southwestern
Garduño's
Mesa Grill
Roadrunner
Z'Tejas Grill

Spanish/Tapas
Cafe Ba Ba Reeba!
Firefly

Steakhouses
AJ's Steak
Alan Albert's
Austin's Steak
Bally's Steak
Becker's Steak
Billy Bob's
Binion's Steak
Blackstone's Steak
Boa Steak
Bob Taylor's
Broiler
Canal Street
Capital Grille
Charlie Palmer
Como's
Craftsteak
Dan Marino's
Del Frisco's Steak
Delmonico Steak
Envy
Fiore Steak
Fleming's Prime
Gallagher's Steak
Golden Steer Steak
Hank's
Hilton Steak
Joe's Sea/Steak
Lawry's Prime Rib
Les Artistes Steak
Luxor Steak
Marc's
Mon Ami Gabi
Morton's Steak

Neros
N9ne Steak
Outback Steak
Palm
Pampas Churrascaria
Prime Steak
Pullman Grille
Range Steak
Redwood B&G
Rosewood Grille
Ruth's Chris
Samba Brazilian
Sir Galahad's
Smith & Wollensky
Sonoma Cellar
Stack
Steak House (Circus)
Steak House (Treasure Is.)
Steakhouse46
StripSteak
Stuart Anderson's
SW Steak
T-Bones Chophouse
Tillerman
Vic & Anthony's
Yolie's Brazilian

Tex-Mex
Chili's G&B

Thai
Archi's Thai
Lotus of Siam
Thai Spice

Vegetarian
Origin India

LOCATIONS

Central
Capriotti's
Doña Maria
Florida Cafe
Tony Roma's

Downtown
André's
Binion's Steak
Buffet (Golden Nugget)
Carson St. Cafe
Center Stage
Chicago Brewing
Chicago Joe's
El Sombrero Café
Garden Court
Hugo's Cellar
Makino
Paradise Buffet
Pullman Grille
Redwood B&G
Rincon Criollo
Second St. Grill
Tinoco's Bistro
Tony Roma's
Triple George Grill
Triple 7
Vic & Anthony's

East of Strip
AJ's Steak
Andiamo
Battista's
Benihana
Buffet (Hilton)
Cafe Heidelberg
Coco's
Cottage Café
Dan Marino's
Del Frisco's Steak
Envy
Firefly
Gandhi India
Hamada
Hard Rock Cafe
Hilton Steak
India Palace
Lawry's Prime Rib
Lotus of Siam
MargaritaGrille
Marrakech
McCormick & Schmick
Metro Pizza
Morton's Steak
Mr. Lucky's 24/7
Nobu
Origin India
Pamplemousse
Paymon's Med. Café
P.F. Chang's
Piero's Trattoria
Pink Taco
Quark's
Roy's
Ruth's Chris
Simon Kitchen
Togoshi Ramen
Tokyo
Yolie's Brazilian

East Side
Amlee Gourmet
Applebee's
Baja Fresh
Big Dog's
Billy Bob's
Broiler
Capriotti's
Carluccio's
Chili's G&B
Chipotle
Crown & Anchor
Fatburger
Feast, The
Fellini's
Firelight Buffet
Guadalajara B&G
Hush Puppy
In-N-Out Burger
La Salsa

Memphis BBQ
Metro Pizza
Outback Steak
Pasta Shop
Roadrunner
Swiss Cafe
TGI Friday's
Tillerman

Henderson

Anna Bella
Applebee's
Black Mtn. Grill
Bonefish Grill
Chandelier
Cheesecake Factory
Chevys Fresh Mex
Chianti Café
Chili's G&B
Chipotle
Coco's
Costa del Sol
Elephant Bar
El Jefe's Mexican
Fatburger
Feast, The
Feast Around World
Festival Buffet
Gaetano's
Guadalajara B&G
Hank's
Il Fornaio
I Love Sushi
In-N-Out Burger
Japengo
Kathy's Southern
King's Fish House
La Salsa
Lucille's BBQ
Melting Pot
Osaka Bistro
Outback Steak
P.F. Chang's
Roadrunner
Romano's Macaroni
Rubio's Mexican
Sammy's Pizza

Sonoma Cellar
Stuart Anderson's
TGI Friday's
Todd's Unique Dining
Tony Roma's
Ventano
Viaggio

Lake Las Vegas

Auld Dubliner
Bistro Zinc
Cafe Tajine
Como's
Luna Rossa
Medici Café
MiraLago

North Las Vegas

Austin's Steak
Fatburger
Feast Around World
Memphis BBQ
Outback Steak

Northwest/Summerlin

Agave
Applebee's
Baja Fresh
Becker's Steak
Big Dog's
Bob Taylor's
Capriotti's
Cheesecake Factory
Chianti Café
Chili's G&B
Doña Maria
Enrico's
Famous Dave's
Fatburger
Feast, The
Festival Buffet
Full Ho
Garduño's
Grape St. Cafe
Hannah's
Hilltop House
In-N-Out Burger
Kona Grill

Restaurant Locations

Marché Bacchus
Marc's
Montesano's
Nora's
Osaka Cuisine
Outback Steak
P.F. Chang's
Roadrunner
Romano's Macaroni
Rubio's Mexican
Salt Lick Bar-BQ
Spiedini
T-Bones Chophouse
Tenaya Creek
Tony Roma's
Z'Tejas Grill

Out of Town

Lake Mead Cruises
Pahrump Valley

South of Strip

Applebee's
Bootlegger Bistro
Chili's G&B
In-N-Out Burger
Outback Steak
Panevino
Roadrunner

Southwest

Applebee's
Baja Fresh
Capriotti's
Coco's
Roadrunner
Sushi Avenue

Strip

Ah Sin
Alan Albert's
al Dente
Alex
America
André's
AquaKnox
Aureole
Bally's Steak

Bartolotta
Bay Side Buffet
Bellagio Buffet
Bertolini's
Big Kit. Buffet
Blackstone's Steak
Boa Steak
Border Grill
Bouchon
Bradley Ogden
Burger Bar
Cafe, The
Cafe Ba Ba Reeba!
Café Bellagio
Cafe Lago
California Pizza
Canaletto
Canter's Deli
Canyon Ranch
Capital Grille
Caribe Café
Carnegie Deli
Chang's
Charlie Palmer
Cheesecake Factory
China Grill
Chin Chin
Chinois
Chipotle
Chocolate Swan
Commander's Palace
Courtyard Buffet
Craftsteak
Cravings
Daniel Boulud
Delmonico Steak
Diego
Dragon Noodle
Drai's
Eiffel Tower
808
Emeril's
Empress Court
Ethel's Chocolate Lounge
Fatburger
Fellini's
Fiamma Trattoria

Fin
Fix
Flavors Buffet
Fleur de Lys
Francesco's
Fusia
Gallagher's Steak
Giorgio Caffè
Grand Lux Cafe
Guy Savoy
Hamada
Harley-Davidson
Hyakumi
Il Fornaio
Il Mulino NY
Isla
Japonais
Jasmine
Jean Philippe
Jimmy Buffett's
Joël Robuchon
Joe's Sea/Steak
La Salsa
L'Atelier/Joël Robuchon
Le Cirque
Le Provençal
Les Artistes Steak
Le Village Buffet
Lombardi's
Lutèce
Luxor Steak
Maggiano's
Market City
Mesa Grill
MGM Grand Buffet
Michael Mina
Michael's
Ming's Table
Mix
Mon Ami Gabi
Neros
Nine Fine Irishmen
Nobhill
Noodles
Noodle Shop
Okada
Olives

Onda
Ortanique
Osteria del Circo
Outback Steak
Palm
Pampas Churrascaria
Paradise Garden
Pearl
Penazzi
P.F. Chang's
Picasso
Pinot Brasserie
Planet Hollywood
Postrio
Prime Steak
Raffles Cafe
Rainforest Cafe
Range Steak
r bar cafe
Red 8 Asian Bistro
Red, White & Blue
rm
Rosewood Grille
Roxy's Diner
Samba Brazilian
Seablue
Sensi
Shanghai Lilly
Shibuya
Shintaro
Sir Galahad's
Smith & Wollensky
Social House
Spago
Spice Mkt. Buffet
Stack
Stage Deli
Steak House (Circus)
Steak House (Treasure Is.)
Steakhouse46
Sterling Brunch
StripSteak
Sushi Roku
SW Steak
Tableau
Tamba
Tao

Taqueria Canonita
Tintoretto Bakery
Toby Keith's B&G
Todai
Top of the World
Trattoria del Lupo
Tremezzo
Valentino
Verandah
Victorian Room
'wichcraft
Wing Lei
Wolfgang Puck
Zeffirino

West of Strip

Alizé
All-American B&G
Antonio's
Bamboleo
Big Al's Oyster
Broiler
Buzio's
Canal Street
Capriotti's
Carnival World
Chang's
Coffee Pub
Don Miguel's
Feast, The
Fiore Steak
French Mkt. Buffet
Garduño's
Gaylord's
Golden Steer Steak
Guadalajara B&G
Hamada
In-N-Out Burger
Little Buddha
N9ne Steak
Nove Italiano
Outback Steak
Ping Pang Pong
Romano's Macaroni
TGI Friday's
Village Seafood
VooDoo Cafe

West Side

Applebee's
Archi's Thai
Baja Fresh
Bella Luna
Bertolini's
Big Dog's
Café Wasabi
Capriotti's
Cathay House
Chang's
Chicago Brewing
Chili's G&B
Egg & I
Eliseevsky
Fatburger
Fellini's
Ferraro's
Fleming's Prime
Hash House
Hush Puppy
Joyful House
Lou's Diner
Makino
Mama Jo's
Mayflower Cuisinier
Melting Pot
Memphis BBQ
Metro Pizza
Montesano's
Nora's
Osaka Bistro
Outback Steak
Pasta Mia
Paymon's Med. Café
Rosemary's
Roy's
Rubio's Mexican
Ruth's Chris
Sammy's Pizza
Sam Woo BBQ
Sapporo
Sen of Japan
Stuart Anderson's
Swish
TGI Friday's
Thai Spice
Viva Mercado's

SPECIAL FEATURES

(Indexes list the best in each category. Multi-location
restaurants' features may vary by branch.)

Additions

(Properties added since the
last edition of the book)
Auld Dubliner
Becker's Steak
Bella Luna
Bistro Zinc
Bonefish Grill
Chandelier
Cottage Café
Dan Marino's
El Jefe's Mexican
Ethel's Chocolate Lounge
Fin
Guy Savoy
Hash House
I Love Sushi
Japonais
Lou's Diner
Luna Rossa
Nove Italiano
Origin India
Pampas Churrascaria
Penazzi
Rincon Criollo
Salt Lick Bar-BQ
Sapporo
Sen of Japan
Social House
Stack
StripSteak
Sushi Avenue
Swish
Tamba
T-Bones Chophouse
Triple George Grill
Vic & Anthony's

Breakfast

Bellagio Buffet
Big Dog's
Black Mtn. Grill
Bootlegger Bistro
Bouchon
Café Bellagio
Chicago Brewing
Chocolate Swan
Coco's
Coffee Pub
Crown & Anchor
Egg & I
Fatburger
Jean Philippe
Le Village Buffet
Medici Café
Mr. Lucky's 24/7
Roadrunner
Tintoretto Bakery
Verandah

Brunch

Bellagio Buffet
Café Bellagio
Cheesecake Factory
Commander's Palace
Feast, The
Le Village Buffet
Medici Café
Mesa Grill
Ortanique
Steak House (Circus)
Sterling Brunch
Zeffirino
Z'Tejas Grill

Buffet Served

(Check availability)
Bay Side Buffet
Bellagio Buffet
Big Kit. Buffet
Buffet (Golden Nugget)
Buffet (Hilton)
Cafe Lago
Carnival World

Restaurant Special Features

Courtyard Buffet
Cravings
Feast, The
Feast Around World
Festival Buffet
Firelight Buffet
Flavors Buffet
French Mkt. Buffet
Gandhi India
Garden Court
Gaylord's
India Palace
Joyful House
Lake Mead Cruises
Le Village Buffet
Lotus of Siam
Makino
MGM Grand Buffet
MiraLago
Paradise Buffet
Paradise Garden
Spice Mkt. Buffet
Sterling Brunch
Tamba
Todai
Verandah
Village Seafood
Zeffirino

Business Dining
Alan Albert's
Aureole
Bouchon
Bradley Ogden
Capital Grille
Charlie Palmer
Commander's Palace
Craftsteak
Delmonico Steak
808
Fiore Steak
Fleming's Prime
Gaetano's
Hannah's
Hilton Steak
Joe's Sea/Steak
Lawry's Prime Rib

Michael's
Morton's Steak
Neros
Palm
Pearl
Postrio
Prime Steak
rm
Rosemary's
Roy's
Ruth's Chris
Shintaro
Smith & Wollensky
Sonoma Cellar
Spago
Spiedini
Steak House (Treasure Is.)
SW Steak
Todd's Unique Dining
Tremezzo
Valentino
Verandah

Catering
Aureole
Bouchon
Charlie Palmer
Chocolate Swan
Fellini's
Firefly
Grape St. Cafe
Hamada
Marché Bacchus
Mayflower Cuisinier
Morton's Steak
Nobu
Nora's
Ortanique
Paymon's Med. Café
Postrio
Rosemary's
Roy's
Sensi
Spago
Spiedini
Valentino
'wichcraft

Celebrity Chefs

Alex, *Alex Stratta*
Aureole, *Charlie Palmer*
Bartolotta, *Paul Bartolotta*
Bouchon, *Thomas Keller*
Bradley Ogden, *Bradley Ogden*
Burger Bar, *Hubert Keller*
Charlie Palmer, *Charlie Palmer*
Chinois, *Wolfgang Puck*
Craftsteak, *Tom Colicchio*
Daniel Boulud, *Daniel Boulud*
Delmonico Steak, *Emeril Lagasse*
Emeril's, *Emeril Lagasse*
Fleur de Lys, *Hubert Keller*
Giorgio Caffè, *Piero Selvaggio*
Guy Savoy, *Guy Savoy*
Isla, *Richard Sandoval*
Joël Robuchon, *Joël Robuchon*
L'Atelier/Joël Robuchon, *Joël Robuchon*
Mesa Grill, *Bobby Flay*
Michael Mina, *Michael Mina*
Mix, *Alain Ducasse*
Nobhill, *Michael Mina*
Nobu, *Nobu Matsuhisa*
Okada, *Takashi Yagahashi*
Olives, *Todd English*
Ortanique, *Cindy Hutson*
Picasso, *Julian Serrano*
Pinot Brasserie, *Joachim Splichal*
Postrio, *Wolfgang Puck*
Prime Steak, *J.-G. Vongerichten*
r bar cafe, *Rick Moonen*
rm, *Rick Moonen*
Seablue, *Michael Mina*
Simon Kitchen, *Kerry Simon*
Spago, *Wolfgang Puck*
StripSteak, *Michael Mina*
Trattoria del Lupo, *W. Puck*
Valentino, *Piero Selvaggio*
'wichcraft, *Tom Colicchio*
Wolfgang Puck, *W. Puck*

Cheese Trays

Alex
Alizé
André's

Aureole
Bistro Zinc
Bouchon
Bradley Ogden
Daniel Boulud
Fleur de Lys
Grape St. Cafe
L'Atelier/Joël Robuchon
Mon Ami Gabi

Chef's Table

AquaKnox
Delmonico Steak
Emeril's
Medici Café
Mix
Nobhill
Olives
rm
Smith & Wollensky

Child-Friendly

(Alternatives to the usual
fast-food places; * children's
menu available)
America*
Applebee's*
Bay Side Buffet
Bellagio Buffet
Black Mtn. Grill*
Bootlegger Bistro*
Border Grill*
Bouchon
Burger Bar*
Cafe Heidelberg*
Cafe Lago*
Cafe Tajine*
California Pizza*
Capriotti's*
Caribe Café
Cheesecake Factory
Chicago Brewing*
Chili's G&B*
Chipotle*
Chocolate Swan
Coco's*
Coffee Pub

Restaurant Special Features

Cravings
Doña Maria*
Don Miguel's
Egg & I*
Fatburger*
Feast, The
Festival Buffet
Firelight Buffet*
Flavors Buffet*
Florida Cafe
Full Ho
Garden Court
Garduño's*
Grape St. Cafe
Guadalajara B&G
Hard Rock Cafe*
Harley-Davidson*
Hilltop House*
Hush Puppy*
In-N-Out Burger
Jimmy Buffett's*
Kathy's Southern*
King's Fish House*
Kona Grill*
La Salsa*
Lombardi's
Mama Jo's*
Market City
Medici Café*
Memphis BBQ*
Mesa Grill
Metro Pizza*
MGM Grand Buffet*
MiraLago*
Montesano's*
Mr. Lucky's 24/7*
Neros
Nora's
Outback Steak*
Paradise Garden*
Pasta Mia
Pasta Shop*
Paymon's Med. Café*
Pearl
P.F. Chang's
Planet Hollywood*
Quark's*
Raffles Cafe
Rainforest Cafe*

Red, White & Blue*
Roadrunner*
Romano's Macaroni*
Roxy's Diner*
Roy's*
Rubio's Mexican*
Sammy's Pizza*
Second St. Grill
Sir Galahad's*
Stage Deli*
Swiss Cafe*
Tenaya Creek*
TGI Friday's*
Tony Roma's*
Ventano
Viaggio*
Viva Mercado's*
Z'Tejas Grill*

Children Restricted
Alex
Alizé
Becker's Steak
Chicago Brewing
Daniel Boulud
Fin
Fix
Francesco's
Joël Robuchon
Le Cirque
Onda
Osteria del Circo
Samba Brazilian
Sensi
Steak House (Treasure Is.)

Cigars Welcome
AJ's Steak
Alan Albert's
André's
Becker's Steak
Carluccio's
Charlie Palmer
Chicago Brewing
Chili's G&B
Como's
Craftsteak
Crown & Anchor
Del Frisco's Steak

Delmonico Steak
Fellini's
Ferraro's
Fiore Steak
Firefly
Golden Steer Steak
Hank's
Harley-Davidson
Isla
Medici Café
Mix
Morton's Steak
Palm
Pink Taco
Pinot Brasserie
Pullman Grille
Quark's
Ruth's Chris
Simon Kitchen
Smith & Wollensky
Sonoma Cellar
Spiedini
Tao
Tenaya Creek
Tillerman
Tony Roma's
Tremezzo
Yolie's Brazilian

Delivery/Takeout

(D=delivery, T=takeout)
Alizé (T)
Austin's Steak (T)
Bootlegger Bistro (D)
Burger Bar (T)
Cafe Ba Ba Reeba! (T)
Capriotti's (D)
Chocolate Swan (D)
Fellini's (T)
Ferraro's (T)
Fiamma Trattoria (T)
Firefly (T)
Fix (T)
Gaetano's (T)
Grape St. Cafe (T)
Jean Philippe (T)
Joe's Sea/Steak (T)
King's Fish House (T)
Lawry's Prime Rib (T)

Lotus of Siam (T)
Lucille's BBQ (D)
Makino (T)
Mayflower Cuisinier (D)
Metro Pizza (D)
Mon Ami Gabi (T)
N9ne Steak (T)
Osaka Bistro (D)
Palm (T)
Rosemary's (T)
Roy's (T)
Sam Woo BBQ (T)
Shanghai Lilly (T)
Smith & Wollensky (T)
Todd's Unique Dining (T)
Tremezzo (D)
Valentino (T)

Entertainment

(Call for days and times of performances)
AJ's Steak (piano)
Bootlegger Bistro (varies)
Cafe Ba Ba Reeba! (Spanish)
Cafe Lago (piano)
Charlie Palmer (piano)
Commander's Palace (jazz)
Crown & Anchor (bands)
Del Frisco's Steak (piano/vocals)
Delmonico Steak (piano)
Drai's (DJ)
Egg & I (dinner theater)
Eiffel Tower (piano)
Fellini's (piano/vocals)
Ferraro's (varies)
Firefly (DJ)
Golden Steer Steak (piano)
Hank's (piano)
Jimmy Buffett's (band)
Le Provençal (singing waiters)
Little Buddha (DJ)
Lucille's BBQ (blues)
Medici Café (piano)
Nine Fine Irishmen (Irish)
N9ne Steak (DJ)
Nora's (swing trio)
Onda (piano)

Ortanique (jazz)
Osaka Bistro (jazz)
Range Steak (jazz/piano)
Redwood B&G (piano)
Ruth's Chris (jazz)
Simon Kitchen (varies)
VooDoo Cafe (varies)
Yolie's Brazilian (piano)
Zeffirino (guitar/piano)

Fireplaces

André's
Black Mtn. Grill
Bob Taylor's
Canal Street
Chicago Brewing
Fiamma Trattoria
Fiore Steak
Guy Savoy
Joël Robuchon
Lawry's Prime Rib
McCormick & Schmick
Memphis BBQ
Nobhill
Panevino
Roadrunner
Ruth's Chris
Tillerman
Z'Tejas Grill

Game in Season

Alex
Alizé
Aureole
Black Mtn. Grill
Bouchon
Canaletto
Craftsteak
Daniel Boulud
Delmonico Steak
Japonais
Joël Robuchon
L'Atelier/Joël Robuchon
Osteria del Circo
Picasso
Pinot Brasserie
Postrio
Rosemary's
Todd's Unique Dining

Valentino
Zeffirino

Historic Places

(Year opened; * building)
1930 André's*
1946 El Sombrero Café
1955 Bob Taylor's
1958 Golden Steer Steak

Hotel Dining

Aladdin Resort
  La Salsa
  P.F. Chang's
  Spice Mkt. Buffet
  Tremezzo
Bally's Las Vegas Hotel
  al Dente
  Bally's Steak
  Big Kit. Buffet
  Chang's
  Sterling Brunch
Barbary Coast Hotel
  Drai's
  Michael's
  Victorian Room
Bellagio Hotel
  Bellagio Buffet
  Café Bellagio
  Fix
  Jasmine
  Jean Philippe
  Le Cirque
  Michael Mina
  Noodles
  Olives
  Osteria del Circo
  Picasso
  Prime Steak
  Sensi
  Shintaro
Binion's Hotel
  Binion's Steak
Boulder Station Hotel
  Broiler
  Feast, The
  Guadalajara B&G

Caesars Palace
  Bradley Ogden
  Cafe Lago
  808
  Empress Court
  Guy Savoy
  Hyakumi
  Mesa Grill
  Neros
California Hotel
  Redwood B&G
Casino Royale Hotel
  Outback Steak
Circus Circus Hotel
  Steak House
Desert Passage at Aladdin
  Commander's Palace
  Lombardi's
  Pampas Churrascaria
  Todai
Ellis Island Casino & Brewery
  Metro Pizza
Excalibur Hotel
  Sir Galahad's
Fiesta Henderson Hotel
  Festival Buffet
Fiesta Rancho Hotel
  Festival Buffet
  Garduño's
Flamingo Las Vegas
  Hamada
  Jimmy Buffett's
  Paradise Garden
  Steakhouse46
Forum Shops at Caesars Palace
  Bertolini's
  Boa Steak
  Cheesecake Factory
  Chinois
  Il Mulino NY
  Joe's Sea/Steak
  La Salsa
  Palm
  Planet Hollywood
  Spago
  Stage Deli
  Sushi Roku

Four Queens Hotel
  Chicago Brewing
  Hugo's Cellar
Four Seasons Hotel
  Charlie Palmer
  Verandah
Fremont Hotel
  Paradise Buffet
  Second St. Grill
  Tony Roma's
Gold Coast Hotel
  Ping Pang Pong
Golden Nugget Hotel
  Buffet
  Carson St. Cafe
  Vic & Anthony's
Green Valley Ranch
  Fatburger
  Feast Around World
  Hank's
  Il Fornaio
Hard Rock Hotel
  AJ's Steak
  Mr. Lucky's 24/7
  Nobu
  Pink Taco
  Simon Kitchen
Harrah's Las Vegas
  Flavors Buffet
  Ming's Table
  Penazzi
  Range Steak
  Toby Keith's B&G
Hilton Hotel
  Andiamo
  Benihana
  Buffet
  Hilton Steak
  MargaritaGrille
  Quark's
Hooters Hotel
  Dan Marino's
Hotel at Mandalay Bay
  Cafe, The
  Mix

Howard Johnson Hotel
  Florida Cafe
Hyatt Regency Lake Las Vegas
  Cafe Tajine
  Japengo
JW Marriott
  Spiedini
Luxor Hotel
  Fusia
  La Salsa
  Luxor Steak
Main Street Station Hotel
  Garden Court
  Pullman Grille
  Triple 7
Mandalay Bay Resort
  Aureole
  Bay Side Buffet
  Border Grill
  China Grill
  Fleur de Lys
  Noodle Shop
  Raffles Cafe
  Red, White & Blue
  Shanghai Lilly
  StripSteak
  Trattoria del Lupo
Mandalay Place
  Burger Bar
  Chocolate Swan
  Giorgio Caffè
  r bar cafe
  rm
MGM Grand Hotel
  Craftsteak
  Diego
  Emeril's
  Fiamma Trattoria
  Joël Robuchon
  L'Atelier/Joël Robuchon
  MGM Grand Buffet
  Nobhill
  Pearl
  Rainforest Cafe
  Seablue
  Shibuya
  Stage Deli
  'wichcraft
  Wolfgang Puck

Mirage Hotel
  California Pizza
  Caribe Café
  Carnegie Deli
  Cravings
  Fin
  Japonais
  Onda
  Samba Brazilian
  Stack
Monte Carlo Resort
  André's
  Blackstone's Steak
  Dragon Noodle
  Market City
New York-New York Hotel
  America
  Chin Chin
  Gallagher's Steak
  Il Fornaio
  Nine Fine Irishmen
Orleans Hotel
  Big Al's Oyster
  Canal Street
  Don Miguel's
  French Mkt. Buffet
  TGI Friday's
Palace Station Hotel
  Broiler
  Chang's
  Feast, The
  Guadalajara B&G
Palms Casino Hotel
  Alizé
  Garduño's
  Little Buddha
  N9ne Steak
  Nove Italiano
Paris Las Vegas
  Ah Sin
  Eiffel Tower
  Le Provençal
  Les Artistes Steak
  Le Village Buffet
  Mon Ami Gabi
  Ortanique

Plaza Hotel
  Center Stage
Red Rock Casino
  Feast, The
  Rubio's Mexican
  Salt Lick Bar-BQ
  T-Bones Chophouse
Renaissance Las Vegas Hotel
  Envy
Rio All-Suite Hotel
  All-American B&G
  Antonio's
  Bamboleo
  Buzio's
  Carnival World
  Fiore Steak
  Gaylord's
  Hamada
  Village Seafood
  VooDoo Cafe
Ritz-Carlton, Lake Las Vegas
  Medici Café
Riviera Hotel
  La Salsa
Sam's Town Hotel
  Billy Bob's
  Fellini's
  Firelight Buffet
Santa Fe Station Hotel
  Fatburger
Stratosphere Hotel
  Courtyard Buffet
  Fellini's
  Roxy's Diner
  Top of the World
Sunset Station Hotel
  Costa del Sol
  Fatburger
  Feast, The
  Guadalajara B&G
  Sonoma Cellar
Texas Station Hotel
  Austin's Steak
  Fatburger
  Feast Around World

Treasure Island Hotel
  Canter's Deli
  Francesco's
  Isla
  Social House
  Steak House
Venetian Hotel
  AquaKnox
  Bouchon
  Canaletto
  Canyon Ranch
  Delmonico Steak
  Grand Lux Cafe
  Lutèce
  Pinot Brasserie
  Postrio
  Tao
  Taqueria Canonita
  Tintoretto Bakery
  Valentino
  Zeffirino
Wynn Las Vegas
  Alex
  Bartolotta
  Daniel Boulud
  Okada
  Red 8 Asian Bistro
  SW Steak
  Tableau
  Wing Lei

Late Dining

(Weekday closing hour)
Agave (24 hrs.)
All-American B&G (6 AM)
America (24 hrs.)
Becker's Steak (24 hrs.)
Big Al's Oyster (12 AM)
Big Dog's (24 hrs.)
Black Mtn. Grill (24 hrs.)
Bootlegger Bistro (24 hrs.)
Broiler (12 AM)
Café Bellagio (24 hrs.)
California Pizza (12 AM)
Canter's Deli (12 AM)

Restaurant Special Features

Caribe Café (24 hrs.)
Carnegie Deli (2 AM)
Carson St. Cafe (24 hrs.)
Chang's (varies)
Chianti Café (varies)
Chicago Brewing (varies)
Coco's (24 hrs.)
Cottage Café (12 AM)
Crown & Anchor (24 hrs.)
Drai's (12 AM)
Eliseevsky (1 AM)
Fatburger (varies)
Firefly (3 AM)
Fix (12 AM)
Grand Lux Cafe (24 hrs.)
Hamada (varies)
Il Fornaio (varies)
In-N-Out Burger (1 AM)
Isla (4 AM)
Jimmy Buffett's (1 AM)
Joyful House (3 AM)
La Salsa (varies)
Metro Pizza (varies)
Mr. Lucky's 24/7 (24 hrs.)
Noodles (2 AM)
Noodle Shop (3 AM)
Osaka Bistro (varies)
Osaka Cuisine (varies)
Outback Steak (varies)
Paymon's Med. Café (1 AM)
P.F. Chang's (varies)
Ping Pang Pong (3 AM)
Raffles Cafe (24 hrs.)
Rainforest Cafe (12 AM)
Roadrunner (24 hrs.)
Ruth's Chris (varies)
Smith & Wollensky (3 AM)
Stage Deli (24 hrs.)
Tao (12 AM)
Tenaya Creek (12 AM)
TGI Friday's (varies)
Tintoretto Bakery (12:30 AM)
Toby Keith's B&G (2 AM)
Triple 7 (7 AM)
Victorian Room (24 hrs.)
Zeffirino (12 AM)

Meet for a Drink

Agave
AJ's Steak
Alan Albert's
André's
Aureole
Bertolini's
Boa Steak
Cafe Ba Ba Reeba!
Capital Grille
Charlie Palmer
Chicago Brewing
Chinois
Craftsteak
Crown & Anchor
Delmonico Steak
Drai's
Eiffel Tower
808
Elephant Bar
Envy
Fiore Steak
Fleming's Prime
Gaetano's
Hannah's
Joe's Sea/Steak
Le Cirque
Lutèce
Michael Mina
Mix
Nobu
Olives
Osteria del Circo
Palm
Paymon's Med. Café
P.F. Chang's
Picasso
Piero's Trattoria
Postrio
Prime Steak
Range Steak
Roadrunner
Roy's
Ruth's Chris
Simon Kitchen
Spago
Spiedini

Taqueria Canonita
Tenaya Creek
TGI Friday's
Tillerman
Tremezzo
Valentino
Viaggio
Viva Mercado's
VooDoo Cafe
Wing Lei
Yolie's Brazilian
Z'Tejas Grill

Outdoor Dining

(G=garden; P=patio;
S=sidewalk; T=terrace;
W=waterside)
Agave (P)
Ah Sin (P)
Alex (W)
André's (P)
Baja Fresh (P,S)
Bartolotta (P,W)
Bertolini's (P)
Black Mtn. Grill (P)
Boa Steak (P)
Border Grill (P)
Bouchon (P)
Cafe Ba Ba Reeba! (P)
Cafe Lago (P)
Cafe Tajine (P)
Canaletto (P)
Cheesecake Factory (P)
Chicago Brewing (P)
Chipotle (P)
Chocolate Swan (P)
Coffee Pub (P)
Como's (P)
Daniel Boulud (W)
Egg & I (P)
Elephant Bar (P)
Empress Court (P)
Enrico's (P)
Fatburger (P,S)
Fellini's (P)
Fiore Steak (T)
Firefly (P)

Garduño's (P)
Grape St. Cafe (P)
Hannah's (P)
Harley-Davidson (P)
Il Fornaio (P)
Il Mulino NY (P)
Jimmy Buffett's (P)
Joël Robuchon (G)
King's Fish House (P)
Kona Grill (P)
Le Provençal (P)
Little Buddha (P)
Lucille's BBQ (P)
Lutèce (P)
Maggiano's (P)
Mama Jo's (P)
Marché Bacchus (T,W)
Marc's (P)
Mayflower Cuisinier (P)
McCormick & Schmick (P)
Medici Café (P)
Memphis BBQ (P)
Metro Pizza (P)
MiraLago (P)
Mix (T)
Mon Ami Gabi (P)
Nine Fine Irishmen (P)
Okada (G)
Olives (P,W)
Pahrump Valley (P)
Pasta Mia (P)
Paymon's Med. Café (P,S)
P.F. Chang's (P,W)
Picasso (P)
Pink Taco (P,S)
Postrio (P)
r bar cafe (P)
Roadrunner (P)
Romano's Macaroni (P)
Roy's (P)
Rubio's Mexican (P)
Sammy's Pizza (P)
Shintaro (P)
Simon Kitchen (P)
Smith & Wollensky (P,S)
Spiedini (P)
Swiss Cafe (P)

SW Steak (P)
Tableau (P)
Taqueria Canonita (P)
TGI Friday's (P)
Tremezzo (T)
Ventano (P)
Verandah (P)
Viaggio (P)
VooDoo Cafe (T)
Z'Tejas Grill (P)

People-Watching

Agave
AJ's Steak
Alex
Aureole
Bartolotta
Bertolini's
Boa Steak
Bootlegger Bistro
Charlie Palmer
Chinois
Coffee Pub
Commander's Palace
Craftsteak
Daniel Boulud
Delmonico Steak
Drai's
808
Eliseevsky
Fiamma Trattoria
Joe's Sea/Steak
Kona Grill
Le Cirque
Little Buddha
Michael Mina
Michael's
Mon Ami Gabi
Mr. Lucky's 24/7
N9ne Steak
Nobu
Olives
Osteria del Circo
Palm
Pearl
Picasso
Piero's Trattoria
Pink Taco
Postrio

r bar cafe
Red 8 Asian Bistro
Ruth's Chris
Seablue
Sensi
Simon Kitchen
Spago
Spiedini
Steak House (Circus)
SW Steak
Tao
Taqueria Canonita
Tillerman
Tintoretto Bakery
Trattoria del Lupo
Valentino
VooDoo Cafe
Wolfgang Puck
Z'Tejas Grill

Power Scenes

André's
AquaKnox
Aureole
Bradley Ogden
Charlie Palmer
Chinois
Coffee Pub
Commander's Palace
Craftsteak
Drai's
Eiffel Tower
Fellini's
Joël Robuchon
Le Cirque
Michael Mina
Mix
Nobu
Olives
Palm
Pearl
Picasso
Piero's Trattoria
Postrio
Prime Steak
Rosemary's
Ruth's Chris
Spago

Spiedini
SW Steak
Tillerman
Trattoria del Lupo
Valentino

Quiet Conversation

Alizé
Bartolotta
Boa Steak
Capital Grille
Charlie Palmer
Chianti Café
Craftsteak
Envy
Gaetano's
Golden Steer Steak
Guy Savoy
Hannah's
Hugo's Cellar
Joe's Sea/Steak
King's Fish House
Le Cirque
Lutèce
Marché Bacchus
Marc's
Ming's Table
Okada
Pearl
Red 8 Asian Bistro
Second St. Grill
Sensi
Shibuya
Steak House (Circus)
Sushi Roku
SW Steak
Tinoco's Bistro
Todd's Unique Dining
Verandah
Viaggio
Wing Lei

Raw Bars

Big Al's Oyster
Bistro Zinc
Bouchon
Broiler
Buzio's
Cravings
Daniel Boulud
Emeril's
King's Fish House
Makino
Mon Ami Gabi
Paradise Garden
Penazzi
r bar cafe
Seablue
Ventano
Zeffirino

Romantic Places

Alex
Alizé
André's
Aureole
Bartolotta
Becker's Steak
Cafe Ba Ba Reeba!
Canaletto
Chianti Café
Chicago Joe's
Daniel Boulud
Eiffel Tower
Fleur de Lys
Hannah's
Hugo's Cellar
Le Cirque
Marché Bacchus
Marc's
Michael's
Mix
Nobhill
Ortanique
Pamplemousse
Pearl
Picasso
Prime Steak
Sensi
Top of the World
Valentino
Viaggio
Wing Lei
Zeffirino

Senior Appeal
Applebee's
Benihana
Bootlegger Bistro
Center Stage
Cheesecake Factory
Coco's
Coffee Pub
Egg & I
Festival Buffet
Fleming's Prime
Florida Cafe
Garden Court
Hilltop House
Hugo's Cellar
Hush Puppy
Mama Jo's
Pasta Shop
Piero's Trattoria
Redwood B&G
Stuart Anderson's
Swiss Cafe
Tintoretto Bakery
Todai
Tony Roma's
Verandah
Victorian Room
Village Seafood
Wolfgang Puck

Singles Scenes
Agave
AJ's Steak
Benihana
Cheesecake Factory
Drai's
808
Fiamma Trattoria
Fleming's Prime
Gaetano's
Hamada
Harley-Davidson
Jimmy Buffett's
Kona Grill
Little Buddha
Mama Jo's
Marrakech

Mr. Lucky's 24/7
N9ne Steak
Nobu
Panevino
Paymon's Med. Café
Pearl
P.F. Chang's
Piero's Trattoria
Pink Taco
Roadrunner
Roy's
Sapporo
Sensi
Simon Kitchen
Smith & Wollensky
Spago
Taqueria Canonita
TGI Friday's
Todai
Trattoria del Lupo
Triple 7
Viaggio
Village Seafood
Viva Mercado's
VooDoo Cafe
Z'Tejas Grill

Sleepers
(Good to excellent food, but little known)
Anna Bella
Antonio's
Archi's Thai
Austin's Steak
Bartolotta
Café Wasabi
Ferraro's
Fiore Steak
Gaetano's
Gaylord's
India Palace
Japengo
Joyful House
Kathy's Southern
Marc's
Mayflower Cuisinier
Medici Café

Nora's
Okada
Ortanique
Osaka Bistro
Osaka Cuisine
Pasta Shop
Second St. Grill
Sonoma Cellar
Steak House (Treasure Is.)
Tableau
Thai Spice
Todd's Unique Dining
Viva Mercado's

Tasting Menus

André's
Aureole
Eiffel Tower
808
Emeril's
Guy Savoy
Joël Robuchon
Le Cirque
Lutèce
Medici Café
Michael Mina
Mix
Nobhill
Nobu
Osaka Cuisine
Pinot Brasserie
rm
Rosemary's
Shibuya
Tableau
Valentino
Wing Lei

Teen Appeal

Benihana
Cheesecake Factory
Chevys Fresh Mex
Coco's
Florida Cafe
Grand Lux Cafe
Hard Rock Cafe
Harley-Davidson

In-N-Out Burger
Jean Philippe
La Salsa
Mama Jo's
Melting Pot
Mr. Lucky's 24/7
Osaka Bistro
Paradise Garden
Pink Taco
Planet Hollywood
Quark's
Rainforest Cafe
Roxy's Diner
Tao
Taqueria Canonita
Tintoretto Bakery
Todai
Top of the World
Victorian Room
Village Seafood
Viva Mercado's
Wolfgang Puck

Trendy

Agave
Ah Sin
AJ's Steak
Alex
AquaKnox
Aureole
Boa Steak
Bradley Ogden
Cafe Ba Ba Reeba!
China Grill
Daniel Boulud
Drai's
Elephant Bar
Fiamma Trattoria
Firefly
Guy Savoy
Hannah's
Joe's Sea/Steak
Kona Grill
Little Buddha
Mix
Mr. Lucky's 24/7
N9ne Steak

Nobu
Olives
Osteria del Circo
Pearl
Piero's Trattoria
Pink Taco
Postrio
Rosemary's
Roy's
Seablue
Simon Kitchen
Spago
Tao
Trattoria del Lupo
VooDoo Cafe

Views

Alex
Alizé
Bamboleo
Binion's Steak
Bouchon
Café Bellagio
Cafe Tajine
Capital Grille
Center Stage
Daniel Boulud
Eiffel Tower
Fellini's
Guy Savoy
Japengo
Japonais
Jasmine
Jimmy Buffett's
Lake Mead Cruises
Le Cirque
Maggiano's
Marché Bacchus
Medici Café
Michael Mina
MiraLago
Mix
Mon Ami Gabi
Nove Italiano
Okada
Olives
Osteria del Circo

Outback Steak
Pahrump Valley
Picasso
Prime Steak
Range Steak
Shintaro
Social House
Tableau
Top of the World
Tremezzo
Ventano
Viaggio
VooDoo Cafe

Visitors on Expense Account

Alex
Aureole
Bartolotta
Boa Steak
Capital Grille
Charlie Palmer
Commander's Palace
Craftsteak
Daniel Boulud
Delmonico Steak
Eiffel Tower
808
Envy
Fiore Steak
Guy Savoy
Hilton Steak
Hugo's Cellar
Il Mulino NY
Joe's Sea/Steak
Le Cirque
Lutèce
Michael Mina
Mix
Morton's Steak
Neros
N9ne Steak
Nobu
Okada
Osteria del Circo
Palm
Prime Steak

Red 8 Asian Bistro
rm
Rosemary's
Rosewood Grille
Roy's
Ruth's Chris
Sensi
Shintaro
Smith & Wollensky
Steak House (Treasure Is.)
Sterling Brunch
SW Steak
Tableau
Tillerman
Top of the World
Tremezzo
Wing Lei
Yolie's Brazilian

Winning Wine Lists

Alan Albert's
Alex
Alizé
André's
Aureole
Bartolotta
Boa Steak

Capital Grille
Charlie Palmer
Craftsteak
Daniel Boulud
Drai's
Envy
Fiore Steak
Grape St. Cafe
Guy Savoy
Joe's Sea/Steak
Le Cirque
Marché Bacchus
Michael Mina
Mix
Osteria del Circo
Picasso
Postrio
rm
Sensi
Smith & Wollensky
Spago
SW Steak
Tableau
Valentino
Viaggio
VooDoo Cafe

Nightlife

Most Popular

Central Las Vegas

95 · 93 · 95 · 515
Fremont St.

Las Vegas

95 · 15 · 515 · 93 · 95

Area of detail

NEVADA

Henderson
15

160
215
★ The Whiskey

0   Miles   5

Martin Luther King Blvd.

Bonneville Ave.

Main St.
Casino Center Blvd.

Charleston Blvd.

0   Mile   1/2

Oakey Blvd.

Rancho Dr.

Wyoming Ave.

Olympic
★ Garden

Cheetah's ★

Top of the
★ World
Stratosphere

Las Vegas
"The Strip"

Crazy Horse
★ Too

Western Ave.

Industrial Rd.

Circus
Circus Dr.

Las Vegas Blvd. S. "The Strip"

St. Louis Ave.

Sahara Ave.

Karen Ave.

Las Vegas
Country Club

15

Peppermill
★ Fireside

Convention Ctr. Dr.

The Beach
★

Convention
Center

Valley View Blvd.

Desert Inn Rd.

Spearmint
★ Rhino

Spring Mountain Rd.

Treasure
Island

Lure
★
Wynn

Paradise Rd.

Cleopatra's Barge
Pure
Pussycat Dolls
Shadow

Tangerine ★

Harrah's

Venetian

Sands Ave.

Twain Ave.

VooDoo
Lounge ★
Rio
All-Suite

Caesars
Palace

★ V Bar
Carnaval
Court

Barbary
Coast ★

Barbary Coast
Drai's After Hours

Flamingo Rd.

2 ★ Palms
Hotel

┌ ghostbar
└ Rain

Bellagio

Paris

Napoleon's Lounge
Risqué

Hard
Rock ★

Body
★ English

Caramel
Light
Fontana Bar

"The Strip"

Harmon Ave.

Ice ★

University
of Nevada,
Las Vegas

MGM Grand

Studio 54
Tabú

New York-New York

Bar at Times Square
Coyote Ugly
ESPN Zone
Nine Fine Irishmen

Tropicana Ave.

Paradise Rd.

Nefertiti's
Lounge

Luxor

McCarran
International
Airport

Hacienda Ave.

15

Mandalay Bay

Coral Reef
House of Blues
Ivan Kane's Forty Deuce
Red Square
rumjungle

Las Vegas Blvd. S.

Russell Rd.

Most Popular

Each surveyor has been asked to name his or her five favorite places. This list reflects their choices.

1. rumjungle
2. Light
3. Red Square
4. ghostbar
5. House of Blues
6. Rain
7. Studio 54
8. Coyote Ugly
9. Drai's After Hours
10. Pure
11. ESPN Zone
12. Caramel
13. Bar at Times Sq.
14. Fontana Bar*
15. VooDoo Lounge
16. Olympic Garden
17. Body English
18. Tabú
19. Crazy Horse Too
20. V Bar
21. Pussycat Dolls
22. Cleopatra's Barge
23. Whiskey, The
24. Tangerine
25. Nefertiti's Lounge
26. Nine Fine Irishmen
27. Spearmint Rhino
28. Top of the World
29. Shadow
30. Coral Reef
31. Risqué*
32. Beach, The
33. Lure*
34. Cheetah's
35. Ice
36. Peppermill Fireside
37. Napoleon's Lounge
38. Barbary Coast
39. Carnaval Court*
40. Ivan Kane's Forty Deuce

* Indicates a tie with place above

Top Rated Nightlife Spots

Excluding places with low voting.

Appeal

27 Pure
26 Lure
   ghostbar
   Ivan Kane's Forty Deuce
   Body English

25 Top of the World
   Fontana Bar
   VooDoo Lounge
   Drai's After Hours
24 Spearmint Rhino

Decor

26 Lure
   Pure
24 Whiskey, The
   Red Square
   Fontana Bar
   Ivan Kane's Forty Deuce
23 Rain

Service

24 Lure
22 Peppermill Fireside
   Fontana Bar
21 Whiskey, The
   Spearmint Rhino
   Body English
20 Crazy Horse Too

By Category
Listed in order of Appeal rating

Dance Clubs
27 Pure
26 Body English
25 Drai's After Hours
24 Rain
   Light

Drink Specialists
26 ghostbar
25 Top of the World
   Fontana Bar
   VooDoo Lounge
24 Red Square

Live Music
25 Fontana Bar
   VooDoo Lounge
22 Napoleon's Lounge
21 House of Blues
   Joint, The

Lounges
26 Lure
   ghostbar
   Ivan Kane's Forty Deuce
25 Top of the World
   Fontana Bar

Newcomers/Unrated
   Cherry
   Jet
   Moon
   Playboy Club
   Tryst

Open 24 Hours
21 Peppermill Fireside
   Bar at Times Sq.
20 Breeze Bar
17 Beach, The
   Big Apple Bar

Strip Clubs
24 Spearmint Rhino
   Crazy Horse Too
23 Olympic Garden
21 Cheetah's
   Club Paradise

Views
26 ghostbar
25 Top of the World
   Fontana Bar
   VooDoo Lounge
22 Tangerine

Ratings & Symbols

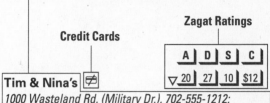

Name, Address, Phone Number & Web Site

Zagat Ratings

Credit Cards

A	D	S	C
▽ 20	27	10	$12

Tim & Nina's 🚫

1000 Wasteland Rd. (Military Dr.), 702-555-1212; www.zagat.com

"Party like there's no tomorrow" at this desert venture by a "couple of pesky New Yorkers" whose "watches must have stopped mid-flight" to Vegas; it's "always 'round midnight" at this 24/7 club in a "decommissioned missile silo" on the "outskirts" of town where "subterranean scenesters" get "lost for days", "subsisting on the garnish" in their "crazily high-cost" cocktails while the "DJs drop sonic bombs" on the dance floor; retire to the "sexy ultra-lounge" in the "old control room" where the "crew once waited to hit the launch button."

Review, with surveyors' comments in quotes

Top Spots: Places with the highest overall ratings, popularity and importance are listed in BLOCK CAPITAL LETTERS.

Credit Cards: 🚫 no credit cards accepted

Ratings are on a scale of **0** to **30**.

A	Appeal	D	Decor	S	Service	C	Cost
20		27		10		$12	

0–9 poor to fair	**20–25** very good to excellent
10–15 fair to good	**26–30** extraordinary to perfection
16–19 good to very good	▽ low response/less reliable

Cost (C): Reflects our surveyors' average estimated price of a typical single drink and is a benchmark only.

For newcomers or survey write-ins listed without ratings, the price range is indicated as follows:

I	below $5	**E**	$9 to $11
M	$5 to $8	**VE**	more than $11

Nightlife Directory

Addison's Lounge   _｜_｜_｜ M
Rampart Casino, 221 N. Rampart Blvd. (Summerlin Pkwy.),
702-507-5900; www.rampartcasino.com
For older cocktailers, this "little lounge" in Summerlin's
Rampart Casino is a quiet alternative to the ear-splitting DJ
blasts and noisy crowds at higher-priced competitors; affordable drinks and live music (from rock to hip-hop) help
make the nondescript spot "better than you would expect."

Art Bar ⊅   _｜_｜_｜ I
1511 S. Main St. (bet. Charleston Blvd. & Wyoming Ave.),
702-437-2787
Young hipsters belly up to the "lit-up cocktail tables and
the luminous bartop" at this pub on the fringe of
Downtown's burgeoning Arts District, which doubles as a
hip concert space for local rockers; the paintings on the
bright walls are "interesting", but given its location, bohos
might have to stumble over hobos to get in.

Artisan Lounge   _｜_｜_｜ E
Artisan Hotel, 1501 W. Sahara Ave. (I-15), 702-214-4000;
www.theartisanhotel.com
A "great place to have a glass of wine and relax" is this
plush, moody lounge in a non-casino boutique hotel west of
the Strip; it's done up in dark, polished woods and decorated with replicas of master painters' work, with an overall
chill vibe that appeals to tipplers who are all gamed out.

Bahama Breeze   ∇ 19 ｜ 19 ｜ 21 ｜ $13
375 Hughes Center Dr. (bet. Flamingo & Paradise Rds.),
702-731-3252; www.bahamabreeze.com
The "food is good and so are the cocktails" at this East Side
Caribbean chain themester offering a "nice environment in
which to enjoy" a breezy after-work luau with a "large
group"; though its specialty "girl drinks" can be especially
"yummy" outside on the patio when the reggae band is
jamming, mainlanders mash the place as "generic kitsch."

Bar at Times Square   21 ｜ 18 ｜ 17 ｜ $11
New York-New York Hotel, 3790 Las Vegas Blvd. S.
(Tropicana Ave.), 702-740-6969; www.nynyhotelcasino.com
Just like in its namesake Manhattan square, "everyone
cuts loose" at this "energetic" 24/7 "place for bachelor
and bachelorette parties" in the Strip's New York-New
York; with "hysterical dueling pianos" stoking the "rowdy"
sing-alongs, the scene can get "hectic", but "crowds" of
"approachable" types make for a "fun time."

Barbary Coast Lounge   15 ｜ 12 ｜ 18 ｜ $8
Barbary Coast Hotel, 3595 Las Vegas Blvd. S. (Flamingo Rd.),
702-737-7111; www.barbarycoastcasino.com
"Frat boys" "drown their sorrows" at this Strip "dive"
that's "what Vegas should be all about": "cheap drinks",

decor that's "just a touch shabby about the edges" and "fantastic" if "marginal entertainment" – i.e. the substantial person of "Pete Vallee as Big Elvis", a "must-see" 500-pound hunka burnin' love.

Beach, The 17 15 17 $8
365 Convention Center Dr. (Paradise Rd.), 702-731-1925; www.beachlv.com
"Sirens, confetti, beer-bong competitions, whipped-cream body shots – need I say more?" ask the "rowdy", "clinging-to-college" patrons of this "sex-charged" "frat party" east of the Strip that's also rife with "cheesy pickup lines" and "scorchingly beautiful" "thong-bikini-clad kamikaze pushers"; as for the upstairs 24-hour bar, "when the sun comes up and you're still alone and desperate, there's only one place left to go."

Beauty Bar – – – E
517 Fremont St. (bet. Las Vegas Blvd. & 6th St.), 702-598-1965; www.beautybar.com
As part of the ongoing project to beautify Downtown, this faux beauty parlor franchise with roots in LA, SF and NY aims its Aquanet at Fremont Street, plying Sin City's hip set with hairy hooch and teaching them how to paint their nails all pretty at the Wednesday–Friday happy hour; the colorful, '60s-inspired space includes a patio where lookers let their locks down for monthly DJ do's and concerts by national rock bands.

Big Apple Bar 17 16 16 $9
New York-New York Hotel, 3790 Las Vegas Blvd. S. (Tropicana Ave.), 702-740-6969; www.nynyhotelcasino.com
The "cheesy Vegas act is included" in the ambiance at this "ok mid-casino bar" in New York-New York where live bands jam just "a step away" from the gaming tables; if you're thirsty, it can be "hard to get a drink" given "sporadic waitress service" and "limited seating" at the rail, and even Gotham-aholics who "love themed places" are "not sure about that red-apple disco ball."

Body English 26 23 21 $12
Hard Rock Hotel, 4455 Paradise Rd. (bet. Flamingo Rd. & Harmon Ave.), 702-693-4000; www.bodyenglish.com
The former club "Baby's is all grown up", with "great DJs" spinning "nutty rip-ups", "plenty of celebrities to gawk at" and enough "crazy-hot" bartenders who "know how to pour a real drink" to make this "off-the-hook" Hard Rock revamp "hot, hot, hot"; "pretty people" flock to the downstairs dance floor "to shake their money-makers under the crystal chandelier" or cruise the "fantastic" upstairs ultra-lounge – "with such eye candy, who can even remember the prices, and who cares?"

Breeze Bar
20 | 18 | 19 | $13

Treasure Island Hotel, 3300 Las Vegas Blvd. S.
(Spring Mountain Rd.), 702-894-7111; www.treasureisland.com
This 'round-the-clock Treasure Island lounge may be "a little cheesy in terms of decor", but at 4 AM, even design divas aren't so discriminating when they dive into the drink; it's a "good meeting place" and if your date is late, you can pass the time playing "video poker in the bar."

Brendan's Irish Pub
– | – | – | M

Orleans Hotel, 4500 W. Tropicana Ave. (Arville St.),
702-365-7111; www.orleanscasino.com
"A little Irish music goes a long way" toward "great fun any night" at this wee bit o' the old sod in the Orleans west of the Strip; the varied entertainers who "play here regularly" are "wonderful", and "the crowd gets totally involved", particularly after they've had a taste (or two or three) from the top-notch selection of Emerald Isle whiskeys and ales.

Bunkhouse Saloon NEW
– | – | – | I

124 S. 11th St. (bet. Carson Ave. & Fremont St.), 702-384-4536;
www.bunkhouselv.com
Have a Pabst with The Duke at this Downtown Western-themed watering hole where John Wayne photos line the walls alongside antique spurs and saddles; its cheap beer and shots rope in plenty of budget-minded cowpokes, and it fills up on weekends when rising local rock bands put on free shows.

Caramel
22 | 22 | 20 | $13

Bellagio Hotel, 3600 Las Vegas Blvd. S. (Flamingo Rd.),
702-693-8300; www.lightgroup.com
With a look "as smooth and rich as the name implies", this "swanky", "darkly lit" club in the middle of the Bellagio casino floor straddles the divide between "kicked-back cool" and "hot and horny"; it's "good for chilling" earlier on with "those who are too old" for raving ("but not old enough to be in bed by 10 PM"), and it gets "bumping after midnight" with "chic young fashionistas" on a "pre-game warm-up" before "bouncing over to Light."

Carnaval Court
20 | 15 | 18 | $8

Harrah's Las Vegas, 3475 Las Vegas Blvd. S. (Flamingo Rd.),
702-369-5000; www.harrahs.com
Stop in for "flowing drinks" from the "most flamboyant" "flair bottle-slingers" on the Strip at this "trashy Mardi Gras–themed" outdoor bar at Harrah's, and you too might end up on the "conga line" clutching the back end of an "older" "frat partier" bunny-hopping to the "lively cover band"; "gorgeous blackjack dealers" on weekends, plus quintessential lounge act Cook E. Jarr on Tuesdays and Wednesdays "make it even better", though the mod squad calls it "so '80s, it's not funny."

Celebrity Las Vegas
- - - M

201 N. Third St. (Ogden Ave.), 702-384-2582; www.celebritylv.com
Pumping up the volume in Downtown's Entertainment District, this hopping club cranks out a free-ranging roster of parties nightly; live music runs from Dixieland jazz to rock 'n' roll, and when the bands aren't onstage, the DJs lay down tracks for wannabe celebrities of the dance floor.

Cellar Lounge
- - - M

3601 W. Sahara Ave. (Valley View Blvd.), 702-362-6268
You never have to see daylight again when you descend into this 24/7 sipping cellar on the West Side; "I like this place" say molelike hepcats, who groove to the sounds of live blues and jazz until the wee hours and then some; there's also a separate subterranean wedding room where vampiric couples can celebrate hooking up for all eternity.

Champagnes Cafe ⊅
- - - I

3557 S. Maryland Pkwy. (Dumont Blvd.), 702-737-1699
Stray off the beaten path and pop the cork at this gritty East Side adventure, a dive bubbling with local characters, red studded Naugahyde, dangling Christmas bulbs and decrepit flocked wallpaper; rock-bottom pricing, a Sinatra-friendly juke and a weekend karaoke scene make it a magnet for the town's smoothest off-shift and retired lounge talents.

Cheetah's
21 13 19 $10

2112 Western Ave. (bet. Sahara & Wyoming Aves.), 702-384-0074
"When you just want to get your freak on", this all-hours "gentlemen's palace" west of the Strip is "purrrfect"; the "beautiful" gals "put extra effort into making you smile", and "they don't hustle": a "polite refusal of a lap dance is not met with scorn" here; though the "chairs make it hard to bounce multiple ladies" on your knee, attempting it is still a "great" workout – "just don't be too shocked if the morning sun is blasting when you leave."

Cherry NEW
- - - E

Red Rock Casino, 11011 W. Charleston Blvd. (Hwy. 215), 702-797-7777; www.mocbars.com
Starting with its mirrored tunnel entrance, this ritzy West Side nightclub from nightlife impresario Rande Gerber boasts plenty of fab flourishes, including red leather walls, a floating dance floor and an outdoor pool deck; private alcoves allow for cozy canoodling, and even the men's room is sultry, with urinals shaped like pairs of pouting lips.

Cheyenne Saloon ⊅
- - - I

3103 N. Rancho Dr. (Cheyenne Ave.), 702-645-4139
This gritty hangout may be parked on the city's Far North Side, but the punk, metal and hard rock bands that hold court here play loud enough to be heard for miles around;

even though it may be hard on your hearing, it's easy on the wallet with enough low-priced pops to ease the throbbing in your temples.

Chrome Showroom
– | – | – | M

Santa Fe Station Hotel, 4949 N. Rancho Dr.
(bet. Lone Mountain Rd. & Rainbow Blvd.), North Las Vegas,
702-658-4900; www.stationcasinos.com

Testifying to the kind of top-shelf talent that it attracts, this spacious North Side showroom displays autographed basses and guitars from the likes of Ray Price and Stanley Clarke, and its performers range from country stars to the Prince tribute act Purple Reign; Wednesday's blues night draws the biggest crowds, showcasing leading names in the genre at no cover charge.

Cleopatra's Barge
17 | 19 | 18 | $11

Caesars Palace, 3570 Las Vegas Blvd. S. (Flamingo Rd.),
702-731-7110; www.caesarspalace.com

A "funky cross between a Liz Taylor movie and a Vegas lounge", this "old-school" "schmaltz" ship run aground "in the middle of an aisle" in Caesars Palace "is not a place to see the pretty people", but it is a "standby for the LV veterans"; even the saltiest sinners "look seasick", though, when this "cheeseball" boat rocks – the hydraulics-and-hooch combination might lead you to ask "is this thing moving, or did I have one too many?"

Club, The
– | – | – | I

Cannery Hotel, 2121 E. Craig Rd. (Losee Rd.), North Las Vegas,
702-507-5700; www.cannerycasinos.com

Aging gadflies get their funk on at this Cannery venue in North Las Vegas while The Archies' Ron Dante ladles out 'Sugar, Sugar' or The Surfaris ride the 'Wipe Out' wave onto the stage; the ample joint doubles in size when the back wall is dismantled to create an outdoor theater for stargazing in both senses of the word.

Club Madrid
– | – | – | M

Sunset Station Hotel, 1301 W. Sunset Rd. (Stephanie St.),
Henderson, 702-547-7777; www.sunsetstation.com

"Good acts come through on a regular basis", so "if you time it right", you're in for some "great entertainment" at this Henderson performance lounge; best of all, you don't have to "worry about tourists", since it's something of a "Vegas secret."

Club Paradise
21 | 18 | 19 | $12

4416 Paradise Rd. (bet. Flamingo Rd. & Harmon Ave.),
702-734-7990

The "zealous" natives "circulate constantly", which probably is what keeps them in such "very good shape" at this east-of-the-Strip club, a "nice place" to get a load of the "hottest" "naked girls dancing around for your money"; its "pretty talent" and "easy access to the Hard Rock" lead to "standing-room-only weekend nights" in the "cramped main room", so if you're looking to spread out, "splurge on the outrageously marked-up champagne and get into the larger VIP area."

Club Rio
20 | 20 | 20 | $12

Rio All-Suite Hotel, 3700 W. Flamingo Rd. (bet. I-15 & Valley View Blvd.), 702-777-6875; www.riovegasnights.com
"Action, activity" and who-knows-what-acts "going on in the dark corners" make this "longtime" dance club west of the Strip "fun, fun, fun"; sweat it to Latin and hip-hop amid the "great crowd" of "tourists", and try to ignore the snobs who say it "was much better" years before.

Cooler Lounge ⊅
– | – | – | I

1905 N. Decatur Blvd. (bet. Concord Village Dr. & W. Lake Mead Blvd.), 702-646-3009; www.coolerlounge.com
Despite the aesthetic appeal of a graffiti-covered subway stop, this bustling West Side rock club draws crowds with acts ranging from indie hip-hop to rampaging death metal bands; cheap beer helps blot out the band-stickers-and-cigarette-butts decor, but after 25 years on the scene, obviously nobody minds much.

Coral Reef
21 | 20 | 18 | $12

Mandalay Bay Resort, 3950 Las Vegas Blvd. S. (Mandalay Bay Rd.), 877-632-7800; www.mandalaybay.com
Get hooked on the "excellent, relaxed atmosphere" of this "cool" casino bar and sushi joint, a "great place to meet for an afternoon cocktail" inside Mandalay Bay; by midnight, though, it's "packed" with swingers flipping their tail fins to "very solid" Top 40 and rock acts, and cruising against the tide to get to the bar can be "like warfare."

Coyote Ugly
16 | 15 | 15 | $11

New York-New York Hotel, 3790 Las Vegas Blvd. S. (Tropicana Ave.), 702-740-6969; www.nynyhotelcasino.com
"You rented the video, now drink" at this New York-New York "takeoff" on the namesake movie, a "hangout" where "hundreds" of dudes get "dumb" over "hot chicks" pouring hooch and "dancing on the bar"; "middle-aged" "oglers" whimpering over "sore necks the next day" from a night of "looking up" at the "poorly choreographed" hoedown howl "don't forget your crackers" 'cuz "this place has all the cheese you need."

Crazy Armadillo
– | – | – | M

Stratosphere Hotel, 2000 Las Vegas Blvd. S. (north of Sahara Ave.), 702-383-5230; www.stratospherehotel.com
The flair skills of the "bartenders make it all worthwhile", even when the live bands, DJs or boozed-up karaoke talent are having an "off night" at this dance club and cantina in the Stratosphere, where tequila-laced oyster shooters

combine the menu's featured items; it's "not much to look at in terms of decor", but the "attractive" waitresses "give you plenty more visual stimulation."

Crazy Horse Too 24 15 20 $13
2476 Industrial Rd. (bet. Northbridge St. & Sahara Ave.), 702-382-8003; www.crazyhorsetoo.com
Mustangs snort "ditch your wife" and join the "bachelor-party" herd to gallop after the gals at this nudie corral west of the Strip – or be rounded up by them: the "women remain a bit pushy", and management "could spend a little money updating the decor"; still, with a "strong staff-to-guest ratio" and "talent to suit any taste", unloading "mad cash" here leads to "decadence at its best."

Curve 21 21 15 $11
Aladdin Resort, 3667 Las Vegas Blvd. S. (Harmon Ave.), 702-785-5525; www.aladdincasino.com
A "big entryway" and "high ceilings" make this "Aladdin's version of an ultra-lounge" "a little more grand" than its competitors, but there are still plenty of "secluded alcoves" to "cuddle up" in; it runs from hits to "misses", though: the dance floor is a "sexy" spot to "let loose" "without pretensions", but "empty" rooms can make it "dull on some evenings."

Dino's Lounge ⍯ – – – I
1516 S. Las Vegas Blvd. (Wyoming Ave.), 702-382-3894; www.dinoslv.com
In a city known for its turnover, this popular Downtown neighborhood dive has been a favorite watering hole 24 hours a day for more than 45 years; it offers up a laid-back, non-flashy vibe for anyone who wants to dress down, get down (to the jukebox or karaoke and live bands during the Arts District's First Friday block parties) and pound 'em down on the cheap, courtesy of the buy-four-get-one-free card.

Divebar NEW – – – I
3035 E. Tropicana Ave. (McLeod Dr.), 702-435-7526; www.vegasdivebar.com
Anything goes at this rock club east of the Strip where the raucous mood is set by the bras and panties dangling from a pair of deer antlers; the steady lineup of regional and national bands is mostly free, and on Wednesday nights a rotating cast of Elvis impersonators takes the stage, adding some kitsch notes to this choice locals' hang.

Double Down Saloon ⍯ ▽ 21 16 18 $8
4640 Paradise Rd. (Naples Dr.), 702-791-5775; www.doubledownsaloon.com
"End an evening of debauchery" (or start one) at this "delightfully seedy" 24/7 "biker bar" east of the Strip where "the perfect combination of crappy pool tables, stale beer smell" and "live rock, punk and metal" has a certain

THE VEGAS MAP

ATTRACTIONS

Bellagio
The **Fountains of Bellagio** dance in front of the hotel, enhanced by light and music. *Showtimes: Mon.–Fri.: 3 p.m. to 8 p.m., every 30 minutes, 8 p.m.–midnight every 15 minutes; Sat.–Sun, Holidays: noon to 8 p.m., every 30 minutes, 8 p.m. to midnight every 15 minutes.* **Bellagio Conservatory** is a 13,573-square-foot, indoor, garden extravaganza. *Open 24 hours daily.* 702.693.7111

Caesars Palace
Fall of Atlantis Fountain and Aquarium. *10 a.m.–11 p.m. daily. Every hour on the hour.* 702.731.7110

Circus Circus
The **Adventuredome** is open *Mon.–Thurs.,10 a.m.–6 p.m.; Fri.–Sat., 10 a.m.–midnight; Sun., 10 a.m.–8 p.m. Tickets range from $4–$7. Unlimited pass: $14.95 (visitors 33–47 inches tall); $22.95 (48 inches or taller).* 702.794.3939

Flamingo
Jimmy Buffett's Margaritaville features five bars and live entertainment nightly. *Open 10:45 a.m.–2 a.m., Sun.–Thurs. and 10:45 a.m.–2:30 a.m. Fri. and Sat.* The **Flamingo Wildlife Habitat** is home to a variety of exotic animals, including live Chilean Flamingos and more than 300 birds. *Open 24 hours daily. Free.*

Fremont Street Experience
A unique light and sound show presenting more than 2 million lights and 550,000 watts of concert-quality sound that come alive each night beginning at dusk to midnight on the hour. 702.678.5777

Gameworks
Inside the Showcase Mall, this fantasy land of video games offers, gift shop and food court. *Prices from 50 cents–$4, hourly game play available Open Sun.–Thurs., 10 a.m.–midnight; Fri.–Sat., 10 a.m.–2 a.m.* 702.432.4263

Harrah's
Carnaval Court features live music and flair bartenders who sing, dance, juggle and spit fire, as well as pour drinks. *Open noon to 2 a.m. daily.* 702.369.5000

Imperial Palace
The **Auto Collections** features more than 300 antique, classic and special interest vehicles on display and for sale. *Hours: 9:30 a.m.–9:30 p.m. daily. $6.95 (adults), $3 (children 5-12 and seniors 65 and over), free admission for children under 5.* 702.794.3174

Las Vegas Hilton
Star Trek: The Experience transports visitors into the 24th-century world of Star Trek. *Opens daily at 11 a.m. Tickets are $42.99 (adults), $35.99 (seniors and children 12 and under), $14.99 museum only.* 702.697.8700

Liberace Museum
Houses Liberace's costumes, jewelry, customized cars, rare pianos and personal mementos. *Open: Tues.–Sat. 10 a.m.–5 p.m.; Sun. noon–4 p.m. Closed Thanksgiving, Christmas, New Year's. $12.50 (adults), $8.50 (seniors and students), children under 10 admitted free when accompanied by an adult.* 1775 E. Tropicana Ave. 702.798.5595

M&M's World
A brilliant spectrum of the candy-coated treats and various logo items. *Opens daily at 9 a.m.* 3785 Las Vegas Blvd. S. inside Showcase Mall. 702.736.7611

Madame Tussauds
At The Venetian, Madame Tussauds Las Vegas offers more than 100 stars. *$24 (adults), $18 (seniors and students), $14 (children 6–12), children under 5 admitted free. Open daily.* 702.862.7800

Mandalay Bay
Shark Reef has dozens of sharks, piranha, eels, rays and crocodiles. *Open daily, 10 a.m.–11 p.m., last admission at 10 p.m. Adults: $15.95; children (5–12 years): $9.95, children under 4 are free.*

The Mirage
The **Mirage Volcano** erupts at the top of every hour, from *6 p.m. until midnight. Free.* **White Tiger Habitat** *open 24 hours daily. Free.* **Siegfried & Roy's Secret Garden and Dolphin Habitat** is home to six rare animal breeds. *Open daily. Hours vary seasonally.* 702.632.7777

MGM Grand
Lion Habitat showcases a variety of lions and cubs. *Open daily, 11 a.m.–10 p.m. Free.* 702.891.1111

New York-New York
Manhattan Express roller coaster is open *10:30 a.m–midnight daily.*

"charm"; of course, the "decor is nonexistent", but it sports one of the "best jukes in Vegas", and the bartender will mix you up a bacon martini infused with the real smoked Tennessee stuff; note: "tattoos may be required for entry."

Drai's After Hours
25 | 20 | 17 | $12

Barbary Coast Hotel, 3595 Las Vegas Blvd. S. (Flamingo Rd.), 702-737-0555; www.barbarycoastcasino.com

"Shake your thang" with "locals, Hollywood celebs" and "all the strippers after they're done working" at this "sexy, chic" dance "maze" in the Barbary Coast that may be the "hottest after-hours scene" in town; fans "don't know if it's the oxygen, the alcohol" or "enough silicone to raise the Titanic" that makes it so "awesome", but "party" animals say it's "wild", so dress up really "pretty" and be "patient" to get in the door "when the rest of the city has gone to sleep."

Drop Bar
∇ 23 | 24 | 21 | $9

Green Valley Ranch, 2300 Paseo Verde Pkwy. (Green Valley Pkwy.), Henderson, 702-221-6560; www.greenvalleyranchresort.com

Drop some change at this circular watering hole that "ups the ante" on Henderson nightlife; "if you don't want to deal with door policies and lines", the "small but exciting retro spot" in Green Valley Ranch is a "hip place to meet for drinks" and "chill" at the central bar or on the leather sofas by the windows overlooking the casino; given servers poured into white go-go boots, short shorts and bikini tops, you "can't argue" with the jaw-dropping view either.

Ellis Island Lounge
– | – | – | I

Ellis Island Casino & Brewery, 4178 Koval Ln. (Flamingo Rd.), 702-733-8901; www.ellisislandcasino.com

"Sinatra would be impressed with the old-time crooners" at this "classic" karaoke lounge in the same-named hotel east of the Strip; with nightly croaking fueled by "inexpensive drinks" and "great" housemade beer, it's a "primo dive" where the "truly hip" can have a "genuinely funky" time with the "locals."

Emergency Room Lounge
– | – | – | I

3550 S. Decatur Blvd. (Spring Mountain Rd.), 702-227-6363; www.emergencyroomlounge.com

There's nothing fancy about this locals' club west of the Strip, but blue-collar rock and blues fans don't need to hang with the jet-setters; they just need 24/7 cheap drinks, video poker and hot Friday and Saturday night tunes from area legends like John Earl and the Boogie Man Band.

Empire Ballroom
– | – | – | E

3765 Las Vegas Blvd. S. (Tropicana Blvd.), 702-737-7376; www.empireballroom.com

Slithering into the desert after shedding their gigs at LA's Viper Room, the smooth crew at this megaclub pump up the glamour and the volume in the former Utopia space with bottle service, live bands and a state-of-the-art sound system; sweat it on the elegant dance floor, then chill on the balcony overlooking the Strip.

ESPN Zone   18 | 18 | 16 | $10

New York-New York Hotel, 3790 Las Vegas Blvd. S. (Tropicana Ave.), 702-933-3776; www.espnzone.com

At this "sports nut's dream" in New York-New York, you can even watch the tube in the john; grab a "booth with a TV-channel changer" or a "big chair" near the wide-screens and indulge in fried food while watching some ball; if you're a guy looking to score for yourself, it's "not a great girl scene", but you can "entertain your girlfriend's 12-year-old kid" with "full-size interactive" video games.

Fadó Irish Pub   ∇ 21 | 20 | 22 | $9

Green Valley Ranch, 2300 Paseo Verde Pkwy. (Green Valley Pkwy.), Henderson, 702-407-8691; www.fadoirishpub.com

"If you want a relaxing Irish bar", this Green Valley "link in a chain" of Gaelic pubs is "a great place for a pint" of Guinness, or any of the other 15 brews on tap that go hand-in-hand with traditional fare like fish 'n' chips and "fried pickles, possibly one of the best hangover foods ever"; groove to live Celtic sounds or curse at soccer on the "large-screen TV", depending on the evening.

Flirt   – | – | – | E

Rio All-Suite Hotel, 3700 W. Flamingo Rd. (bet. I-15 & Valley View Blvd.), 702-777-7777; www.riovegasnights.com

For the ultimate girls' night out, gaggles of gals swarm the Chippendales Theater in the Rio All-Suite west of the Strip to be tantalized by muscle-bound hotties – but first, to assure they're in the mood when the men bare almost all, they pass through this sleek little lounge where waiters fawn over them and get them properly liquored up; you can stop in whether you're on your way to the hunkfest or not.

FONTANA BAR   25 | 24 | 22 | $13

Bellagio Hotel, 3600 Las Vegas Blvd. S. (Flamingo Rd.), 702-693-7111; www.bellagio.com

"Old-world Vegas is alive" and well at this "classy", "romantic" lounge in the Bellagio, where "slightly older" types with "cash to burn" sip "pricey" specialty drinks like fresh-peach Bellinis and glide "serenely" around the room to "fantastic live music" by Dian Diaz and other "solid" singers; for a particularly "stylish" experience, head out to the terrace and "dance with the fountains."

Freakin' Frog   – | – | – | M

4700 S. Maryland Pkwy. (Tropicana Ave.), 702-597-3237; www.freakinfrog.com

When you're thirsting for a rare Russian ale or a hard-to-find Brazilian pilsner, this collegiate pub near the UNLV campus boasts one of the best beer selections in town, with more than 500 choices; those seeking something a bit stiffer head to the Whisky Attic upstairs, which pours over 350 varieties of the stuff.

GHOSTBAR
| 26 | 23 | 19 | $13 |

Palms Casino Hotel, 4321 W. Flamingo Rd., 55th fl. (Arville St.), 702-942-7777; www.n9negroup.com
"Get decked out in your best designer duds", ride to the Palms' 55th floor and "wait an eternity" to wade into a "diverse sea of eye candy" rockin' the dance floor at this "glamorous" club with a "bird's-eye view of the Strip"; "A-list celebrities" mingle with "beautiful people" over "expensive", "creative" cocktails best enjoyed on the "fabulous outdoor deck" whose transparent "plexi floor" will have you feeling like a ghost floating above "the pool way below."

Gilley's Dance Hall & Saloon
| 19 | 16 | 18 | $7 |

Frontier Hotel, 3120 Las Vegas Blvd. S. (N. Pecos Rd.), 702-794-8434; www.gilleyslv.com
"Anyone who's ever dreamed of stepping onto the set of *Urban Cowboy*" should mosey into this "honky-tonk" bar in the Frontier, complete with a "mechanical bull" and "sawdust on the floor"; it's "alive and kicking" with country-music bands, "line dancing", "female mud wrestling" and "bikini bull-riding", not to mention "cold beer and good barbecue", all of which have "rowdy cowboys and cowgirls" hollering "yeehaw."

Gipsy
| ▽ 20 | 16 | 19 | $11 |

4633 Paradise Rd. (Naples Dr.), 702-731-1919; www.gipsylv.net
This "hometown" gay watering hole east of the Strip features "one of the most entertaining drag shows" around, plus "affordable" drinks, an "uncommonly friendly" crowd and hot go-go dancers; down-to-earth types boast that it might even give Krave "a run for its money."

Girls of Glitter Gulch
| 16 | 12 | 14 | $10 |

20 Fremont St. (Main St.), 702-385-4774
If you're "easily distracted by the girls of Sin City", this Downtown gentleman's joint can be a "feast for your eyes", but more discriminating clientele "yawn" at the "less-than-quality talent", calling it "tame for Vegas standards"; indeed, the vibe is so "PG-rated", "you could bring your mother-in-law" (especially given the "free admission"), though "once inside, you'll be told of the two-drink minimum" for what some call "overpriced, watered-down" cocktails.

Gold Coast Lounge ⌀
| – | – | – | I |

Gold Coast Hotel, 4000 W. Flamingo Rd. (bet. Valley View Blvd. & Wynn Rd.), 702-367-7111; www.goldcoastcasino.com
When you're longing for Dixieland, come to the desert and spend your weekday afternoons in this 24/7 music lounge west of the Strip where the Royal Dixie Jazz Band has

been blowing Big Easy sets for fans of all ages, including local nursing home residents; at night, Top 40 outfits keep the joint jumping.

Gordon Biersch   19 16 19 $9
3987 Paradise Rd. (Flamingo Rd.), 702-312-5249; www.gordonbiersch.com
"Strippers and porn stars mingle with post-convention businessmen" at this "supersized version of a San Fran brewpub" that offers "more beer than a frat-house basement" along with burgers and "reliable garlic fries"; this "yuppie hangout" "tends to close un-Vegas-ly early", but it's a popular "after-work" scene for "upscale Midwestern singles", so "dress well if you want to get lucky here."

Hofbrauhaus Las Vegas   ▽ 19 19 19 $10
4510 Paradise Rd. (Harmon Ave.), 702-256-5500; www.hofbrauhauslasvegas.com
For "real German beer, bands and food", "grab a stein" and head to the *schwemme* (main hall) for "pure drunken fun" at this east-of-the-Strip "exact replica" of the Munich original, where a "loud, loud, loud atmosphere" means no one will notice when you "sing and dance on the tables"; those less enthused by "oompah chic" advise "save your money for a flight" to Deutschland.

Hogs & Heifers ⊘   – – – M
201 N. Third St. (Ogden Ave.), 702-676-1457
It didn't take long for locals to discover this Downtown knockoff of a Manhattan Meatpacking District institution; almost from day one, closet biker-bar denizens have been ripping off their ties, banging on the vintage Pac-Man and ordering cool ones from the busty bartenders who jump up on the rail and dance to raunchy country classics.

Hootie & the Blowfish's   – – – I
Shady Grove Lounge
Silverton Casino & Lodge, 3333 Blue Diamond Rd. (Industrial Rd.), 702-263-7777; www.silvertoncasino.com
Hootie and the Blowfish only wanna be with you when they play this eponymous spot at the revamped Silverton south of the Strip; if your tastes don't run to mid-'90s blues-rock, you can bowl in the two-lane alley set in an old Airstream, belt back a few shots and slam 'em in the pool-table pockets 24 hours a day at a place that wins some locals' vote for "best improvement for a bar."

House of Blues   21 20 18 $12
Mandalay Bay Resort, 3950 Las Vegas Blvd. S. (Mandalay Bay Rd.), 702-632-7600; www.hob.com
"If you like live music", this "lively" Mandalay Bay venue offers a "raucous good time" featuring acts from "your favorite rock star" to that "rare blues guitarist"; a variety of late-night activities – "fun go-go dancers", "theme"

events and live-band karaoke – make for a "different crowd" each time, unless you find yourself in the members-only Foundation Room where the "extremely attractive" attend to their "tabloid-worthy" antics; P.S. "when you're hungover", there's no better cure than their "great Sunday gospel brunch."

Ice
19 | 19 | 18 | $14

200 E. Harmon Ave. (Koval Ln.), 702-699-9888; www.icelasvegas.com
"Get away from the casinos and into a real nightspot" at this free-standing "experience" east of the Strip where the "cool ambiance" comes with a literal "chill", courtesy of a climate-control system that uses liquid nitrogen to tame the temperature; a "smart" setup with a lounge and dance floor is paired with "top-notch sound" and the spinnings of "world-class DJs", though some "don't get the appeal" of "soaring" cover charges and "ridiculous lines."

Images Cabaret
– | – | – | M

Stratosphere Hotel, 2000 Las Vegas Blvd. S. (north of Sahara Ave.), 702-380-7777; www.stratospherehotel.com
You don't always know who's going to be performing at this small lounge on the bottom floor of the Stratosphere, but you can be sure it will be a cut above most other Vegas acts; a frequently changing, late-night lineup of pop, rock and R&B – including the Huck Daniels Revue on Mondays – draws the type of blue-collar, standing-room-only crowd that keeps its distance from the trendier joints farther down the Strip.

Indigo Lounge
– | – | – | M

Bally's Las Vegas Hotel, 3645 Las Vegas Blvd. S. (Flamingo Rd.), 702-967-4111; www.ballyslasvegas.com
The indigo chairs may be plush at this Bally's lounge, but you won't be tempted to get too comfortable as you swing nightly to its "very good entertainment"; this throwback to old Las Vegas draws a "relatively older", touristy crowd – plus a few music-savvy locals – looking to "get happy" after winning (or losing) their ducats at the nearby gaming tables.

IVAN KANE'S FORTY DEUCE
26 | 24 | 18 | $14

Mandalay Place, 3930 Las Vegas Blvd. S. (Mandalay Bay Rd.), 702-632-9442; www.fortydeuce.com
"Va-va-va-voom!" – "when every place else kicks you out", the "high-energy striptease show" is "just getting good" at Mandalay Bay's "very cool" partner in crime to Ivan Kane's LA original; "old-time" "burlesque is hot", and "no one does it better" than the "in-shape" bump-and-grinders here; the drinks are "expensive" and it can get "a little cramped", so pony up and "get there early for a coveted bar seat" in the "small", "sexy" venue.

J. C. Wooloughan's　　　– | – | – | M |
JW Marriott, 221 N. Rampart Blvd. (Summerlin Pkwy.),
702-869-7725
"Built in Ireland, dismantled and reconstructed in a hall-
way" between the Rampart Casino and the JW Marriott in
Summerlin, this "authentic" pub "never fails to deliver" on
ample tipples, "surprisingly tasty" grub and "cheerful"
blarney; it's an "especially good place to go on a chilly win-
ter evening" ("we do get a few of those in Vegas") for "a
hearty meal, a pint or two", a "good selection of whiskeys"
and "some great Celtic music."

Jet NEW　　　　– | – | – | VE |
Mirage Hotel, 3400 Las Vegas Blvd. S. (Spring Mountain Rd.),
702-693-8300; www.jetlv.com
Just touched down on the Strip with much fanfare, this
sweeping club in the Mirage with three dance floors and
four bars arranged over different levels boasts enough
high-tech lights and positive energy to make it a magnet
for rock stars, jock stars, frock stars and A-listers of all
stripes; expect long, chaotic lines if you want to fly high at
one of Vegas' hottest hangs.

Jillian's　　　　18 | 17 | 16 | $13 |
Neonopolis Entertainment Complex, 450 S. Fremont St.
(Las Vegas Blvd.), 702-759-0450; www.jillians.com
Providing a "blend of adult and juvenile entertainment"
within a "nonthreatening atmosphere", this "fun place"
Downtown is a combination sports cafe, concert venue,
video arcade, bowling alley, dance club and billiard room
("insert pun about huge racks here"); still, those who don't
see the point of coming to Sin City to "play games you can
legally play anywhere else in the world" ask its patrons
"what the hell are you doing in Vegas then?"

Joint, The ♥　　　21 | 19 | 16 | $12 |
Hard Rock Hotel, 4455 Paradise Rd. (bet. Flamingo Rd. &
Harmon Ave.), 702-693-5000; www.hardrockhotel.com
A "cool" crowd of "rock 'n' rollers" ranging from your average "wild child" to "thirtysomething hipsters" hails this
"jam-packed" Hard Rock hangout as an "exciting place"
to get "up-close and personal" with "top-drawer" talent in
a "relatively intimate space"; factor in an "awesome bar"
and "great people-watching", and it's no wonder some
feel the "only issue" is that it's "too far from the Strip."

Kahunaville　　　17 | 17 | 18 | $10 |
Treasure Island Hotel, 3300 Las Vegas Blvd. S.
(Spring Mountain Rd.), 702-894-7390; www.kahunaville.com
"Come in a bad mood" and you'll "leave with a grin and a
buzz" say supporters of the "strong drinks" and "great
entertainment" provided by "fantastic" flair bartenders at
this "friendly" Treasure Island spot; still, the "unim-

pressed" proclaim that its "fair fare" and "corny" Hawaiian decor make it a merely "decent option", "rather than a destination" in its own right.

Krave   ▽ 24 22 19 $12
3663 Las Vegas Blvd. S. (Harmon Ave.), 702-836-0830; www.kravelasvegas.com
Packed "wall-to-wall" with a "mixed crowd" of "sexy" boys-who-dig-boys and girls-who-get-with-girls, this "cool" omni-sexual club on the Strip "has something for everybody"; outfitted with "lots of tables and VIP booths", it's "definitely the place to be seen", and the dance floor pulsing with "upbeat music" is "great for people-watching" and then some.

La Scena Lounge   ▽ 20 21 19 $14
Venetian Hotel, 3355 Las Vegas Blvd. S. (bet. Flamingo & Spring Mountain Rds.), 702-414-1000; www.venetian.com
You wouldn't think of the Venetian, with its Old Italy theme, as a place to rock the night away, but this "posh lounge" is a popular spot with a young crowd looking to get randy to the sounds of "great live bands" instead of taking a leisurely cruise down the faux-canal listening to a gondolier crooning love songs.

LIGHT   24 23 19 $14
Bellagio Hotel, 3600 Las Vegas Blvd. S. (Flamingo Rd.), 702-693-8300; www.lightgroup.com
"Dance, dance, dancing" divas descend upon this "hip" club, "another impossible-to-get-into Bellagio spot" where "beautiful" types decked out in "designer duds" "hook up" and "boogie down" to "fantastic music"; "have plenty of $$$" on hand, though, to handle the "hefty cover" and "top-shelf drinks" – provided you can get by the "rude doormen" ("good luck if you're an unaccompanied male").

LURE   26 26 24 $16
Wynn Las Vegas, 3131 Las Vegas Blvd. S. (Desert Inn Rd.), 702-770-3633; www.wynnlasvegas.com
Steve "did a great job" with this "beautiful hot spot" "overlooking the waterfall and fountain at the Wynn" say "attractive" scenesters who not only "love its looks" (it's one of the "nicest ultra-lounges in town", earning the Top Decor rating for Las Vegas Nightlife), but who also dig the "phenomenal" care from the "accommodating staff" (it's rated tops for Service too); proponents predict it's "going to become *the* place" to "relax with friends old and new."

Mermaid Lounge   – – – M
Silverton Casino & Lodge, 3333 Blue Diamond Rd. (Industrial Rd.), 702-263-7777; www.silvertoncasino.com
Imagine how relaxed you'll feel when you sit back in a comfortable chair beneath the funky, sea-creature-shaped lighting at this Silverton Casino lounge south of the

Strip and gaze while 5,000 tropical fish swim around in a 117,000-gallon tank; on the flip side are the fine-finned femmes who perform an aquatic show behind the glass hourly Wednesday–Sunday nights.

Mist   20 | 20 | 19 | $11

Treasure Island Hotel, 3300 Las Vegas Blvd. S.
(Spring Mountain Rd.), 702-894-7330; www.mistbar.com
"Good music, fast service", "beautiful atmosphere" and a "hot crowd" add up to an "awesome" experience for admirers of this "cozy"-but-"cool" club on the Strip; even thrill-seekers who find it "boring" concede it's a "nice place to start or end an evening if you're staying at Treasure Island", especially since you can ogle the steamy Sirens of TI show from the bar.

Mix Lounge   – | – | – | VE

The Hotel at Mandalay Bay, 3950 Las Vegas Blvd. S., 64th fl.
(Mandalay Bay Rd.), 702-632-7777; www.chinagrillmgt.com
Drink decadently at a dizzying height atop the Hotel at Mandalay Bay, where Alain Ducasse and the China Grill team have unveiled this spacious, high-style lounge, with low banquette seating, a *Clockwork Orange*-esque bar, sculptural drink stands ripe for voguing and a balcony that opens onto the night; given its wraparound panorama of the valley, not only is a sip of a signature cocktail a sky-high sensation, but so is a trip to the loo.

Monte Carlo Pub & Brewery   – | – | – | M

Monte Carlo Resort, 3770 Las Vegas Blvd. S. (bet. Harmon &
Tropicana Aves.), 702-730-7777; www.montecarlo.com
With fermented-on-the-spot suds like Winner's Wheat and High Roller Red, a beer blast isn't a gamble at this micro-brewery in the Monte Carlo on the Strip; the staff is friendly, and the high-ceilinged room provides ample space to belly up while the DJ spins or a live band jams.

Moon NEW   – | – | – | E

Palms Casino Hotel, 4321 W. Flamingo Rd., 53rd fl. (Arville St.),
702-942-6832; www.n9negroup.com
This big-budget new penthouse atop the Fantasy Tower at the Palms lives up to its name with a retractable roof as well as spacey embellishments like hostesses clad in shiny silver outfits, a tiled floor that changes color when you walk on it and laser light show illuminating the mammoth dance floor; a spectacular 53rd-floor view of the Strip ices the cake.

Napoleon's Lounge   22 | 23 | 20 | $12

Paris Las Vegas, 3655 Las Vegas Blvd. S. (bet. Flamingo Rd. &
Harmon Ave.), 702-946-7000; www.parislasvegas.com
"Jazz, jazz and more jazz" used to make the scene here, but dueling pianos and rock bands have displaced the combos and transformed the mood at this "swanky cigar

bar" in the Paris; it's still an "amazing place" where patrons "kick back and enjoy a glass of bubbly" amid "upscale European" decor, though some say its "stereotypically French" service is its "weakest aspect."

Nefertiti's Lounge 18 19 19 $10
Luxor Hotel, 3900 Las Vegas Blvd. S. (Tropicana Ave.),
702-262-4000; www.luxor.com
You'll "feel like King Tut (pre-burial)" at this "tacky" but "fun" theme bar in the Luxor; fans feel it's one of the "best values in Vegas" with relatively "cheap drinks", a "relaxing ambiance" and "soothing music" that make it a "great club to hang out in"; foes retort that management "really needs to liven up the atmosphere" and "update" the setting if they want to "draw back" return visitors.

New York Café ⊟ – – – I
4080 Paradise Rd. (Flamingo Rd.), 702-796-0589
Home away from home for many Vegas rockers, this dark tavern east of the Strip has a distinct tattoo parlor feel jazzed up by black-and-white-checkered booths and a portrait of James Dean over the jukebox; a Pabst and a shot of Wild Turkey can be had for four bucks, and local bands take the stage on the weekends.

Nine Fine Irishmen 21 22 19 $9
New York-New York Hotel, 3790 Las Vegas Blvd. S.
(Tropicana Ave.), 702-740-6969; www.ninefineirishmen.com
"There's not a leprechaun in sight", but patrons proclaiming "another pint of Guinness, please!" assert the "authenticity" of this Irish pub, which was moved piecemeal from its original location on the Emerald Isle to New York-New York; some say it "lost a little in the translation", but those who "love it" insist that "good food", "good music and a good vibe" make it a "great place."

Olympic Garden 23 14 20 $13
1531 Las Vegas Blvd. S. (Wyoming Ave.), 702-385-8987;
www.ogvegas.com
"It doesn't get more Olympian in size" than this "monstrous" "coed strip club" on the Strip, a "sleazy" "Greek-themed" "garden of delights" offering "something for everyone" on "multiple stages": "luscious ladies" on the "large floor downstairs" and "hot" hunks upstairs in the "male revue" (Wednesday–Sunday); "everyone goes home broke and happy" after this "quintessential sybaritic" experience, since "the only thing missing is a machine to turn you over and shake the money out of you."

OPM ∇ 15 16 17 $16
Forum Shops at Caesars Palace, 3500 Las Vegas Blvd. S.
(Flamingo Rd.), 702-369-4998; www.o-pmlv.com
For "a change from the norm", check out this club "atop Wolfgang Puck's Chinois in the Forum Shops at Caesars

Palace"; "primarily frequented by the hip-hop crowd", it also offers a second dance floor where DJs "play good music" of the R&B variety and big-name rappers stop by from time to time; still, those who find it "lame" proclaim "oh, puh-lease!"

Palomino Club 19 12 15 $17

1848 Las Vegas Blvd. N. (bet. Oakley Blvd. & St. Louis Ave.), North Las Vegas, 702-642-2984; www.palominolv.com
"What a dive . . . but it's great!" exclaim fans of this "above-average" skin spot in North Las Vegas that's "supposedly the only fully nude club in town that serves alcohol"; respondents report that the "mouthwatering" gals "would turn a gay bishop straight", though those who feel "the product is disappointing" fail to see the "allure" of the joint, adding "there's a reason it's so far away from its competitors."

PEPPERMILL FIRESIDE LOUNGE 21 21 22 $9

2985 Las Vegas Blvd. S. (bet. Convention Center Dr. & Riviera Blvd.), 702-735-7635
"Friendly bartenders" mix up "cheap, well-made drinks" at this "cozy" Strip "classic", a "romantic", "Rat Pack–style" outpost of the "old-school" that "takes you back to a time when the gin was cold and the cocktail waitresses were hot"; "gigantic booths", "glowing light-filled" faux foliage and a "huge fire pit" make it the "perfect place to chill out with friends" while watching vintage Sin City performers on the ubiquitous monitors.

Petrossian Bar – – – VE

Bellagio Hotel, 3600 Las Vegas Blvd. S. (Flamingo Rd.), 702-693-7111; www.bellagio.com
If the dealers haven't cracked your nest egg yet, you can dig into ova of a different species at this lounge just a step from the action of the Bellagio casino; caviar service, appropriate sips and a fine follow-up stogie compose a luxe break from the losses, while the guy at the baby grand tickles out your swan song.

Playboy Club NEW – – – E

Palms Casino Hotel, 4321 W. Flamingo Rd. (Arville St.), 702-942-6832; www.n9negroup.com
Skin is in at this posh new nightspot from the iconic men's magazine set in the Fantasy Tower at the Palms, where bunnies and betting collide in a space that doubles as both a lounge and a gaming room; in addition to Philippe Starck–designed chandeliers and video screens depicting *Playboy*'s best-known covers, the loos are wallpapered with every centerfold in the publication's history.

Pleasures – – – E

6370 Windy Rd. (bet. W. Post Rd. & W. Teco Ave.), 702-873-8800
"Beautiful women" and an "opulent setting" "make you feel like a king" at this boob room in an industrial area west

of the Strip, where the "nice girls" are not only "attractive" but also a bit more 'natural' than their counterparts up north (some may even "talk about their kids at home"); still, regulars recommend that you "be sure to come on a busy night or else you'll leave disappointed."

Pogo's Tavern ⊭ — — — I
2103 N. Decatur Blvd. (bet. Sawyer & Stacey Aves.), 702-646-9735
A throwback to the days when Sinatra's name dominated Caesars' marquee, this small West Side bar is one of the best spots for old-school jazz in Vegas; though the bowling-trophy-and-beer-sign decor hardly matches the artful sounds issuing from the stage, it still attracts a following on Friday nights, when wizened beboppers get together for jam sessions.

PURE 27 26 19 $15
Caesars Palace, 3570 Las Vegas Blvd. S. (Flamingo Rd.), 702-731-7873; www.purelv.com
"Big, brash" and "beautiful", this "stunning nightclub" in Caesars Palace (rated No. 1 for Appeal in the *Las Vegas Nightlife Survey*) is "smoking hot", regularly "packing the who's who" of Sin City into its "minimalist", multilevel space containing "a variety of rooms", "each with different music" (don't miss the "massive upstairs deck" "overlooking the Strip"); "get there early", or "wait in line for a long time" to reach the "less-than-friendly security staff" at the "tough door."

Pussycat Dolls Lounge 23 21 20 $15
Caesars Palace, 3570 Las Vegas Blvd. S. (Flamingo Rd.), 702-731-7873; www.purelv.com
"Glamorous sex kittens" "swing from the ceiling", bathe "in a giant cocktail glass" and "vamp and camp" across the stage at this "swanky lounge attached to Pure" in the Strip's Caesars Palace, where the "entertaining shows" are "a throwback to an earlier era" of "fun burlesque"; occasional "celebrity guests" are another reason supporters "love the venue", but some "hot-blooded males" craving "more action" complain that the "brief" performances "should last longer."

Railhead, The — — — M
Boulder Station Hotel, 4111 Boulder Hwy. (Lamb Blvd.), 702-432-7777; www.stationcasinos.com
A "must when in Las Vegas", this "great showroom" inside Boulder Station draws music lovers to the East Side to sample sounds from some of the nation's best; no-cover offerings include blues sessions on Thursday nights and classic rock cover band "Yellow Brick Road on the weekends", while those looking to spend their winnings can wager on big-name acts from Merle Haggard to Nazareth to John Corbett.

Rainbow Bar & Grill

| – | – | – | M |

4480 Paradise Rd. (Harmon Ave.), 702-898-3525;
www.rainbowbarandgrilllv.com

Mötley Crüe cravers kickstart their hearts and Van Halen
fans jump for this Vegas cover of the fabled LA hair-band
hang, appropriately positioned east of the Strip opposite
the Hard Rock; get back in black and get in with the young-
sters reliving (or rather living for the first time) the heavy-
metal lifestyle of the '80s; 24/7 rock kitsch, choppers, pizza,
cold beer and, of course, headbanging bands "can be fun
for the right crowd."

Rain Nightclub

| 24 | 23 | 18 | $13 |

Palms Casino Hotel, 4321 W. Flamingo Rd. (Arville St.),
702-942-7777; www.n9negroup.com

"Packed to the rafters" with "beautiful people and
celebs", this "high-energy" "hot spot" at the Palms west
of the Strip is "made even hotter" by 14-ft. flames shooting
above the dance floor and a VIP level with "private sky-
boxes" and cabanas; "great-to-watch go-go dancers" and
a water wall add to the "mesmerizing effect", though
stormy sorts "wish it would rain in the desert" to water
down the "out-of-control lines" and "overcrowding."

RED SQUARE

| 24 | 24 | 20 | $13 |

Mandalay Bay Resort, 3950 Las Vegas Blvd. S.
(Mandalay Bay Rd.), 702-632-7407; www.mandalaybay.com

"Serious cocktail enthusiasts" salute Mandalay Bay's
"red, red, red" restaurant bar whose "kitschy" concept –
"complete with Lenin statue" outside – draws "posh, so-
phisticated" sorts to relinquish rubles, don "Natasha-style
fur coats" and head "into the freezer to taste high-end
vodkas" from a 150-plus selection that's "the biggest this
side of Moscow"; all in all, this "Communist den" is "oh-
so-cool", especially the "ice-topped bar" designed "to
keep your martini cold."

Rehab

| 23 | 21 | 19 | $12 |

Hard Rock Hotel, 4455 Paradise Rd. (bet. Flamingo Rd. &
Harmon Ave.), 702-693-5000; www.rehablv.com

"Bombdigity!" – "one of the greatest spots in North
America on a Sunday afternoon" (it's closed the other six
days) is this "happening" "pool party" in the Hard Rock;
"attracting some of the hotter women" (and guys) in the
city to "rub elbows and bodies" in the water, this "not-to-
be-missed" mecca also boasts "great music" and "fairly
priced drinks" May–September from noon to 8 PM.

Risqué

| 18 | 18 | 17 | $12 |

Paris Las Vegas, 3655 Las Vegas Blvd. S. (bet. Flamingo Rd. &
Harmon Ave.), 702-946-4589; www.risquelasvegas.com

A "step up from normal Strip fare", this "part lounge", part
"dance place" in the Paris is a "hip hangout" that's "not an

ordeal to get into", drawing a "small but nice crowd" with its "colorful" Sunday burlesque show featuring the Vamps Girlie Review; hard-core clubbers "disappointed" by the often "quiet" scene say "there's nothing risqué" about it.

RUMJUNGLE | 22 | 23 | 18 | $12 |
Mandalay Bay Resort, 3950 Las Vegas Blvd. S.
(Mandalay Bay Rd.), 702-632-7408; www.chinagrillmgt.com
"It's certainly a jungle" at this "exotic" Mandalay Bay club (voted Most Popular in the *Las Vegas Nightlife Survey*) that "visually stimulates" with "waterfalls", "fire walls" and "acrobatic women" "flipping and flying across the ceiling" to "primitive drum beats"; "get there for dinner to avoid cover charges and lines" or "reserve a table to people-watch" the "packed" "meat market" while savoring a bottle from the 140-plus rum list; yes, the "drinks are pricey here, but think of it as paying for the view."

Sand Dollar Blues Lounge | – | – | – | I |
3355 Spring Mountain Rd. (Polaris Ave.), 702-871-6651;
www.sanddollarblues.com
The "best dive bar for good blues" in Sin City might just be this "local" hang at a west-of-the-Strip crossroads; the bands are blowing seven nights a week, and Monday and Tuesday jam sessions are free, with a mere Lincoln getting you in the door on other nights; sets generally start at 10 PM and 2 AM, but you can sling 'em back 24/7 at this juke joint.

Sapphire | 22 | 19 | 19 | $15 |
3025 S. Industrial Rd. (Desert Inn Rd.), 702-796-6000;
www.sapphirelasvegas.com
"Far too big" refers not so much to the wares on the "attractive girls" but to the size of this "gargantuan" gent's joint west of the Strip – at over 70,000 sq. ft., it's "touted as the world's largest strip club" complete with VIP sky boxes; the "great eye candy" meets your "expectation of behavior" in such an establishment, but with "expensive" pricing and "tip-oriented" talent, your tab might be huge as well.

Scores | – | – | – | M |
3355 Procyon (Desert Inn Rd.), 702-367-4000;
www.scoreslasvegas.com
This two-story passion palace west of the Strip could very well raise the standard (or lower the standard, depending upon your point of view) for adult entertainment in Las Vegas with its elegant restaurant, classy atmosphere and stable of gorgeous women; perks include cigars, a sports bar and an extra twist: occasional contortionists.

Seahorse Lounge | – | – | – | E |
Caesars Palace, 3570 Las Vegas Blvd. S. (Flamingo Rd.),
702-731-7110; www.caesarspalace.com
Go Cousteau at this aquatically themed lounge that's just washed into Caesars Palace on the Strip; those Australian

Potbelly namesakes in the 1,700-gallon, 360-degree tank
sure are cool to look at (if you can spot them), particularly
after a few Tanqueray-spiked Poseidon martinis or one of
20 champagnes, accompanied by seafood nibbles, natch.

Sedona | – | – | – | M |
9580 W. Flamingo Rd. (I-215), 702-320-4700;
www.sedonaclub.com
Andre Agassi's Summerlin lounge lobs a "relaxed, who-
cares-if-I'm-trendy vibe" with "hip, modern" decor featuring cushy seating and "dark, romantic" lighting that
"would be more beautiful if not for the hideous glow of
video poker machines"; a fire pit stokes the "yuppie"
flames out on the deck, where you might want to go to
actually "hear people"; foodies who slam the chow say the
tennis star "should eat here" more often to coax "improve-
ments from the kitchen."

Shadow | 21 | 19 | 18 | $11 |
Caesars Palace, 3570 Las Vegas Blvd. S. (Flamingo Rd.),
702-731-7110; www.caesarspalace.com
The "only thing hotter" than the "topless" talent writhing
in silhouette behind screens are the "hot girls inside the
bar itself" – but even women "can hang out" and "not feel
like pieces of meat" at this "sexy but not trashy" Caesars
casino lounge; "world-class flair" mixologists getting
"over the top" on the bartop and an easy door "without the
commitment of a cover charge" "don't hurt either."

Sidebar NEW | – | – | – | E |
201 N. Third St. (Ogden Ave.), 702-259-9700; www.sidebarlv.com
Downtown Vegas may be synonymous with urban grit and
deep-fried Twinkies, but this small, tastefully appointed
lounge stands apart from the crowd with its sleek white
couches and plasma screens; premium imported cigars
and nibbles like oysters and truffles work well with its signature 'American Beauty' cocktail, a fizzy pink concoction
served with an edible rose petal.

Sin | ▽ 16 | 15 | 15 | $13 |
3525 W. Russell Rd. (Polaris Ave.), 702-673-1700
In-the-know fans of fauna say this recently opened
sin scene south of the Strip employs "some of the best-
looking women at any strip bar in the country"; the
converted warehouse space features three stages
equipped with poles, VIP rooms, cozy sofas, a gift shop, an
attached sports bar and original artwork in its edifying
Museum of Erotica.

Spearmint Rhino | 24 | 19 | 21 | $13 |
3340 Highland Dr. (Spring Mountain Rd.), 702-796-3600;
www.spearmintrhino.com
"Totally refurbished" and enlarged, this "hot, hot, hot"
west-of-the-Strip skin spot (the Top strip club in the *Las*

Vegas Nightlife Survey) is "dark" but "opulently" decorated, which can make it "a better fit for businessmen";
yet the "results are mixed" say regulars: the "talent" can
"take the cake" for "attractiveness" or be "pushy"
and "awful", while the scene morphs from "laid-back"
"party" during the week to "wild" "lap-dance manufacturing
operation" on weekends.

Studio 54   20 | 19 | 17 | $12

MGM Grand Hotel, 3799 Las Vegas Blvd. S. (Tropicana Ave.),
702-891-7254; www.studio54lv.com
"It's a flashback moment" and then some at the MGM
Grand's "nice adaptation" of the legendary Manhattan
original where the "drinks are strong and you can dance
all night long"; "acrobatic", "hot chicks" "coming down
wires" and "jumping through hoops", plus "music genres
that rotate every 20–30 minutes" make for an "overload of
interesting sights and sounds"; still, scenesters sink its
"older" "tourist" following, deadpanning "Steve Rubell
must be turning in his grave."

Tabú   23 | 23 | 20 | $12

MGM Grand Hotel, 3799 Las Vegas Blvd. S. (Tropicana Ave.),
702-891-7183; www.tabulv.com
"Not too big, not too small, but just right" say club-going
Goldilocks of this "sleek and sexy" ultra-den in the
MGM Grand, where the ubiquitous "awesome visual
displays" even beam from the "sooo cool interactive tables"; "loungey" and "saucy" all at once, it draws so many
"chic tourists and high-rollin' celebs" that it can be "difficult to get into unless you know someone who can get you
on the list."

Take 1 Nightclub   – | – | – | I

707 Fremont St. (bet. Las Vegas Blvd. & Maryland Pkwy.),
702-433-8253; www.take1lasvegas.com
Set on a seedy stretch of Fremont Street, this spacious
Downtown nightclub exudes a vague B-movie air via
framed film posters, but it's definitely designed for local
rockers, not movie stars, especially on weekends when
bands perform beneath its mirrored ceiling.

Tangerine   22 | 21 | 17 | $13

Treasure Island Hotel, 3300 Las Vegas Blvd. S.
(Spring Mountain Rd.), 702-212-8140;
www.treasureisland.com
The "young, wild and crazy" squeeze into this "small" club
at TI, where the "burlesque show with live band" and "outdoor bar overlooking the Sirens" performance make for a
juicy scene; "waitresses in skimpy outfits" skirt the dance
floor where "good hip-hop" pumps amid "very cool" decor
featuring the namesake color, while "techno grooves create a chill environment" on the patio.

Tao   – | – | – | VE

Venetian Hotel, 3355 Las Vegas Blvd S. (bet. Flamingo &
Spring Mountain Rds.), 702-388-8588; www.taorestaurant.com
A popular Pan-Asian New Yorker has landed a spin-off
inside the Venetian, and locals say they might as well
change the name from Tao to Wow; wind through the dark-
red mazelike space past sex-pot models, Buddhist monk
statues, a hook-up bar, a boogie-down dance floor,
exhibitionist restrooms and fully loaded VIP sky boxes
till you find yourself breathless on the balcony
overlooking the Strip.

32 degrees   20 | 17 | 15 | $13

MGM Grand Hotel, 3799 Las Vegas Blvd. S. (Tropicana Ave.),
702-891-1111
"Icy sticky drinks" keep things cool at this "fab" and fruity
fill-'er-upper in the MGM Studio Walk where an "eclectic
crowd" sucks down adult-oriented slurpees (and beer)
before a meal at adjacent Pearl or Seablue; though some
melt over the brightly hued modernist decor, the service
isn't so hot: "32 degrees describes the cold shoulder the
staff gives customers parched from the desert sun" who
are "just trying to get a drink."

Toby Keith's   – | – | – | M
I Love This Bar & Grill

Harrah's Las Vegas, 3475 Las Vegas Blvd. S. (Flamingo Rd.),
702-369-5000; www.harrahs.com
Sure, the name of the venue is a mouthful, but just tell
everyone you're headed to TK's (the initials of one of country music's top performers) and they'll know you're in for a
rip-roarin' night of live C&W, two-stepping and down-
home guzzles and grub; the warm, polished-wood space
inside Harrah's features 22 plasma TVs and a giant screen
blaring music videos by you-know-who.

Tommy Rocker's Mojave Beach   – | – | – | I

4275 Dean Martin Dr. (bet. Flamingo Rd. & Tropicana Ave.),
702-261-6688; www.tommyrocker.com
"Dance while you're laughing your ass off" during weekend sets by the eponymous, um, rocker himself at his
revamped "Buffett beach-style bar" west of the Strip; it's
"not much of a scene for the under-30 crowd", but the
"super-friendly staff", a "music volume that permits conversation" and a "very comfortable" vibe make it the place
"where local bartenders and cocktail servers go to get
sloppy" off-shift.

Top of the World Lounge   25 | 22 | 20 | $12

Stratosphere Hotel, 2000 Las Vegas Blvd. S., 109th fl. (north of
Sahara Ave.), 702-380-7777; www.stratospherehotel.com
Maybe, it's "a bit tacky" inside, but it's "lively and friendly"
and just "happens to be on the 109th floor" of the

Stratosphere; this "rotating lounge" boasts – what else? – "awesome views over Vegas" to devour while you sip your "excellent" specialty martini; with a vista this "breathtaking", the "good lounge acts" are just icing on the cake, though the atmosphere's still not sweet enough for those who think "it's not worth the cost" of the cover charge.

Tryst NEW – | – | – | VE

Wynn Las Vegas, 3131 Las Vegas Blvd. S. (Desert Inn Rd.), 702-770-3375; www.trystlasvegas.com

A $40 million renovation of the club formerly known as La Bête, this new, ultrasvelte nightspot in the Wynn is best remembered for its nine-story waterfall that crashes down into a bubbling lake – and a 'European bottle service' policy where a bottle of Hardy Perfection Cognac will set you back 60 grand; in addition, there's a mirror-covered lounge, a stripper pole–equipped VIP room and a large patio appointed with plush sofas.

V Bar 21 | 21 | 20 | $13

Venetian Hotel, 3355 Las Vegas Blvd. S. (bet. Flamingo & Spring Mountain Rds.), 702-414-3200; www.arkvegas.com

"Hard to define", this "classy" feng-shui'd lounge in the Venetian "can go from a laid-back" "place to relax" to a "dance party in the blink of an eye"; the "DJ spins a good beat" in a "stylish, dark room", making it a "great way to start off the evening" with "cocktails and conversation" or "wind down after a night of debauchery."

VooDoo Lounge 25 | 23 | 19 | $11

Rio All-Suite Hotel, 3700 W. Flamingo Rd., 51st fl. (bet. I-15 & Valley View Blvd.), 702-777-6875; www.riovegasnights.com

Set in a "nice location" on the 51st floor of the Rio, this "fun and funky lounge" with an "incredible" two-story outdoor patio "overlooking the entire Strip" boasts the "ghostbar view without the wannabes" (or "the wait"); "less hype" makes for an "interesting crowd" that's "a little mellower", at least till they sample the sounds of the "talented house band" or the flair bartenders' "unbelievable cocktails" – "beware the Witch Doctor."

WHISKEY, THE 24 | 24 | 21 | $10

Green Valley Ranch, 2300 Paseo Verde Pkwy. (Green Valley Pkwy.), Henderson, 702-617-7560; www.greenvalleyranchresort.com

"Expect some snoot" at Rande Gerber's "fabulous, fantastic" "place to party" at the off-Strip Green Valley Ranch ("celebs stay here for privacy, need I say more?"), a "sophisticated" spot that's "solid for a night out"; "relax" on "comfortable" sofas and beds on the outdoor deck, or down an "excellent drink" at the "very hip bar" inside – either way, you'll enjoy what could be the "best ambiance in town."

Nightlife A | D | S | C

Zingers   _ | _ | _ | M
1000 E. Sahara Ave. (bet. Maryland Pkwy. &
Commercial Center Dr.), 702-736-9464
Perhaps one of the most democratic clubs in town, this upscale gay joint in a downscale neighborhood just east of the
Strip (and across the street from a plaza noted for its boy
bars and swingers clubs) is a friendly place to kick back
and be yourself, whether you're cross-dressing or playing
it straight; stop by for the live entertainment nightly.

Zuri   ∇ 19 | 22 | 25 | $13
MGM Grand Hotel, 3799 Las Vegas Blvd. S. (Tropicana Ave.),
702-891-1111
"After a busy day [or night] of shopping and gambling",
"come in for a cocktail" and a cigar from the humidor at
this 24/7 martini bar off the main lobby of the MGM Grand;
"good service" and "plush chairs" make it easy to "really
enjoy your drink", while a selection of fruit-infused spirits,
specialty beers and a 'morning after' liquid brunch menu
add to its "cool" quotient.

Nightlife
Indexes

LOCATIONS
SPECIAL APPEALS

LOCATIONS

Downtown
Art Bar
Beauty Bar
Bunkhouse Saloon
Celebrity Las Vegas
Dino's Lounge
Girls of Glitter Gulch
Hogs & Heifers
Jillian's
Sidebar
Take 1 Nightclub

East of Strip
Beach, The
Body English
Club Paradise
Divebar
Double Down
Ellis Island
Freakin' Frog
Gipsy
Gordon Biersch
Hofbrauhaus
Ice
Joint, The
New York Café
Rainbow B&G
Rehab
Zingers

East Side
Bahama Breeze
Champagnes Cafe
Railhead, The

Henderson
Club Madrid
Drop Bar
Fadó Irish Pub
Whiskey, The

North Las Vegas
Chrome Showroom
Club, The
Palomino Club

Northwest/Summerlin
Addison's Lounge
Cherry
Cheyenne Saloon
J. C. Wooloughan's
Sedona

South of Strip
Hootie & the Blowfish's
Mermaid Lounge
Sin

Strip
Bar at Times Sq.
Barbary Coast
Big Apple Bar
Breeze Bar
Caramel
Carnaval Court
Cleopatra's Barge
Coral Reef
Coyote Ugly
Crazy Armadillo
Curve
Drai's After Hours
Empire Ballroom
ESPN Zone
Fontana Bar
Gilley's Dance Hall
House of Blues
Images Cabaret
Indigo Lounge
Ivan Kane's Forty Deuce
Jet
Kahunaville
Krave
La Scena Lounge
Light
Lure
Mist
Mix Lounge
Monte Carlo Pub
Napoleon's Lounge
Nefertiti's Lounge
Nine Fine Irishmen
Olympic Garden
OPM
Peppermill Fireside
Petrossian Bar
Pure
Pussycat Dolls
Red Square
Risqué
rumjungle
Seahorse Lounge
Shadow
Studio 54
Tabú

Tangerine
Tao
32 degrees
Toby Keith's B&G
Top of the World
Tryst
V Bar
Zuri

West of Strip
Artisan Lounge
Brendan's Irish Pub
Cheetah's
Club Rio
Crazy Horse Too
Emergency Room
Flirt

ghostbar
Gold Coast Lounge
Moon
Playboy Club
Pleasures
Rain
Sand Dollar Blues
Sapphire
Scores
Spearmint Rhino
Tommy Rocker's
VooDoo Lounge

West Side
Cellar Lounge
Cooler Lounge
Pogo's Tavern

SPECIAL APPEALS

(Indexes list the best in each category. Multi-location nightspots' features may vary by branch. For some categories, schedules may vary; call ahead or check Web sites for the most up-to-date information.)

Additions
(Properties added since the last edition of the book)
Bunkhouse Saloon
Cherry
Cheyenne Saloon
Chrome Showroom
Divebar
Freakin' Frog
Jet
Moon
New York Café
Playboy Club
Sidebar
Take 1 Nightclub
Tryst

After Work
Art Bar
Artisan Lounge
Bahama Breeze
Bar at Times Sq.
Beauty Bar
Celebrity Las Vegas
Cleopatra's Barge
Dino's Lounge
ESPN Zone
Fadó Irish Pub
Gordon Biersch
Hogs & Heifers
Images Cabaret
Indigo Lounge
Kahunaville
Mix Lounge
Monte Carlo Pub
Nine Fine Irishmen
Pogo's Tavern
Red Square
Scores
Seahorse Lounge
Zingers

Asian
Tao

Bachelor Parties
Body English
Cheetah's
Club Paradise
Crazy Horse Too
Girls of Glitter Gulch
Hogs & Heifers
Ivan Kane's Forty Deuce
Olympic Garden
Pure
Scores
Shadow
Sin
Spearmint Rhino
Tao

Bachelorette Parties
Body English
Flirt
Hogs & Heifers
Olympic Garden
Pure
Tao

Beautiful People
Beach, The
Beauty Bar
Body English
Coyote Ugly
Curve
Drai's After Hours
Drop Bar
ghostbar
Gordon Biersch
Ice
Ivan Kane's Forty Deuce
La Scena Lounge
Light
Lure
Mix Lounge
Moon
Playboy Club
Pure
Pussycat Dolls
Rain
Red Square
rumjungle

Studio 54
Tao
V Bar
VooDoo Lounge

Blues

Cellar Lounge
Chrome Showroom
Divebar
Emergency Room
Hootie & the Blowfish's
House of Blues
Railhead, The
Sand Dollar Blues

Bottle Service

(Bottle purchase sometimes
required to secure a table)
Beach, The
Cherry
Drai's After Hours
Empire Ballroom
Ice
Ivan Kane's Forty Deuce
Jet
Krave
Mix Lounge
Moon
Playboy Club
Pure
Pussycat Dolls
Rain
Red Square
Risqué
rumjungle
Scores
Sidebar
Studio 54
Tabú
Tao
Tryst
V Bar
VooDoo Lounge
Whiskey, The

Burlesque

Ivan Kane's Forty Deuce
Pussycat Dolls
Risqué
Shadow
Tangerine

Cigar-Friendly

Art Bar
Artisan Lounge

Bahama Breeze
Barbary Coast
Breeze Bar
Bunkhouse Saloon
Carnaval Court
Celebrity Las Vegas
Cellar Lounge
Cheetah's
Club Paradise
Coyote Ugly
Crazy Horse Too
Ellis Island
Emergency Room
Fontana Bar
ghostbar
Gilley's Dance Hall
Girls of Glitter Gulch
Gordon Biersch
Hofbrauhaus
Hogs & Heifers
House of Blues
Ice
Indigo Lounge
Ivan Kane's Forty Deuce
J. C. Wooloughan's
Joint, The
Krave
La Scena Lounge
Light
Mist
Mix Lounge
Moon
Napoleon's Lounge
Nefertiti's Lounge
New York Café
Olympic Garden
OPM
Peppermill Fireside
Petrossian Bar
Playboy Club
Pleasures
Rainbow B&G
Rain
Red Square
Rehab
Risqué
Sand Dollar Blues
Sapphire
Scores
Shadow
Sidebar
Sin
Spearmint Rhino
Studio 54

Tabú
Tao
32 degrees
Toby Keith's B&G
Tryst
Zuri

Dancing
Beach, The
Body English
Cherry
Chrome Showroom
Cleopatra's Barge
Club, The
Club Madrid
Club Rio
Coral Reef
Crazy Armadillo
Curve
Drai's After Hours
Empire Ballroom
Fontana Bar
ghostbar
Gilley's Dance Hall
Gipsy
Gordon Biersch
House of Blues
Ice
Jet
Joint, The
Kahunaville
La Scena Lounge
Light
Mist
Moon
Napoleon's Lounge
Nefertiti's Lounge
OPM
Playboy Club
Pure
Pussycat Dolls
Railhead, The
Rain
Risqué
rumjungle
Sand Dollar Blues
Sin
Studio 54
Tangerine
Tao
Tommy Rocker's
Tryst
V Bar
VooDoo Lounge
Whiskey, The

Dives
Barbary Coast
Champagnes Cafe
Cooler Lounge
Dino's Lounge
Divebar
Double Down
Emergency Room
New York Café
Palomino Club
Sand Dollar Blues

DJs
(Call ahead to check nights and times)
Beach, The
Body English
Celebrity Las Vegas
Cheetah's
Cherry
Cleopatra's Barge
Club, The
Club Rio
Crazy Armadillo
Curve
Drai's After Hours
Empire Ballroom
ghostbar
Gipsy
Ice
Jet
Krave
Light
OPM
Pure
Rain
rumjungle
Studio 54
Tangerine
Tao
Tryst
V Bar

Drink Specialists
Beer
(* Microbrewery)
Ellis Island
Fadó Irish Pub
Freakin' Frog
Gordon Biersch*
Hofbrauhaus
J. C. Wooloughan's
Monte Carlo Pub*
Zuri

Champagne
Cherry
Jet
Moon
Napoleon's Lounge
Petrossian Bar
Playboy Club
Seahorse Lounge
Tryst

Cocktails
Cherry
Fontana Bar
ghostbar
Jet
Mix Lounge
Moon
Nefertiti's Lounge
Playboy Club
Sidebar
Tryst
VooDoo Lounge

Martinis
Beauty Bar
Cherry
Jet
Moon
Playboy Club
Red Square
Seahorse Lounge
Top of the World
Tryst
Zuri

Scotch/Single Malts
Playboy Club

Tequila
Crazy Armadillo
Playboy Club

Vodka
Petrossian Bar
Playboy Club
Red Square
Zuri

Whiskey
Brendan's Irish Pub
Fadó Irish Pub
J. C. Wooloughan's
Nine Fine Irishmen

Wine by the Glass
Artisan Lounge

Euro
Beach, The
Club Rio
Curve

Flair Bartenders
Carnaval Court
Coyote Ugly
Crazy Armadillo
Hogs & Heifers
Kahunaville
Shadow
VooDoo Lounge

Frat House
Beach, The
Coyote Ugly
Double Down
ESPN Zone
Freakin' Frog
Hogs & Heifers
House of Blues
Seahorse Lounge

Gay/Lesbian
Gipsy
Krave
Zingers

Happy Hour
Art Bar
Artisan Lounge
Bahama Breeze
Beauty Bar
Celebrity Las Vegas
Gordon Biersch
Napoleon's Lounge
Tommy Rocker's

Hotel Bars
Aladdin Resort
  Curve
Artisan Hotel
  Artisan Lounge
Bally's Las Vegas Hotel
  Indigo Lounge
Barbary Coast Hotel
  Barbary Coast
  Drai's After Hours
Bellagio Hotel
  Caramel
  Fontana Bar
  Light
  Petrossian Bar
Boulder Station Hotel
  Railhead, The

Nightlife Special Appeals

Caesars Palace
  Cleopatra's Barge
  Pure
  Pussycat Dolls
  Seahorse Lounge
  Shadow
Cannery Hotel
  Club, The
Ellis Island Casino & Brewery
  Ellis Island
Forum Shops at Caesars Palace
  OPM
Frontier Hotel
  Gilley's Dance Hall
Gold Coast Hotel
  Gold Coast Lounge
Green Valley Ranch
  Drop Bar
  Fadó Irish Pub
  Whiskey, The
Hard Rock Hotel
  Body English
  Joint, The
  Rehab
Harrah's Las Vegas
  Carnaval Court
  Toby Keith's B&G
Hotel at Mandalay Bay
  Mix Lounge
JW Marriott
  J. C. Wooloughan's
Luxor Hotel
  Nefertiti's Lounge
Mandalay Bay Resort
  Coral Reef
  House of Blues
  Red Square
  rumjungle
Mandalay Place
  Ivan Kane's Forty Deuce
MGM Grand Hotel
  Studio 54
  Tabú
  32 degrees
  Zuri
Mirage Hotel
  Jet
Monte Carlo Resort
  Monte Carlo Pub

New York-New York Hotel
  Bar at Times Sq.
  Big Apple Bar
  Coyote Ugly
  ESPN Zone
  Nine Fine Irishmen
Orleans Hotel
  Brendan's Irish Pub
Palms Casino Hotel
  ghostbar
  Moon
  Playboy Club
  Rain
Paris Las Vegas
  Napoleon's Lounge
  Risqué
Red Rock Casino
  Cherry
Rio All-Suite Hotel
  Club Rio
  Flirt
  VooDoo Lounge
Santa Fe Station Hotel
  Chrome Showroom
Silverton Casino & Lodge
  Hootie & the Blowfish's
    Mermaid Lounge
Stratosphere Hotel
  Crazy Armadillo
  Images Cabaret
  Top of the World
Sunset Station Hotel
  Club Madrid
Treasure Island Hotel
  Breeze Bar
  Kahunaville
  Mist
  Tangerine
Venetian Hotel
  La Scena Lounge
  Tao
  V Bar
Wynn Las Vegas
  Lure
  Tryst

Irish

Brendan's Irish Pub
Fadó Irish Pub
J. C. Wooloughan's
Nine Fine Irishmen

Live Entertainment
(See also Blues, Burlesque, Strip Clubs)
Bahama Breeze (reggae)
Big Apple Bar (varies)
Brendan's Irish Pub (bands)
Carnaval Court (varies)
Champagnes Cafe (karaoke)
Cleopatra's Barge (bands)
Coral Reef (bands)
Coyote Ugly (bartenders)
Crazy Armadillo (bands)
Dino's Lounge (karaoke/bands)
Double Down (punk/rock/metal)
Ellis Island (karaoke)
Empire Ballroom (varies)
Fadó Irish Pub (Irish)
Fontana Bar (vocals)
Gilley's Dance Hall (country)
Gold Coast Lounge (jazz)
Hofbrauhaus (German music)
Hogs & Heifers (bartenders)
Images Cabaret (rock/R&B)
Indigo Lounge (R&B)
J. C. Woolloughan's (varies)
Jillian's (bands)
Kahunaville (reggae)
Krave (adult show)
La Scena Lounge (rock)
Mermaid Lounge (mermaids)
Mist (varies)
Monte Carlo Pub (bands)
Napoleon's Lounge (jazz)
Nefertiti's Lounge (varies)
Nine Fine Irishmen (Irish)
Pogo's Tavern (jazz)
Rainbow B&G (rock/metal)
Rain (dancers)
rumjungle (dancers)
Studio 54 (dancers)
Tao (performers)
Tommy Rocker's (bands)
Top of the World (lounge acts)
VooDoo Lounge (jazz)
Zingers (varies)

Meat Markets
Bahama Breeze
Beach, The
Celebrity Las Vegas
Cherry
Coyote Ugly
Curve
Drai's After Hours

ghostbar
Gipsy
Gordon Biersch
Hogs & Heifers
Jet
Light
Mix Lounge
Moon
Pussycat Dolls
Rain
rumjungle
Shadow
Studio 54
Tryst
V Bar
VooDoo Lounge

Old Las Vegas
(Year opened; * building)
1900 Girls of Glitter Gulch*

Open 24 Hours
Artisan Lounge
Bar at Times Sq.
Barbary Coast
Beach, The
Big Apple Bar
Breeze Bar
Bunkhouse Saloon
Cellar Lounge
Champagnes Cafe
Cheetah's
Cheyenne Saloon
Cooler Lounge
Crazy Horse Too
Dino's Lounge
Divebar
Double Down
Drop Bar
Ellis Island
Emergency Room
Gold Coast Lounge
Hootie & the Blowfish's
Nefertiti's Lounge
New York Café
Olympic Garden
Peppermill Fireside
Petrossian Bar
Rainbow B&G
Sand Dollar Blues
Sapphire
Sin
Spearmint Rhino
Tommy Rocker's
Zuri

Outdoor Spaces

Garden
Lure

Patio/Terrace
Bahama Breeze
Beach, The
Beauty Bar
Carnaval Court
Cherry
Club, The
Empire Ballroom
Fontana Bar
Gordon Biersch
J. C. Wooloughan's
Mix Lounge
Moon
Nine Fine Irishmen
Rainbow B&G
Sedona
Sidebar
Tangerine
Tao
Tommy Rocker's
Tryst
VooDoo Lounge
Whiskey, The

Rooftop
ghostbar
VooDoo Lounge

Waterside
Kahunaville
Rehab
Tryst

People-Watching
Bar at Times Sq.
Beach, The
Carnaval Court
Cleopatra's Barge
Coyote Ugly
Curve
Double Down
Gipsy
Hogs & Heifers
House of Blues
Ivan Kane's Forty Deuce
Joint, The
Kahunaville
La Scena Lounge
Mermaid Lounge
Monte Carlo Pub
Nine Fine Irishmen
Peppermill Fireside
Pussycat Dolls
Rainbow B&G

Red Square
Rehab
Seahorse Lounge
Studio 54
Tao
VooDoo Lounge
Zingers

Quiet Conversation
Addison's Lounge
Artisan Lounge
Mermaid Lounge
Napoleon's Lounge
Nefertiti's Lounge
Petrossian Bar
Sidebar

Roadhouse
Cheyenne Saloon
Coyote Ugly
Double Down
Gilley's Dance Hall
Hogs & Heifers
Rainbow B&G
Sand Dollar Blues
Toby Keith's B&G

Romantic
Caramel
Cherry
Curve
Fontana Bar
Jet
Mix Lounge
Peppermill Fireside
Sidebar
Top of the World
Tryst
V Bar
VooDoo Lounge

Russian
Petrossian Bar
Red Square

Sports Bars
Cellar Lounge
ESPN Zone
Hootie & the Blowfish's
Jillian's
Scores
Sin

Strip Clubs
Cheetah's
Club Paradise

Crazy Horse Too
Girls of Glitter Gulch
Olympic Garden
Palomino Club
Pleasures
Sapphire
Scores
Spearmint Rhino

Swanky

Caramel
Cherry
Drop Bar
Ice
Jet
Joint, The
Light
Mix Lounge
Moon
Playboy Club
Rain
rumjungle
Seahorse Lounge
Sidebar
Studio 54
Tao
Tryst

Tourist Favorites

Bahama Breeze
Carnaval Court
Cleopatra's Barge
Club Paradise
Coyote Ugly
Crazy Horse Too
Curve
Drai's After Hours
ESPN Zone
Flirt
Fontana Bar
Kahunaville
Napoleon's Lounge
Nefertiti's Lounge
Nine Fine Irishmen
Peppermill Fireside
Rain
rumjungle
Toby Keith's B&G
Top of the World

Trendy

Beauty Bar
Cherry
Coyote Ugly
Curve

Drai's After Hours
Drop Bar
ghostbar
Hogs & Heifers
Ice
Jet
Kahunaville
Light
Lure
Mix Lounge
Moon
Playboy Club
Pussycat Dolls
Rain
Rehab
rumjungle
Shadow
Sidebar
Studio 54
Tangerine
Tao
Tryst
V Bar

Velvet Rope

Body English
Cherry
Curve
ghostbar
Ice
Jet
Light
Moon
Playboy Club
Pure
Pussycat Dolls
Rain
Studio 54
Tabú
Tao
Tryst

Views

Cherry
Fontana Bar
ghostbar
Mermaid Lounge
Mix Lounge
Moon
Playboy Club
Tangerine
Tao
Top of the World
VooDoo Lounge

Noteworthy Hotels with Casinos

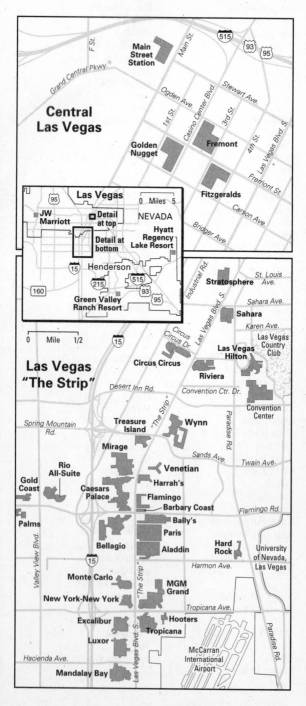

Noteworthy Hotels with Casinos

Aladdin Resort & Casino
3667 Las Vegas Blvd. S., 702-785-5555; 877-333-9474;
www.aladdincasino.com

Bally's Las Vegas Hotel
3645 Las Vegas Blvd. S., 702-967-4111; 888-742-9248;
www.ballyslv.com

Barbary Coast Hotel & Casino
3595 Las Vegas Blvd. S., 702-737-7111; 888-227-2279;
www.barbarycoastcasino.com

Bellagio Hotel
3600 Las Vegas Blvd. S., 702-693-7111; 888-987-6667;
www.bellagiolasvegas.com

Caesars Palace
3570 Las Vegas Blvd. S., 702-731-7110; 800-634-6661;
www.caesarspalace.com

Circus Circus Hotel
2880 Las Vegas Blvd. S., 702-734-0410; 877-224-7287;
www.circuscircus.com

Excalibur Hotel
3850 Las Vegas Blvd. S., 702-597-7777; 877-750-5464;
www.excaliburlasvegas.com

Fitzgeralds Casino & Hotel
301 Fremont St., 702-388-2400; 800-274-5825;
www.fitzgeraldslasvegas.com

Flamingo Las Vegas
3555 Las Vegas Blvd. S., 702-733-3111; 888-308-8899;
www.flamingolasvegas.com

Fremont Hotel & Casino
200 Fremont St., 702-385-3232; 800-634-6182;
www.fremontcasino.com

Gold Coast Hotel & Casino
4000 W. Flamingo Rd., 702-367-7111; 888-402-6278;
www.goldcoastcasino.com

Golden Gate Hotel & Casino
1 Fremont St., 702-385-1906; 800-426-1906;
www.goldengatecasino.net

Golden Nugget Hotel
129 E. Fremont St., 702-385-7111; 800-846-5336;
www.goldennugget.com

Green Valley Ranch Resort & Spa
2300 Paseo Verde Pkwy., Henderson, 702-617-7777;
866-782-9487; www.greenvalleyranchresort.com

Hard Rock Hotel & Casino
4455 Paradise Rd., 702-693-5000; 800-473-7625;
www.hardrockhotel.com

Harrah's Las Vegas
3475 Las Vegas Blvd. S., 702-369-5000; 800-427-7247;
www.harrahs.com

Hooters Casino Hotel
115 E. Tropicana Ave., 866-584-6687;
www.hooterscasinohotel.com

Hyatt Regency Lake Las Vegas Resort
101 Montelago Blvd., Henderson, 702-567-1234;
800-233-1234; www.lakelasvegas.hyatt.com

JW Marriott Resort & Spa
221 N. Rampart Blvd., 702-869-7777; 877-869-8777;
www.jwlasvegasresort.com

Las Vegas Hilton Hotel
3000 Paradise Rd., 702-732-5111; 888-732-7117; www.lv-hilton.com

Luxor Hotel
3900 Las Vegas Blvd. S., 702-262-4000; 888-777-0188;
www.luxor.com

Main Street Station Hotel
200 N. Main St., 702-387-1896; 800-465-0711;
www.mainstreetcasino.com

Mandalay Bay Resort
3950 Las Vegas Blvd. S., 702-632-7777; 877-632-7000;
www.mandalaybay.com

MGM Grand Hotel
3799 Las Vegas Blvd. S., 702-891-7777; 800-929-1111;
www.mgmgrand.com

Mirage Hotel
3400 Las Vegas Blvd. S., 702-791-7111; 800-627-6667;
www.mirage.com

Monte Carlo Resort & Casino
3770 Las Vegas Blvd. S., 702-730-7777; 888-529-4828;
www.monte-carlo.com

New York-New York Hotel & Casino
3790 Las Vegas Blvd. S., 702-740-6969; 888-696-9887;
www.nynyhotelcasino.com

Palms Casino Hotel
4321 W. Flamingo Rd., 702-942-7777; 866-942-7777;
www.palms.com

Paris Las Vegas
3655 Las Vegas Blvd. S., 702-946-7000; 888-266-5687;
www.parislasvegas.com

Rio All-Suite Hotel & Casino
3700 W. Flamingo Rd., 702-777-7777; 888-746-7482;
www.playrio.com

Riviera Hotel & Casino
2901 Las Vegas Blvd. S., 702-734-5110; 800-634-6753;
www.theriviera.com

Sahara Hotel & Casino
2535 Las Vegas Blvd. S., 702-737-2111; 888-696-2121;
www.saharavegas.com

Stratosphere Hotel & Tower
2000 Las Vegas Blvd. S., 702-380-7777; 800-998-6937;
www.stratospherehotel.com

Treasure Island Hotel
3300 Las Vegas Blvd. S., 702-894-7111; 800-288-7206;
www.treasureisland.com

Tropicana Hotel
3801 Las Vegas Blvd. S., 702-739-2222; 800-468-9494;
www.tropicanalv.com

Venetian Hotel
3355 Las Vegas Blvd. S., 702-414-1000; 877-283-6423;
www.venetian.com

Wynn Las Vegas Casino Resort
3131 Las Vegas Blvd. S., 702-770-7100; 888-320-9966;
www.wynnlasvegas.com

Wine Vintage Chart

This chart, based on our 0 to 30 scale, is designed to help you select wine. The ratings (by **Howard Stravitz**, a law professor at the University of South Carolina) reflect the vintage quality and the wine's readiness to drink. We exclude the 1987, 1991–1993 vintages because they are not that good. A dash indicates the wine is either past its peak or too young to rate.

	'86	'88	'89	'90	'94	'95	'96	'97	'98	'99	'00	'01	'02	'03	'04	'05
WHITES																
French:																
Alsace	–	–	26	26	25	24	24	23	26	24	26	27	25	22	24	25
Burgundy	25	–	23	22	–	28	27	24	23	26	25	24	27	23	25	26
Loire Valley	–	–	–	–	–	–	–	–	–	–	24	25	26	23	24	25
Champagne	25	24	26	29	–	26	27	24	23	24	24	22	26	–	–	–
Sauternes	28	29	25	28	–	21	23	25	23	24	24	28	25	26	21	26
German:	–	25	26	27	24	23	26	25	26	23	21	29	27	25	26	26
Austrian:																
Grüner Velt./ Riesling	–	–	–	–	–	25	21	28	28	27	22	23	24	26	26	26
California:																
Chardonnay	–	–	–	–	–	–	–	–	–	24	23	26	26	27	28	29
Sauvignon Blanc	–	–	–	–	–	–	–	–	–	–	–	27	28	26	27	26
REDS																
French:																
Bordeaux	25	23	25	29	22	26	25	23	25	24	29	26	24	25	23	27
Burgundy	–	–	24	26	–	26	27	26	22	27	22	24	27	24	24	25
Rhône	–	26	28	28	24	26	22	24	27	26	27	26	–	25	24	–
Beaujolais	–	–	–	–	–	–	–	–	–	–	24	–	23	27	23	28
California:																
Cab./Merlot	–	–	–	28	29	27	25	28	23	26	22	27	26	25	24	24
Pinot Noir	–	–	–	–	–	–	–	24	23	24	23	27	28	26	23	–
Zinfandel	–	–	–	–	–	–	–	–	–	–	–	25	23	27	22	–
Oregon:																
Pinot Noir	–	–	–	–	–	–	–	–	–	–	–	26	27	24	25	–
Italian:																
Tuscany	–	–	–	25	22	24	20	29	24	27	24	26	20	–	–	–
Piedmont	–	–	27	27	–	23	26	27	26	25	28	27	20	–	–	–
Spanish:																
Rioja	–	–	–	–	26	26	24	25	22	25	24	27	20	24	25	–
Ribera del Duero/Priorat	–	–	–	–	26	26	27	25	24	25	24	27	20	24	26	–
Australian:																
Shiraz/Cab.	–	–	–	–	24	26	23	26	28	24	24	27	27	25	26	–

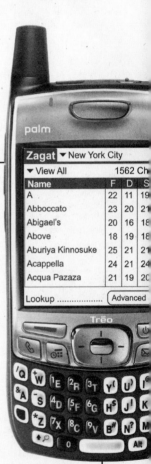